The Political Thought of
Henry David Thoreau

The Political Thought of HENRY DAVID THOREAU

Privatism and the Practice of Philosophy

JONATHAN McKENZIE

UNIVERSITY PRESS OF KENTUCKY

Copyright © 2016 by The University Press of Kentucky

Scholarly publisher for the Commonwealth,
serving Bellarmine University, Berea College, Centre College of Kentucky,
Eastern Kentucky University, The Filson Historical Society, Georgetown College,
Kentucky Historical Society, Kentucky State University, Morehead State
University, Murray State University, Northern Kentucky University, Transylvania
University, University of Kentucky, University of Louisville, and Western
Kentucky University.
All rights reserved.

Editorial and Sales Offices: The University Press of Kentucky
663 South Limestone Street, Lexington, Kentucky 40508-4008
www.kentuckypress.com

Cataloging-in-Publication data is available from the Library of Congress.

ISBN 978-0-8131-6630-8 (hardcover : alk.paper)
ISBN 978-0-8131-6631-5 (epub)
ISBN 978-0-8131-6632-2 (pdf)

This book is printed on acid-free paper meeting
the requirements of the American National Standard
for Permanence in Paper for Printed Library Materials.

♾

Manufactured in the United States of America.

Member of the Association of
American University Presses

To Christina, for the heart,

and

Frederic Homer, for the *psyche*

Contents

INTRODUCTION

The Philosophical Risks of Politics

> The man of wild habits
> Partridges and Rabbits
> Who has no cares
> Only to set snares
> Who liv'st all alone
> Close to the bone—
> And where life is sweetest
> Constantly eatest.
> —Thoreau, *Journal*, July/August 1850[1]

Henry Thoreau's legacy as one among the many polymaths of the American Renaissance still opens vistas into new interpretations of his thought that take seriously his forays into geology, language, political theory, history, and ecology. This work aims to position Thoreau between disciplinary boundaries, as a burgeoning philosopher who espouses a political theory of privatism as a way of managing the damaging effects of democratic participation. In this sense I take "politics" to refer primarily to the engagement of the self with constituted public values, using discursive tools to espouse and understand public problems. This is a relatively modern and uncomplicated concept of politics, one I employ in order not to complicate the way in which Thoreau himself sees politics.[2] My argument, simply stated, is that Thoreau's work, particularly his *Journal* and correspondence, demonstrate repeated exercises in philosophical maturation similar to those found in Socratic writings of the later Stoics, and that Thoreau uses his writings to shape a philosophical personality that can withstand the seductions of democratic political participation.

This work positions Henry Thoreau within the often misunderstood political philosophy of privatism, the elective detachment of the self from political life that serves to insulate the philosophical personality against the sway of the public. This oft-maligned political theory, I argue, is as old as organized political thinking in the West and can, in fact, be traced back to Plato's *Apology* and Socrates's famous act of political defiance in refusing to arrest Leon of Salamis: "For that government, with all its power, did not frighten me into doing anything unjust, but when we came out of the rotunda, the other four went to Salamis and arrested Leon, but I simply went home."[3]

Although we are wont to see Socrates as actively engaged in civil disobedience, the text offers little to support that claim. In fact, we could argue that Socrates's choice to "simply" return home exhibits a much more uncomfortable virtue: political indifference.[4] Socrates's admission to his indifference comes at the heels of his explanation of his *daimon* to the jury, where he argues that "something divine and spiritual comes to me," and that "it is what opposes my engaging in politics."[5] Finally, Socrates argues that his detachment from politics is what makes it possible for him to "speak the truth."[6]

Socrates establishes the philosophical risk of political participation in *Apology*, orienting his philosophical task or calling against the public aggregation of sentiments and mores that inhabit the political sphere. Socrates's speech develops two trains of thought that I would like to follow with Thoreau: first, that Thoreau, like Socrates, makes a virtue out of political indifference. My reading of Thoreau's "reform papers" relies on establishing that Thoreau's goal is not the reorientation or reform of nineteenth-century Concord, but that he instead strives to overcome his own concern with political action. There is a great deal of ambiguity in Socrates's "objection" to the arrest of Leon of Salamis, and Thoreau will magnify that ambiguity in "Resistance to Civil Government," "Slavery in Massachusetts," and "A Plea for Captain John Brown." While Socrates finds himself still tied to the concept of justice, Thoreau attempts to abandon the concept and invoke a standard of personal choice.

The second strain of Socratic thought that helps us to understand Thoreau is Socrates's interesting diversion from democracy: Socrates argues that an intensely private life is the way to live philosophically, and that engaged public life leads one away from the truth. The promise of democracy lies in the notion that reciprocally engaged actors in the public sphere bring forward truth either from aggregation or mutual full disclosure. Socrates's counter is that the aggregation of untruth remains untruth, and that the dangerous seductions of democratic political participation come from persuasion, delusion, and the realm of belief. Socrates places the self's philosophical constitution above the demands of the city and works hard to establish an inner life that reflects the difficult demands of a self-reflective life. Thoreau's political theory is engaged in a similar tension, attempting to carve a meaningful philosophical existence from the everyday observations and entrenchments in private life. Thoreau's political indifference rests ultimately on his attempt to create a robust philosophical self.

Efforts have been made to read Thoreau as an important inheritor of the Socratic philosophical legacy. Dana Villa's *Socratic Citizenship* opens space for considering the valuative aspects of moral individualism in new and important ways. Viewing Socrates as the founder of "conscientious citizenship," Villa argues that Socrates provides the only form of citizenship "truly compatible with moral individualism—itself a phenomenon or mode of being one could say was invented by Socrates."[7] Villa locates the active and engaged "avoidance of injustice" as the core of the concept of care for the self, arguing that Socrates's sustained attention to himself performs both an important philosophical and political purpose. As such, Socrates rethinks citizenship as a practice of "dissent and noncompliance," becoming one "who devotes his entire life to engaging his fellow citizens on the question of how one should live."[8] Socrates's thought, upon this reading, is not antidemocratic but takes advantage of the opened private realm that democracy offers citizens for the "possibility of individual self-fashioning."[9]

Socratic citizenship is disengaged and inwardly focused but maintains an eye on the public sphere, if only to maintain an absence of injustice in one's own life. Villa argues that Socrates, while disengaging himself in the pursuit of self-care, still performs the vital service of elevating fellow citizens through the *elenchus:* "The 'gadfly' rouses, persuades, and reproves them in order to prevent them from sleeping till the end of their days in a state of moral self-satisfaction."[10] While care for one's soul takes "priority" over care for the citizenry, Socrates does not recede into privatism, but both elements remain important in contextualizing Socrates's approach to the moral demands of citizenship. This interesting argument posits that "the most important part of citizenship is *not* found in participation in the deliberation of the courts and the assembly but in the kind of 'private' activity Socrates makes his lifework."[11]

Villa's analysis of *Apology* and *Gorgias* locates harmony with Thoreau, whom he sees as an intensifier of Socrates's form of alienated citizenship. Taking his reading of Thoreau from "Resistance to Civil Government," Villa argues that "Thoreau's essay extends and, in many respects, deepens the Socratic idea of conscientious individualism, yet it also goes beyond that idea insofar as it is an unabashed call to action."[12] Villa reads Thoreau as one who is willing to make a greater existential commitment to the eradication of injustice: "It does not lead [Socrates], as it does Thoreau, to demand the attempted abolition of an evil, regardless of its worldly consequences."[13] If we attend to this reading, we see that Villa characterizes Thoreau's citizenship as disengaged or alienated in only a minor fashion. The reading of "Resistance" seems to merit an understanding of a more engaged, practiced Thoreau, one who is willing to sacrifice his self-fashioning (and indeed the existence of his country) to the eradication of injustice.

George Kateb's "Socratic Integrity" attempts to formulate a similar appreciation of Socratic citizenship. Kateb's reading of Socrates centers on his negativity: "Socrates practices negativity . . . in the sense that he says no to the doctrines of others without producing one of his own."[14] This negativity is what separates Socratic integrity from a more common moral philosophy. Kateb also finds that this negativity exists in Thoreau: "Thoreau, for example, is powerfully inspired by Socrates and equally negative."[15] Kateb uses this reading of Socrates to claim that the eradication of justice from his life is Socrates's most important mission (and, by proxy, perhaps Thoreau's as well). This reading is interesting, primarily because it posits an intellectually complicated picture of Socratic philosophy while maintaining a narrow interpretation of the nuances of his thought. This negativity, Kateb concludes, leads to the only positivity that characterizes Socratic thought: "He was driven irresistibly and from the beginning . . . Driven by what? By the one positivity that perhaps can be attributed to him: that he was driven by affection and compassion for others."[16] This generous reading of Socrates makes important moral headway in the interpretation of his thought and his conduct as an alienated citizen; indeed, it is not surprising that Kateb concludes with very similar affirmations of Thoreau, Emerson, and Whitman.

These Socratic readings of moral individualism make possible an appreciation of Thoreau's alleged "apolitical individualism." Villa and Kateb defend the moral quality of disengaged citizenship, while providing a reading of Socrates and Thoreau that allows us to glean a positive vision of communal life. My reading also argues that Thoreau obeys a basically Socratic practice in his thought, but that we are too quick to assign the high moral status to Thoreau's thought based upon readings of "Resistance to Civil Government" alone. Indeed, if we attend to the bulk of Thoreau's thought, we find a Socratic philosophy that combines continuous work on the self with the constant desire to avoid engagements in politics. Thoreau's desire to remove injustice, upon this reading, is more complicated—we see Thoreau attempting to engage politically in the smallest possible way in order to maintain his grip on his own work of the self. More than any other source, Thoreau's *Journal* bears this conclusion.

Thoreau not only works on himself philosophically through the *Journal*, but he also demonstrates evidence of his progress in his correspondence as well as in *Walden*, which I read as a Socratic manual for philosophical education. In fact, one could take my reading of *Walden* as a following-through of Cavell's notion that "*Walden* is meant to establish [Thoreau's] claim as a philosopher."[17] Thoreau's letters to H. G. O. Blake, a dedicated follower and minor figure in nineteenth-century American thought, show evidence of his having mastered basic philosophical concepts. Take, for example, Thoreau's letter of August 10, 1849: "Mr. Blake . . . I might say . . . be not anxious to avoid poverty. . . . Let our meanness be our footstool, not our cushion. In the midst of this labyrinth let us live a *thread* of life. We must act with so rapid and resistless a purpose in *one* direction, that our vices will necessarily trail behind."[18]

Thoreau's letters to Blake carry a voice that is unique in his correspondence—a patient teacher planting maxims in his student, repeating teachings and admonishing that student to take a few basic propositions of the philosophical life and carry them forward. Thoreau takes the role of the sage in his dealings with Blake, evidence of his robust and hard-earned philosophical voice. Of course, as we will also see in "The Bean-Field," Thoreau is an uncertain sage. Toward the end of his letter to Blake, Thoreau writes, "These things I say; other things I do."[19] Thoreau's incompleteness as a philosopher requires a still-constant vigilance through the writing of the *Journal*.

Thoreau's *Journal: Askesis* and the Risks of Politics

Thoreau's philosophical goal of maximizing the vital value of private life leads him to severely question the existential value of politics, given the propensity of political engagement as popularly understood to interfere with the upward path of philosophical work. Recent literature on Thoreau aims to reconstruct a view of America's "bachelor uncle," a committed antislavery reformer whose seminal life events—the two years ensconced at Walden Pond, the night in jail for refusal to pay poll tax, the friendship with and spirited defense of John Brown—contribute to a positive vision of politics.[20] This reconstructive surgery accomplishes a great deal toward solidifying Thoreau's significance as a political theorist but unfortunately minimizes the complexity of his broader philosophy. In order to remedy this incomplete reading of Thoreau, I offer a comprehensive view. My interpretation merges Thoreau's more popular works—*Walden*, the natural history essays, the *Reform Papers*—with the Thoreau of the journals and correspondence. The view of Thoreau's politics I advance—privatist, provincial, tense, unsure, Stoic—argues for Thoreau's importance as one of modernity's best interpreters of the Socratic vision of philosophy, a theory of earned selfhood that keeps constant watch over one's seductions and will.

Thoreau's *Journal* offers a comprehensive account of his philosophical growth, using the written word to work out his continual *askesis*, relying on persistent exercises of simplification, experimentation, and naturalization. The *Journal* offers us the clearest picture of Thoreau's philosophical sensibility, providing entrée into the purpose behind his published statements on philosophy and politics. Without the work of the *Journal*, we miss Thoreau's philosophical and political origins, strivings, and conclusions. This reading of Thoreau correlates strongly with Michel Foucault's exploration of *askesis* in his late lectures, particularly *The Hermeneutics of the Subject*. "Another major form through which the subject can and must transform himself in order to have access to the truth is a kind of work. This is a work of the self on the self, an elaboration of the self by the self, a progressive transformation of the self by the self for which one takes responsibility in a long labor of ascesis (*askesis*)."[21]

Foucault isolates what he calls "self-writing" as a philosophical method that enhances one's training of oneself and reveals or develops a responsibility for truth through the finality of the written word.[22] Foucault reorients the experience of ancient philosophy as a series of exercises or tests in constituting a self that is capable of accessing and living the truth in a philosophical context. Foucault's use of *askesis* correlates with the repetitive and plodding style of the Roman Stoics and with the ways in which Thoreau's *Journal* transitions from observation to private admonition throughout the pre-*Walden Journal* entries. Foucault's note that *askesis* is a "long labor" resonates with Thoreau's work of putting together not only a long journal but a philosophical persona that is a match for the transformative experiences of everyday life in the nineteenth century.

Foucault clarifies the function of self-writing, noting that "writing has, to use an expression that one finds in Plutarch, an *ethopoietic* function: it is an agent of the transformation of truth into *ethos*."[23] Thoreau's *Journal* demonstrates the apprehension of writing in a similar vein. Thoreau writes not only to record, but to record on himself and through himself the philosophical dicta that he believes will cultivate a self-transformation or upward turn toward a more rich philosophical life. Thoreau's consistent remarks on poverty, solitude, wildness, the natural, and time are written with himself in mind, as admonitions to the self that convince that self of the efficacy of the words and the necessity that those words be written. Put simply, we can watch Thoreau become a philosopher through and by means of his daily writing.

In a journal entry from the early Walden Pond period (fall–winter 1845–1846), Thoreau writes the following: "For every inferior earthly pleasure we forego a superior celestial one is substituted."[24] This small bit of light philosophical advice reads like a truism, but if we contextualize the remark, we can see the employment of Thoreau's *Journal* as a philosophical exercise. The remark is made directly following Thoreau's explanation of the materials he uses to construct his cabin at the pond. Thoreau follows this remark with a separate paragraph: "To purify our lives requires simply to weed out what is foul & noxious—And the sound and innocent is supplied—as nature purifies the blood—if we will but reject impurities."[25] Thoreau is writing primarily to himself, supplying himself with an action principle that will motivate and justify his long excursion into the woods. Thoreau is not writing here as a sage, giving instruction to his students (although his writing will take on this quality), but convincing himself by committing himself to a principle that he knows is true but struggles to live as an ethos.

In an entry from January 16, 1852, Thoreau introduces us to Bill Wheeler, "the town drunk found frozen to death one winter morning."[26] More than a contrarian send-up of a fallen citizen, Thoreau's eulogy explores the notion of the withdrawn hermit—a disappointment to respectable Concord—as a philosophically complex human being: "How low he lived perhaps from a deep principle—that he might be some mighty philosopher greater than Socrates or Diogenes—simplifying life—returning to nature—having turned his back on towns—How many things he had put off—luxuries—comforts—human society even his feet—wrestling with his thoughts. . . . Perchance here is one of sect of philosophers—the only one—so simple—so abstracted in thought & life from his contemporaries."[27]

The Bill Wheeler eulogy is one of the great moments in Thoreau's *Journal*. Thoreau remembers Wheeler as perhaps the Stoics remember Socrates, as the lowly, grungy, self-respecting philosopher of a life lived from deep principle, appearing simple because the complexity persists on the inside. Wheeler's outside judgments—particularly the popular knee-jerk reaction that his life constitutes utter failure—are turned upside down by Thoreau's imaginative remembrance. There is much to learn about Thoreau's philosophical sense from this passage as well. Of particular importance is Thoreau's declaration that Wheeler may be a "mighty" philosopher, greater than Socrates or Diogenes. Placing Diogenes next to Socrates in this context strikes us as strange, given that the Socratic legacy was already well established and that Diogenes's legacy was in question in the nineteenth century. In this case Thoreau displays the strong Socratic tendencies of the late Stoics, particularly Epictetus.[28] As A. A. Long maintains in his seminal study of Epictetus's thought, Socrates and Diogenes sit at the head table of philosophical examples, an unusual pairing for a Stoic.

Long concludes that Epictetus's preference for Diogenes underscores his "need for his students to focus on the primary and transformative message of Stoicism as distinct from its more scholastic developments."[29] Similarly, in Thoreau's case, we see him isolate Socrates and Diogenes because they are the two figures most closely aligned with the practice of philosophy, or what Pierre Hadot terms "philosophy as a way of life." As Robert Richardson, Thoreau's most esteemed biographer, has shown, Thoreau fashions his philosophical ideal after the model of Stoicism: "Thoreau's interest in individual reformation also led him back to the Greek ethical schools, and particularly to Stoicism—the search for self-rule or autarky."[30] Thoreau's philosophical disposition owes much to Epictetus in the sense that he, like Thoreau, rescues Socratic philosophy as a lived practice of the "aesthetics of existence." With the employment of Bill Wheeler, Thoreau imagines a philosophical hero whose life is as intensely lived as it is thoroughly principled.

What gives Wheeler's life value is the principle of "putting things off" in the service of his private pursuits of virtue, artistry, and vitality. Judgments against Wheeler are inevitable, as his simplifying nature alienates him philosophically from his generation. Thoreau is, on one level, transferring his own feelings of philosophical solitude onto Wheeler, providing a safe landing spot for Thoreau's own articulations of his place. But he also identifies simplification as a special type of philosophical work, the work of living, persistently exercising restraint and self-confidence in the "no-saying" of fighting contemporary culture. Thoreau identifies the important virtues of the philosopher—simplifying, returning to nature, turning one's back to the town, wrestling with his thoughts—as a way of immortalizing Wheeler (similarly to the way in which he transforms John Brown into the last Puritan) but also as a way of staking claim to the identity of philosophical work. Wheeler serves as Thoreau's reflection of his understanding of philosophy up to this point and, as such, represents an apex in Thoreau's *Journal*.

Wheeler is the Socratic character whose life causes one to reevaluate one's own: "I felt even as Diogenes when he saw the boy drinking out of his hands—& threw away his cup."[31] Thoreau captures and vitalizes Wheeler's solitude and furthers the case by appealing to its elective nature: "Must he not see things with an impartial eye—disinterested as a toad observes the gardener!"[32] Wheeler's isolation and his death appear to Thoreau as the only possible existential conclusion to a life whose pursuit of principle leaves him outside of consensual realities and mores: "Whose very vividness of perception—clear knowledge & insight have made him dumb."[33] Wheeler's only suffering is in the eyes of the everyday Concordian, the average individual whose allegiance to customary means of evaluating life leaves him unable to properly account for an acute philosophical soul. Thoreau idolizes Wheeler—mentioning more than once in the eulogy his jealousy—perhaps because of his uncommon ability to transcend the social, performing that magnificent act of existential simplification that escapes Thoreau himself.

Thoreau lists Wheeler's many virtues: performing little work, eating little meat, having few communications, unwillingness to do "chores" for others, simplifying, returning to nature, absolving himself of concern with the town, putting off leisure items, ignoring comforts, sacrificing his own feet, going alone, remaining unambitious, ignoring opinions of others, cultivating disinterest and abstraction, wisdom that appears as foolishness, being humble and mortified, vividness of perception, knowledge, lack of common consciousness. Thoreau's familiar trick of divining the low while demonizing the

high certainly colors his description of Wheeler, but Wheeler is no rhetorical foil. Thoreau earnestly "would have liked to know what view he took of
life."[34] Wheeler's life is an example of the humility of the reflectively simple life—Wheeler is no fool but manages through exercising and practice to
live an authentic Socratic philosophy. To look at some of his virtues, Thoreau appears to reconstruct virtue as a sort of minding one's own concern,
to authenticate every portion of life as a vital purpose given to and through
individual life. Wheeler is only one of Thoreau's philosophical heroes, to
which we can add Alek Therien and Joe Polis, all united in the simplification
of a complex social landscape.

Wheeler's Socratic figure is established through his death, which Thoreau casts as an event consonant with his philosophical life: "A month or two
after this, as I heard he was found dead among the brush over back of the
hill—So far decomposed that his coffin was carried to his body & it was put
into it with pitch forks."[35] As the Stoics deify Socrates as the one who dies
philosophically, Thoreau performs a similar service for Wheeler, remaining
hopeful that he died "a Brahmin's death dwelling at the roots of trees at
last."[36] Wheeler's death, the occasion for Thoreau's consideration of him as a
philosopher, cements his concerns with reflectively simplifying his own life,
dying on his own terms as one not willing to sacrifice his hard-earned principles for the cold comforts of a fireplace, warm bed, and the fellow feelings
of the respectable townspeople. Wheeler's death and his life represent a philosophical ideal entirely wrought from the attention paid to simplifying one's
own life, offering a glimpse into the work to which Thoreau puts philosophy.
Wheeler, like the image of Socrates before him, constructs a complete life
that is barren, cold, hard-edged, but also concrete, sincere, internally consistent, and highly principled. The final test of Wheeler's life is the character of
his death, the subject of Thoreau's private eulogy, and the foundation for his
method of reflective simplification.

There is nowhere in Thoreau's published writing an understanding of
his philosophical development that compares to this *Journal* entry. We learn
here, from a simple day's writing, the identification of Thoreau's idea of philosophy with the actions and persona of Socrates. Further, we understand
the complexity of Thoreau's use of simplification as the method of philosophy, uniting the concept with the overcoming of everyday social evaluations
of existence and performing the necessary vitalizing of solitude by deifying
its philosophical origins. Thoreau's *Journal* records the work of philosophy,

the series of tests to one's ownness given in everyday existence. Writing in the same month as the above entry, Thoreau finds himself seduced by a large newspaper, managing to overcome its promises by walking: "My walks were full of incidents. I attended not to the affairs of Europe but to my own affairs in Concord fields."[37] This representative entry finds Thoreau challenged and resolved to continue the upward path of *askesis*. Thoreau's eulogy for Bill Wheeler demonstrates the need to forge characters of solitude in order to make the concept of ownness more robust and livable.

In this sense Thoreau carries much in common with the Roman Stoic Epictetus, who alerts students to the vital value of carrying a prescriptive philosophy of "ownness." Buttressed by Socrates's insistence on maintaining a private life in *Apology*, Epictetus collapses existential choice into a single category: "Stop admiring your clothes, and you are not angry at the man who steals them; stop admiring your wife's beauty, and you are not angry at her adulterer. Know that a thief or adulterer has no place among the things that are your own, but only among the things that are another's."[38]

Epictetus's counsel contracts one's ethical realm to the smallest degree, settling important questions by the standard of existential (and ethical) distance. Epictetus's insistence on ownness as an ethical starting point distinguishes him from other Roman Stoics and provides the most compelling entry point into his consonance with Thoreau's thought. Thoreau's feeling of shame for burning the Concord woods reflects the inability of others to distance themselves from the ownership of external events; indeed, Thoreau's work of admonishing himself is also determined by his inability to distance himself from the events.

Thoreau's sense of ownness is forged through his *Journal*, realized in the repetitive exercises that recall Pierre Hadot's interpretation of Stoic thought. Take, for example, an early entry from April 5, 1841: "I will build my lodge on the southern slope of some hill, and take there the life the gods send me— Will it not be employment enough to accept gratefully all that is yielded me between sun & sun?"[39]

Thoreau's yearning for ownness, for the solitude of personal prerogative, engages him on the practical level of his home and work. Thoreau's lifelong quest for a work that is his own—a problem exaggerated through his association with Emerson, his work in his father's pencil shop, and the alienation of surveying for others—persistently creeps into his *Journal*. In this case, Thoreau ends his thought with a question, clearly aimed at himself: Is it possible for me to train myself to accept what is my own and leave the rest? Thoreau's efforts to challenge himself to affirm what is his own constitute one of the most important ways in which his thought resembles the philosophical discipline of Epictetus.

Thoreau's *Journal* reveals the tensions that animate his philosophy. Writing in the fall of 1851, Thoreau finds himself more in line with the nature in which he so frequently ensconces himself. This, however, provides its own problems: "I seem to be more constantly merged in nature—my intellectual life is more obedient to nature than formerly—but perchance less obedient to spirit. . . . I exact less of myself. . . . O if I could be discontented with myself!"[40]

The tension between the natural and the spiritual is one that creates opportunities for philosophical grounding in Thoreau's thought. The celebrated late excursion essays, like "Walking" or "Wild Apples," demonstrate the degree to which Thoreau merges his identity with his natural surroundings. The tension involved in becoming wholly natural—as Thoreau argues, to exhibit the "animal man"—is that the animal loses the higher or spiritual grade that Thoreau also cherishes. The result of this tension between the natural and the spiritual is Thoreau's philosophy of "half-cultivation" (from his chapter "The Bean-Field" in *Walden*) that apprehends the line between becoming animal and becoming god. Without attention paid to Thoreau's *Journal*, it is difficult to appraise Thoreau's deeply entrenched struggles to develop a comprehensive philosophy of life.

Thoreau's wider corpus, historically ignored by political theorists, provides fruitful ground for understanding the genesis and context of Thoreau's politics. Leading the charge to interrogate Thoreau's comprehensive writings, Jane Bennett's *Thoreau's Nature* (1994) introduces the political value of Thoreau's journals, letters, and natural history writings: "The Thoreau most vocal in these debates is not the Thoreau of 'Resistance to Civil Government' or the antislavery lectures, but the Thoreau of *Walden*, the journals, *The Maine Woods*, *A Week on the Concord and Merrimack Rivers*, and the natural history essays. I find these naturalist writings more engaging than the political writings because they map out a larger project within which, among other things, Thoreau's arts of civil disobedience and political dissent are set."[41]

Bennett's prefatory remark to her excellent work performs a redirection in the presumptions of Thoreau's importance as a political thinker. For Bennett, Thoreau of "Resistance to Civil Government" is not a different Thoreau, necessarily, but an incomplete one. Her insistence that Thoreau's wider works "map out a larger project" leads to her more important claim: that Thoreau's comprehensive philosophy exhibits the development of a "crafting of the self" that inhabits a *"postmodern sensibility,"* thus justifying Bennett's comparative analysis of Thoreau with Foucault in particular, and Haraway, Deleuze, and Kafka as well.[42] Ultimately, Bennett folds the contemporary understanding of Thoreau's affirmative political action into her understanding of his broad philosophical project, arguing that "his dissent is more a means toward self-refashioning than toward societal reform."[43]

Bennett's major accomplishment is to see in Thoreau a process of self-fashioning that expresses itself through repetitive actions aimed at reconstructing a self: "My Thoreau, however, takes one down a somewhat different path—to reflection into the type of self capable of an act of conscientious dissent and into the processes through which that individual may come into being."[44] She argues, in a chapter entitled "Techniques of the Self," that Thoreau's project of self-fashioning carries consonance with deconstructive techniques of postmodern thought. Bennett locates Thoreau's project as one of persistent work on the self: "I describe Thoreau's quest as a series of eight techniques: moving inward, idealizing a friend, keeping quiet, going outside, microvisioning, living doubly, hoeing beans, and eating with care. These exercises are to be practiced daily until they become second nature."[45]

Bennett's understanding of Thoreau's project as a process of self-fashioning, an art of existence that manifests itself through repetitive exercise, establishes a key connection between Thoreau's politics and his wider philosophical goal. To prove her thesis, Bennett focuses on the "non-political" writings, as mentioned above. Bennett's reading of Thoreau draws her to a postmodern thesis of Thoreau's self-creative exercises reflected in the philosophical thought of Foucault, Haraway, and Deleuze. Thoreau represents an early call to destabilize the "natural," heighten our anxiety about the suffocation of social life, and "give the Wild its due . . . to preserve the element of heterogeneity present in any entity."[46]

Bennett succeeds in moving Thoreau away from the narrow, moralist interpretation of Thoreau's politics toward an ethics that reflects the self-creative value of becoming.[47] Bennett argues that Thoreau "writes with ethical purpose, hoping to guide political behavior and modify identity,"[48] but consistently couches this ethics within the boundaries of self-cultivation. A keystone problem in transcendentalist politics is the relation between the

Bildung of appropriating Goethe's self-cultivation and the status of reform projects celebrated by Emerson and the communitarian transcendentalists. Bennett fruitfully complicates Thoreau's contribution to this problem, suggesting that Thoreau's ethical purpose primarily consists of self-fashioning practices that decenter both the publicness of the concept of ethics and the identity of the self over time. Nature, under Bennett's rubric, transitions from the space of respite to the avenue of the irrepressibly other, challenging Thoreau and providing the ground for Thoreau's challenge of spiritual identity.

Thoreau's Nature remains the key text in incorporating Thoreau's philosophy into an understanding of his political theory. Bennett's composition of self-fashioning, apprehending nature, and aestheticizing politics is a key contribution to understanding Thoreau's motives. In each of these cases, my method in this text resonates with Bennett's superb analysis. It is important both to recognize my debt to Bennett's work and to alert myself and others to our fundamental points of departure. Like Bennett, I find the comprehensive view of Thoreau's work essential to understanding his project as a philosophical thinker. My use of the journals and letters, however, builds upon them as documents that demonstrate Thoreau's *askesis,* to borrow a term from Foucault's late lectures. In other words, I will argue that Thoreau's journals and letters document the genesis of a philosophical life, and that we can read the published work (particularly *Walden*) as an account-taking of his philosophical personality. Second, Bennett's argument consistently circles toward challenging and ultimately privileging Thoreau's political dissent and activity as the core of his political thought. Thoreau's political engagement is, undoubtedly, the most difficult portion of his philosophy to appraise within the context of his naturalist writings. Instead of trapping myself with the need to justify and defend Thoreau's intermittent political engagement, I argue that Thoreau's "reform papers" constitute abrupt fits of externality that has to be checked by his desire for inward transformation. This culminates in my broad argument that Thoreau's fullness of life makes necessary a privatist political theory. Finally, while Bennett's thesis that Thoreau's wider work composes a self-fashioning ethic, Thoreau's fit within postmodern discourses of antifoundationalism seems loose. My analysis takes Thoreau back to his own vision of ancient philosophers, whose project of self-fashioning rests on the foundation of a core of overcoming temporality, something altogether uncomfortable for postmodern thought.

My understanding of Thoreau's philosophical development is indebted to another key study of his political thought. Brian Walker's (1998, 2001) reading of *Walden* as a manual in "democratic cultivation" attends to the use of maxims and exercises in the middle chapters of *Walden* in order to tie Thoreau to earlier philosophical treatises on the arts of existence. Walker argues that "some of the best-known works in the history of political theory are written in the advice-giving mode. Much of Stoicism was at least ostensibly cast in this form."[49] Walker leaves the connection at that point, while pointing out in another article, "The idea that ancient philosophy may offer the key to modern work predicaments goes back very far in Thoreau's thought. . . . The key to *Walden* is the way it combines ancient philosophical practices and modern economic calculation to set out a strategy by which citizens may realize their liberty."[50]

Walker categorizes *Walden* as an "experiment in philosophy" and argues that Thoreau aims to enlighten young men by following (and surpassing) the skeletal frame of democratic advice-giving literature. Walker's sensitivity to Thoreau's ancient influences opens a sphere of acknowledgment beyond the scope of Walker's own analysis. Walker's vision of *Walden*'s philosophical purpose, that "Thoreau uses the narrative of his experiment at Walden Pond to show how the resources of ancient philosophy can be used by those who find themselves vulnerable within the modern market system," sells itself short in making a tight connection between ancient philosophy and modern economic concerns.[51]

Walker's distillation of *Walden* into a series of helpful maxims amplifies *Walden*'s connection with Hellenistic thought. Walker establishes this connection in directing the purpose of Thoreau's maxims to the notion of autonomy: "In the Hellenistic schools and in other ancient philosophical traditions . . . adherents memorized maxims that summed up the complex moral and physical attitudes advocated by the school."[52] Walker carries Thoreau's self-cultivation into a "model of ethico-political action that sees a continuity between self-fashioning in the household and the broader shaping of the political community."[53] Walker distills the organization of *Walden*'s advice-giving, then uses this characterization of Thoreau to homogenize the acts of political will in "Resistance to Civil Government" and other texts with the naturalist tinge of "The Bean-Field" chapter of *Walden* and the other, less overtly political aspects of *Walden*. Walker's connection of Thoreau with ancient thought opens fruitful ground for understanding the nature of Thoreau's disparate politics.

Another recent work on Thoreau takes aim at aligning Thoreau's naturalist writings with his positive political contribution. Shannon Mariotti's *Thoreau's Democratic Withdrawal* provides a fruitful reading of Thoreau alongside Theodor Adorno, situating Thoreau within the context of social theories of alienation and withdrawal.[54] Mariotti's major thesis is that "Thoreau's excursions into nature are not apolitical retreats but ways of confronting particular objects that stimulate dissonant, rupturing, negative critiques of modern society and allow him to recuperate the capacities that define truly democratic citizens."[55] Mariotti closely reads Thoreau's microscopic orientation to the natural world as a way of paying particular attention to the critical capacity of things, orienting himself away from the polis and the market in order to reestablish his ground as a part of each. Mariotti reads Thoreau and Adorno within an agonic democratic context, holding that critique grounds and examines the ability of democracy to provide vital value for citizens: "Negative dialectics, walking, and huckleberrying instantiate, perform, and enact the critical negation that democracy depends upon and is defined by."[56] Thoreau's retreats into "leading a huckleberry party" retain particular political significance under this reading.

Importantly, Mariotti establishes that Thoreau's acts of distancing himself are ways of "experimenting with one's life." The purpose of these experiments is to "teach us to think against conventions, to see particular differences instead of perceiving abstractly and generalizing."[57] Mariotti holds that Thoreau requires acts of distancing in order to learn to think against conventions, reading these acts of withdrawal against the common assumption (shared by Emerson, among others) that Thoreau engages in withdrawing acts precisely *because* he thinks against conventions. "To be alienated is to think and say exactly what we are expected to think and say, what everyone else thinks and says, to say 'yes' to conventions. But on the other hand, Thoreau places the greatest value on the part of us that can say 'no,' and think against the grain of common thought."[58] In order to establish the political importance of walking, Mariotti turns the act into a primary mode of democratic activity—the preparatory stage of democratic citizenship. This is a highly nuanced reading of Thoreau's wider work, and Mariotti uses this framework to recuperate Thoreau's political reputation.

Mariotti's thesis depends upon the ability to establish the democratic capability of withdrawal—that is, to make the case that Thoreau not only reaffirms and teaches himself the art of going against convention but puts that newfound political integrity to work: "While Thoreau goes into nature out of a need to regain parts of the self, his withdrawals are not retreats from politics. Rather, Thoreau is trying to carve out a new space for his own variety of politics *within* nature. He may go into nature to reject the alienating village and mainstream politics ('what is called politics'), but he goes there with a mission, a crusade to carve out a new space for a new type of democratic politics."[59]

On this reading of "Walking," Mariotti merges her understanding of Thoreau with Bennett's and Walker's. We see Thoreau not as the staunch moralist, but as the one whose life dedicates itself to the cultivation of a type of self capable of establishing the grounds for his own understanding of democratic intensity and integrity.[60] Mariotti's reading of Thoreau's intentions in "Walking" lessens the emphasis on Thoreau's overtly political participation (in the speech defending John Brown or what becomes "Resistance to Civil Government") and attends to the process of becoming that dictates Thoreau's philosophical life. Notice, in particular, that Mariotti argues that Thoreau is "trying to carve out space" for a new type of politics. She does not claim, rightly I think, that Thoreau's "Walking" represents a new type of politics, but that it constitutes an ongoing effort toward that politics.

Walker and Mariotti each fashion new ground in the ways we understand Thoreau's philosophical debts, his philosophical context, and the ways in which his thought represents an experiment with new ways of understanding democracy in the nineteenth century. Ultimately, Walker stops short of giving Thoreau's *Walden* its philosophical due by keeping it couched within a common understanding of democratic practice and value. Mariotti's work deftly describes Thoreau's withdrawal but is less convincing in its major thesis of making that withdrawal democratic. If Thoreau retires to private space for the purpose of constituting a new type of politics *within* nature, what is the democratic import? If Thoreau does not return to the village with participatory plans (even critical ones), where does withdrawal gain its political purpose?[61] Endeavoring to adhere Thoreauvian critical or self-creative practices to the critical or educative practice of democratic politics distorts the ingenuity of Thoreau's self-cultivation and his critique of democracy. However, while Walker and Mariotti both suffer a shortcoming in their abilities to sufficiently distill Thoreau's cultivation of self as "democratic," this remains insignificant in comparison with the wider sphere they provide to our understanding of Thoreau's thought.

Time and the Dissolving Human: Understanding Thoreau's Journals

Although Thoreau's journals and correspondence are widely overlooked in political theory, literary critics have taken hold of the journals and attempted to read them as a single offering. Two successful readings, Sharon Cameron's *Writing Nature* (1985) and H. Daniel Peck's *Thoreau's Morning Work,* aim to extract a frame of interpretation from Thoreau's lifework. Cameron's major thesis is that Thoreau "is writing his life so that it actually comes to comprise alternate—natural—phenomena."[62] Cameron argues that, while Thoreau's journal entries can, in some sense, constitute an autobiography, the *Journal* "dismisses not just Thoreau's consideration of himself but his consideration of other selves. What remains is just enough of the human to represent the natural."[63] Peck, on the other hand, focuses on the "art of memory" as Thoreau's way of dealing with temporality and the pangs of past wrongs: "What is happening here is a rediscovery, a deepening of awareness, a coming into fuller knowledge of what is already known."[64] While Cameron attends to Thoreau's desire to write the human out of nature, Peck understands Thoreau's *Journal* as an exercise in the phenomenology of phenomena—the reciprocal apprehension of the self and the self's environs.

Cameron's argument rests on the notion that the *Journal* attempts a re-visioning of nature, an "alternative to a visual medium."[65] Thoreau writes the journal in order to develop "an anatomy of seeing nature," merging the concerns of the limitations of vision with the possibilities of literature (and its attendant concerns).[66] As such, Thoreau utilizes the lifelong journal as the only way in which one can carry out the mammoth project of writing nature, reconstituting the eye and pen toward looking "always at what is to be seen."[67] Importantly, Cameron reads the *Journal* against *Walden,* making the argument that the *Journal* contains a purer and more compelling account of Thoreau's literary intentions: "Thoreau's impatience with, and grief over, society are largely a consequence of the concessions required by the *writing* of *Walden.* These concessions are exacting. They also are not easy. It takes seven drafts to cultivate nature, to formalize what Thoreau sees so that others can follow it."[68]

Cameron not only defends the *Journal* as a literary enterprise worthy of attention but argues that *Walden* presents Thoreau with such animosity toward the abstract other that he cultivates antisocial opinions and maxims as a way out of the disappointment of reducing his goal of writing nature. By placing *Walden* below the *Journal* in Thoreau's own corpus, Cameron carves out a privileged space of the *Journal*'s literary accomplishments.

The concessions required to write *Walden* include reducing the distance between the natural and the human and presenting "not nature but the seductive rapprochement of the natural and the social to which, put in the harshest terms, nature is sacrificed."[69] Thoreau succeeds in the *Journal* to produce what, Cameron assumes, is his goal for *Walden* as well: "Thoreau has freed himself from the obligatory engagement with the human."[70] Thoreau accomplishes this disengagement by sticking close to the objects as described: "The emphasis of the question is not on the discrepancy between the partiality of sights and the wholeness to which we convert them; it is rather on the particularity of sights, on why these sounds and sights . . . tug at us with their meaning."[71] Attending to particularity resolves and dissolves the distinction between the human and the natural through a twofold process: first, particularity inhibits Thoreau from categorizing nature. Cameron notes that "naming and identification presume that man, and his categories, are central to the nature that he sees; they also presume his ability to comprehend it."[72] Second, particularity allows Thoreau to see by removing the desire to understand nature: "In the *Journal*, Thoreau strives toward a randomness of impressions."[73] Noting that he can see only when he relinquishes the desire to understand, Thoreau's *Journal* exhibits the purpose of writing nature.

One will notice that Cameron develops a thesis that takes Thoreau's *Journal* away from what is commonly understood as its private purpose: to serve as the rough draft for a number of literary projects. While Cameron acknowledges that the *Journal* contains skeletal visions of *Walden* and *A Week on the Concord and Merrimack Rivers*, as well as the raw material of a number of speeches and papers, the *Journal* itself contains its own public purpose: "Because the work is a journal and because it was published posthumously, we assess it to be private. Yet claims made in the *Journal* explicitly about it— and in fact the nature of its composition—rather suggest that Thoreau hoped for our eventual discovery and assessment of this work *qua* work. Thus I shall argue that the *Journal* confounds the distinction between the private and the public on which our determinations about how to treat discourse conventionally depend."[74]

Cameron persuasively argues that the *Journal* substantiates Thoreau's lifelong aspiration to communicate the language of nature, a project unfulfilled in *Walden* or *The Maine Woods*. The *Journal* sustains contradictions, miscalculations, mood shifts, and the disorienting transformation of parts into wholes (and wholes back into parts) in a way that no ostensibly public work could. Cameron is quick to alert the reader to the fact that Thoreau's *Journal* is a public work, one that aims not for the transformation of one's thoughts into a readable part, but the transmission of the whole on the author's own terms.

One of the most nuanced critiques of Cameron's work is Peck's (1990) *Thoreau's Morning Work*. Peck dissects the *Journal* as well as *Walden* and *A Week on the Concord and Merrimack Rivers* as examples of Thoreau's phenomenology of time. Peck sees Thoreau using the *Journal* as, among other things, a repository that "could preserve for him what otherwise would be lost to the attritions of time and experience."[75] The notion of the *Journal* as a space of preservation of time presents the challenge of the work as the killing of time itself. While Cameron focuses intently on the amplification of the natural and the eclipse of the human in the post-1850 *Journal*, Peck latches on to the *Journal* as a grappling with temporality (and, as a result, spatiality as well), directing his attention to Thoreau's attempt to codify nature through the "Kalendar" and other projects: "These charts . . . are an attempt to lay out all of nature's phenomena on a flat plane, that is, to graph their temporality and make a comprehensive picture of time."[76]

Cameron and Peck converge on the importance of Thoreau's relational philosophy, but Peck situates Thoreau's method as one of seeking phenomena, the merger of the natural object and the mental representation of the object in the mind.[77] Peck's interest in unpacking Thoreau's development of phenomena initiates a theory of the self-awareness of Thoreau's perceptive capacity and its inability to fully apprehend the thing itself. Thoreau's self-awareness becomes a problem, for he desires "to emphasize the primary, defining, phenomenological qualities of the thing in itself."[78] Thoreau's categorical personality, affirmed through the persistent use of relations to amplify the internal qualities of individual things, develops out of a desire in the *Journal* to give continuous credence to objects that shift in themselves and in consciousness.[79] Thoreau's categorizations, calendars, and relations "validate the emergence of 'things' into unity and coherence in a world constantly changing before our eyes."[80] In this sense, Thoreau's emphasis on relations and fitting categories presents the *Journal* as "an intriguingly proto-modern document."[81]

Ultimately, Peck argues that the *Journal* attempts to kill time through preserving, for memory and for understanding, the transitory elements of nature through phenomenologically apprehending their elements and relations: "In another sense of the phrase from *Walden,* this effort is Thoreau's 'morning work'—his lifelong work of legitimating the level of experience that phenomena define. The task of his aesthetic, and of his Journal, is to make a place for phenomena to be real."[82] The struggle of the *Journal,* on this reading, is to transcend the intractable relation between categories of reality and the mind's apprehension of those categories. Unlike Emerson, who ignores the categories of reality, or Melville, who resigns to the inability of the self to apprehend them, Thoreau works at handling the distance between the self and the thing in itself, "search[ing] the world constantly for categories that were, at least provisionally, viable."[83] Thoreau attends to categories as a way of delineating the "drifting continuum of change" and slowing time to allow things to appreciate in our consciousness: "Observing change through the prism of a phenomenological calendar lifts us from the linear and destructive time of history."[84]

Cameron and Peck dissect the *Journal*'s intentions and rebuild the document stressing either the elimination of the human through the attempt to offer a visual medium of nature (in Cameron's case) or the work of preserving memory and building a phenomenological account of nature's shifting foci through a categorical accounting of processes and likenesses (in Peck's reading). The effort to read the *Journal* as a more or less linear document yields incredible fruit for studying Thoreau; in addition to opening the *Journal* for critical appreciation as a public document meant to be part of the author's oeuvre, Cameron and Peck lay the groundwork for appreciating the *Journal* as Thoreau's most comprehensive intellectual enterprise and accomplishment. In each case, we find Thoreau struggling with what he sees and pitting this against what he knows, dramatizing the *Journal* as the effort of an observer trying to come to grips with "looking always at what is to be seen."[85]

A Comprehensive Vision

This work remains indebted to the critical work mentioned above for several reasons, none more important than the expanding horizon of political scholarship on Thoreau, allowing us to view a thinker more complicated than the curmudgeonly or brazenly moralist thinker of early- and mid-twentieth-century perception. My analysis hinges on a particular interpretation of the *Journal* that, while taking into account Thoreau's accounting for nature, explores the philosophical content of the work. Taking cues from Foucault's reading of Hellenistic thought, I argue that the *Journal* confers an *askesis*—a set of exercises and practices in developing a philosophical standpoint. I wish to make clear that I do not renounce the other interpretations of Thoreau's *Journal* but wish to add to them by highlighting the portions of the *Journal* they renounce—specifically, the presence of others and the use of nature as metaphor. Thoreau certainly intends to write nature and to preserve his memory, but he also develops a form of self-writing that has extraordinary resonance with Stoic thought and with Foucauldian interpretations of the practice of philosophy.

To demonstrate this reading of Thoreau's *Journal,* I would like to highlight two journal passages employed as key entries by Cameron and Peck. Cameron's entry, taken from the long missive on September 7, 1851, concerns Thoreau's alleged narcissism and reading the glorification of nature into the dissolution of the self:

> How to live—How to get the most life! as if you were to teach the young hunter how to entrap his game. How to extract its honey from the flower of the world. That is my every day business. I am as busy as a bee about it. I ramble over all fields on that errand and am never so happy as when I feel myself heavy with honey & wax. I am like a bee searching the live-long day for the sweets of nature. Do I not impregnate & intermix the flowers produce rare & finer varieties by transfering my eyes from one to another? I do as naturally & as joyfully with my own humming music—seek honey all the day. With what honied thought any experience yields me I take a bee line to my cell. It is with flowers I would deal. Where is the flower there is the honey—which is perchance the nectareous portion of the fruit—there is to be the fruit—& no doubt flowers are thus colored & painted—to attract & guide the bee. So by the dawning or radiance of beauty are we advertised where is the honey & the fruit of thought of discourse & of action—We are first attracted by the beauty of the flower, before we discover the honey which is a foretaste of the future fruit. Did not the young Achilles (?) spend his youth learning how to hunt? The art of spending a day. If it is possible that we may be addressed—it behoves us to be attentive. If by watching all day & all night—I may detect some

trace of the Ineffable—then will it not be worth the while to watch? Watch & pray without ceasing. . . . I am convinced that men are not well employed—that this is not the way to spend a day.[86]

Cameron's interpretation of this quote centers on the role of the bee toward the middle of the piece, arguing that, contra Perry Miller, Thoreau does not appear an aggrandizing narcissist, but that in the excerpt "self-glorification becomes glorification of nature . . . the emphasis is not on self-aggrandizement but conversely on how the self, like a bee, can learn to draw beauty from nature."[87] This quotation represents one means of establishing Thoreau's primary purpose to lift the veil on natural phenomena in order to keep the focus on nature itself.

If, however, we attend to the way Thoreau brackets his conversation in the sentences previous to the long quotation, we find room for a different reading of the text. Immediately before the quoted passage, Thoreau writes, "Suppose you attend to the hints to the suggestions which the moon makes for one month—commonly in vain—will they not be very diffirent from any thing in literature or religion or philosophy."[88] In this passage, Thoreau is attempting to use the bee not as a means to glorify nature, but to explain the rationale behind his decision to plumb nature for its existential effects. The ambient concern in the day's entries is with what Thoreau calls "the art of life," or the ancient philosophical question of how to live. Thoreau puts this problematic into a sphere of activity: "by what disciplines to secure the most life."[89] The chief disciplines whereby we answer this question—philosophy, literature, religion—are not rejected by Thoreau *tout de suite* but are set aside temporarily as Thoreau engages the question of nature's contribution to the question. When we return to the long passage, we find Thoreau "searching for the sweets of nature" and ecstatic when he is "heavy with honey & wax."[90] While it may appear that Thoreau is extolling the virtues of nature qua nature, Thoreau is using the abundance of nature as an exercise in philosophical methodology, while his gaze remains attendant to the larger concern: "where is the honey & the fruit of thought of discourse & of action."

Toward the end of this train of writing, Thoreau asks: "We are surrounded by a rich & fertile mystery—May we not probe it—pry into it—employ ourselves about it—a little? To devote your life to the discovery of the divinity in Nature or to the eating of oysters would they not be attended with very different results?"[91] Asking the question as a way of defining the answer, Thoreau pits consumptive and reflective uses of nature against each other and compels the reader to compare their respective effects. We might ask, however, for whom the "different results" matter. Thoreau offers two means of utilizing the experience of nature to aid in the preparedness of the self for the tasks of existence. Thoreau couches the entire entry within the auspice of "the art of living," suggesting that for this particular purpose he does not deflate the subject but keeps his own exercise at the forefront of his concern. Later, Thoreau writes, "My profession is to be always on the alert to find God in nature—to know his lurking places."[92] Thoreau appears interested in the object of nature as such, but he shortly qualifies his search, noting, "If the wine which will nourish me grows on the surface of the moon—I will do the best I can to go to the moon for it."[93] The emphasis is on Thoreau's own development, not with a narcissistic glint but with the deep coloration of the complex work of developing a self.

Similarly, Peck locates an important passage in Thoreau's *Journal*: "We need a calendar that can teach us the lesson of the turtle: 'Be not in haste; mind your private affairs. Consider the turtle. . . . Perchance you have worried yourself, despaired of the world, meditated the end of life, and all things seemed rushing to destruction; but nature has steadily and serenely advanced with a turtle's pace. . . . Has not the tortoise . . . learned the true value of time?'"[94]

The long passage quoted in Peck's text connects the hatching of a tortoise to the true value of time, suggestive of Thoreau's interest in using memory to rethink temporality. The larger entry from which the portion quoted above is gleaned, however, offers a distinctly philosophical understanding different from Peck's interpretation. The key to the passage here is "Be not in haste; mind your private affairs." Appealing to Thoreau's admonishment that one "mind one's own business," the tortoise teaches us not only about existential time, but about the occupations to which one devotes oneself and their philosophical consequences. "June, July, and August, the tortoise eggs are hatching a few inches beneath the surface in sandy fields. You tell of active labors, of works of art, and wars the past summer; meanwhile the tortoise eggs underlie this turmoil."[95] The tortoise egg satisfies the ends of its own life despite the tumult of life on the surface.

Thoreau invites us to examine the tortoise as an example of inward development, a process honed in the persistent work of withdrawal toward the end of self-cultivation. Thoreau writes: "What events have transpired on the lit and airy surface three inches above them! Sumner knocked down; Kansas living an age of suspense."[96] Making a virtue of the tortoise's unwillingness to rise before its time, to arise in immaturity to a public frame of understanding and concern, Thoreau's *Journal* entry drives the paramount importance of philosophical exercise in the Hellenistic sense to the forefront of his existential concern.[97] Thoreau notes, "The young turtle spends its infancy in its shell. It gets experience and learns the way of the world through that wall."[98] The importance of the quote is not only the tortoise's understanding of time, but its understanding of itself within its own period of growth. The "wall" of the shell is the key to Thoreau's use of the tortoise as an example of philosophical exercise—it prepares itself with an eye to itself, cultivating a sense of inwardness that acts as a citadel against the distracting and fracturing realities of the "rash schemes" of the everyday world.[99]

The two quoted passages are not intended to disqualify the important readings of Thoreau's *Journal* undertaken by Cameron and Peck, but to indicate a different point of emphasis for my reading of the *Journal*, the correspondence, and Thoreau's canonical works. My argument, very simply, is that Thoreau engages in the ancient practice of practicing philosophical exercises for the purpose of strengthening the self toward public indifference. My reading of the *Journal* emphasizes Thoreau's lessons from nature *and* social life, oriented toward his philosophical development of a sense of self capable of indifference in political and social matters. In this sense, I argue, Thoreau's philosophy aspires toward a type of Stoicism; however, I do not feel that Thoreau is exclusively Stoic, or that Stoicism is *the* key to understanding his philosophy. Thoreau's philosophical work lends itself toward a Socratic interpretation of philosophy best practiced by the Roman Stoic Epictetus. On my reading, this complicates Thoreau's already complicated political theory: I read Thoreau's speeches and scattered writings on political action, most notably "Resistance to Civil Government," "Slavery in Massachusetts," and the John Brown essays, as fits or starts, episodes out of line with the philosophical temperament Thoreau attempts to create throughout his life. Taking political indifference as his apex, Thoreau delves into political activity only when his boundaries of indifference fail him.

Yielding to Privatism: Thoreau's Work of Politics

Understanding Thoreau as a political thinker interested primarily in negating the state's vital contribution to inner life, I characterize Thoreau as an aspiring privatist, an adherent of a political theory that electively dismisses political participation in favor of the amplification of private life. Privatism, as a political philosophy, concerns itself not with the organization of the state or the forms of discourse, but with a fundamental axiology of political participation itself. Privatism contests the *value* of the self's political participation, calling into question the existential worth of discourse, concern, and the everyday forms of nominal political participation. This contestable term has a short history, but it is used by Nancy Rosenblum in her *Another Liberalism: Romanticism and the Reconstruction of Liberal Thought* as a capsule of Thoreau's recalcitrant political thought. Rosenblum's major argument, that romantic individualisms operate according to a set of rules facilitated by liberalism's basic framework, takes special aim at the egregious individualism she finds within privatism. Beginning her argument, Rosenblum claims, "Freedom means just one thing to antipolitical souls: escape from victimhood."[100] Claiming that other forms of romantic individualism make a place for political life, Rosenblum holds that privatism is essentially a theory of individual victimhood, a set of selves too occupied with losing their possession of their own freedom (however it is construed) to constitute themselves as political actors. Under this view, privatism suffers as a sort of immature philosophy, one made for those who fail to outgrow the early stages of adolescence.

Rosenblum argues that "privatism is a condition of uncaring and unconcern."[101] Paying close attention to the detachment performed through the practice of political indifference, Rosenblum attacks the sentiments of privatism as overdrawn, overstated—even perhaps a little trite. It is clear that Rosenblum has no sympathy with the extreme of privatism, preferring the safe haven of liberal self-interest to privatist disinterest. She is correct, however, to point to disinterest as a fundamental segment of the privatist ethos. However, the practice of disinterest is not won out of victimhood, as Rosenblum states, but out of the course of natural events and the length of one's own impact on an increasingly complex political picture. Rosenblum is correct to emphasize the Stoics, whose practice of disinterest in the world is a major precursor to Thoreau's, but she pays insufficient attention to how political indifference (or disinterest) aims to insulate the individual not from becoming a victim, but from extending oneself beyond one's realm of influence. Privatism can exist as an authentic individualist philosophy born of a cognizant struggle with the facts of one's impact, importance, and fate.

Moving toward the Stoics, Rosenblum argues that the "stoic ideal is personal tranquility. There is nothing to be discovered or done; the only thing to achieve is resignation."[102] Using her explanation as an implicit critique, Rosenblum allows the foolishness of the statement to sink in, refusing the enticing offer to criticize Stoic thought with a dramatic dismissal. It appears, however, that this Stoic withdrawal is so absurd as to require rejoinder; indeed, much of Rosenblum's discussion of privatism is couched within the understanding that it does not require any sort of meaningful confrontation. We are not led, by Rosenblum or by other liberal theorists, to challenge the assumption that action morally trumps inaction. When searching for an origin to this study in withdrawal, Rosenblum argues, "One reason antipolitics appeals to some romantic sensibilities is its hatred of the world."[103] Rosenblum paints the picture of the "mortified victim" whose subsequent antipolitics establishes an "elitist ethos" of detachment. The resignation of the privatist becomes the comfort of the Stoic, finding internal peace within a coercive and troubling outside world.

Rosenblum lends several pictures of the privatist—the detached Stoic, the moralist Christian, and the beauty-driven aesthetician.[104] Thoreau could, of course, fit any of these categories at various points of textual analysis, but the overarching concern of his political life is with a theory of privatism that works out of radical simplification of one's life commitments, preparatory to engaging in experiments plumbing life for its vital value. Thoreau's comprehensive philosophy offers the vitalist view of privatism that Rosenblum never encounters in her study of romantic thought; indeed, although she works with and against Thoreau in the text, she never seriously engages his privatism. This work sympathizes with Thoreau's ethos of detachment and resists the urge to carry it back to a theory of democratic politics or a subaltern means of political engagement. Thoreau's philosophical lifework is to live and present to us a vitalist critique of political and social life that engages one's own inner life in a serious and comprehensive way, culminating in an existential personality oriented toward indifference to public matters. As such, Thoreau's thought becomes unique and nuanced within the various means of comprehending inwardness in nineteenth-century thought.

I rely on a generative argument that connects Thoreau's *Journal* and *Walden* in the following way: the *Journal*, on my reading, presents Thoreau's practical exercises in his philosophical ideal—simplification, indifference, vitalism. *Walden*, on the other hand, fulfills Thoreau's desire to enact his philosophy; Thoreau uses *Walden* to goad others toward undertaking acts of self-control and simplification. This use of the journals and the published work pushes the boundary of our understanding of Thoreau's political work. His political goals—sustained indifference amplified by recovering the fruits of freedom as wildness—arise from the repetitive daily work of wringing his valuative world of its external influences and building the inner citadel of self-control. Thoreau's work of becoming a philosopher leads him to nuanced conclusions about the value of political life—for instance, demanding that the gauge of democracy's value is its ability to provide vitality, arguing vehemently for an ever-enclosing provincialism in a communications and democratic revolution, and suggesting that nature can provide the existential benefit of shielding the self as well as the philosophical justification of political examples. Thoreau subjects politics to inquiry, forcing it to come to terms with his own development of the fullness of life.

The state of Thoreau's politics leans toward accepting an affirmative vision of democratic critique and alternative practice. This is nowhere clearer than in *A Political Companion to Henry David Thoreau*, a recent collection summarizing recent research in Thoreau's politics and offering outlines of future work. This work follows in the spirit of this movement forward insofar as Thoreau's politics have, in recent years, been made more complicated and nuanced due to considerations of his alternative practices of political participation, the performativity of his speeches, and his status as prophet of an increasingly secular America. In a sense, the project animating this book seems to be critical or perhaps anachronistic—I am, after all, arguing that Thoreau is not "political" in the complex sense contemporary research suggests. In a more important way, however, this work continues the trend of pushing for a more comprehensive vision of Thoreau's philosophy with respect to the rest of his life and work. The originality of this book resides in the willingness to suggest that Thoreau's major political essays do not occupy privileged space in his political theory, but that they obscure the relationship that Thoreau wishes to cultivate with the state. We can locate a more comprehensive and complicated political vision through Thoreau's wider work, giving us a vision of a theorist heavily invested in cultivating a serious philosophical mind and struggling to place political participation within that comprehensive vision.

My argument that Thoreau creates a political theory of privatism does indeed rely heavily on his "private" writings, particularly his *Journal*. This could, and perhaps should, raise a significant red flag. I would caution against dismissing Thoreau's *Journal* in this way on two fronts. First, to borrow from Sharon Cameron, Thoreau "came to think of the *Journal* as his central literary enterprise."[105] That is to say, Thoreau's *Journal* is not a diary in a pedestrian sense, but a complex production of the literary imagination that deserves its place as Thoreau's masterwork. That Thoreau's *Journal* went unpublished does not signify necessarily that the work was meant to be private; indeed, one could argue that the *Journal* could not have existed as a published manuscript in Thoreau's lifetime. Secondly, there is a fallacy in assuming that one's published or spoken work represents one's truest vision of thought or philosophy. Thoreau's major political speeches include bits of flair given for oratorical effect and survive in a mood of urgency, exasperation, and wonder that is representative of a rhetorical move aimed to create effect. The *Journal*—less distilled, more comprehensive, more imaginative, more varied—provides a clearer picture into the philosophical world of Thoreau's writing. Thoreau's private writings do not present a private philosophy, but they inform the nuance of his *privatism* that is espoused in the major essays.

Read in this light, Thoreau's bedrock contributions in "Resistance to Civil Government," "Slavery in Massachusetts," and "A Plea for Captain John Brown" emerge not as definitive statements of political moralism, but as fits of emotional investment controlled by Thoreau's recommitment to himself.

1

Reflective Simplification

The Questions of a Philosophical Life

One can read the bulk of Plato's treatments of Socrates as a project intended to magnify the importance of Socratic style—that is, the way in which Socrates practices philosophy.[1] For Thoreau, the method of philosophizing is of the first importance, and this chapter argues that reflective simplification serves as Thoreau's fundamental task for philosophy *and* the way in which the richness of one's philosophical life is evaluated. Reading reflective simplification into Thoreau's thought allows us to see the vitality behind his walks, observations, and dwellings in nature and in the town: "Perhaps I may say that I have never had a deeper and more memorable experience of life—its great serenity, than when listening to the trill of a tree-sparrow among the huckleberry bushes after a shower. It is a communication to which a man must attend in solitude and silence, and may never be able to tell his brother."[2]

This entry from September 28, 1843, clarifies the existential importance of the woods and its wildlife to Thoreau's own sense of being. A major purpose of Thoreau's endeavors is to feel life more deeply—and Thoreau devotes ample time in his life to experiencing these feelings of the serenity of life. What is not written in this passage, however, is that Thoreau's philosophical work prepares him for the stripped-down experience of hearing a tree-sparrow and understanding its impact upon him. Thoreau's philosophy may culminate in hearing what is in the world, but it begins with the painstaking process of simplifying his commitments and reflecting upon the necessities of existence. As Thoreau mentions in "Walking," only after one has given up one's life commitments can one be prepared for the sights and sounds of the walk.

Thoreau's employment of ancient philosophy is well known.[3] Pierre Hadot, a revolutionary figure in ancient philosophical interpretation, offers a reading of the first chapter of *Walden* that establishes Thoreau as a mixture of Epicureanism and Stoicism: "Thoreau wanted to devote himself to a certain mode of philosophical life that included, at the same time, manual labor and poverty, but also opened up to him an immensely enlarged perception of the world."[4] Hadot recognizes in Thoreau a conceptualization of philosophy similar to that of the Socratics—Hellenistic and Roman thinkers who inherit Socrates's method of philosophy—with a concentration on the philosophical life, realized through persistent spiritual exercise and constant awareness of the self. Writing about Marcus Aurelius, Hadot argues that Stoicism establishes a central task of philosophy: "It resides neither in sophistry, bookish dissertations, nor pretentious declamations, nor in ostentatiousness, but rather in simplicity."[5] Further enlarging the task of the Stoic philosopher, Hadot writes, "The fundamental attitude that the Stoic must maintain at each instant of his life is one of attention, vigilance, and continuous tension."[6] Hadot finds meaning within the steady and heedful work of maintaining an eye on oneself, aligning the practice of philosophy with the establishment of a few key principles and following them in daily exercise. Hadot notes that the Stoic requires a practice of "unrelaxing vigilance" on one's desires and affirmations, an ever-present eye required to keep one's life in check with itself.

This chapter argues that Thoreau equates philosophy with simplification, and that one overlooked purpose of the *Journal* is to develop and collect practical exercises in reflective simplification. *Walden*, consequently, represents Thoreau's record of having become a philosopher. The early *Journal* abounds with passages such as the following: "How shall I help myself? By withdrawing into the garret, and associating with spiders and mice—determining to meet myself face to face sooner or later."[7] Thoreau makes himself the object of his study and desperately strives to work himself out of the most basic interests of life, experimenting with the means by which he exerts a "constant retiring out of life."[8] Thoreau's *Journal*, viewed as a tool of his philosophical genesis, resembles the *Hupomnemata* discussed in Foucault's essay "Self Writing." Foucault argues: "No technique, no professional skill can be acquired without exercise; nor can the art of living, the *tekhne tou biou*, be learned without an *askesis* that should be understood as a training of the self by oneself."[9] Foucault recognizes that the primary form of self-training in ancient thought was through what he calls "self-writing," the act of using one's writing practices as a way of solidifying one's attention to daily life and the challenges of philosophical austerity. Thoreau endeavors to meet himself "face to face sooner or later," suggesting a taxing and demanding accounting of his own existential progress recorded through the *Journal*. As Thoreau writes *Walden*, however, he writes with the perplexity and the confidence of the budding sage, one whose life has situated itself within the prism of self-reflection and satisfaction with the self. The relationship between the two philosophical states is the subject of this chapter.

The Work of the Self

Thoreau's early interest in self-culture in the *Journal* owes its debt to Goethe, whose occupation with self-culture dominates Thoreau's understanding of the subject in his early productive years. Goethe's major contributions to Thoreau's early thought—a phenomenological disposition and steadfast attention to self-creation as a lived virtue—aid in propelling Thoreau forward as a theorist of self-cultivation. In the early *Journal* entries, Thoreau employs the endlessness of work as a way of developing a theory of working on the self: "Can he not wriggling, screwing, self-exhorting,—self-constraining, wriggle or screw out something that shall live—respected, intact, intangible . . ."[10] Existential labor is Thoreau's focus, and he employs it here (as in *Walden*) as an alternative to the instrumental labor of the large farm or small industry. In a *Journal* entry from May 21, 1839, Thoreau writes: "Who knows how incessant a surveillance a strong man may maintain over himself—how far subject passion and appetite to reason. . . . By a strong effort, may he not command even his brute body in unconscious moments?"[11]

   This rendering of Thoreau's constant watch over himself recalls Foucault's late lectures at the Collège de France, in which he distills an aesthetics of existence through rereading Hellenistic thought. Foucault writes: "Epictetus offers this advice: we should meditate (*meletan*), write (*graphein*), and train (*gumnazein*) . . . simply by writing we absorb the thing itself we are thinking about. We help it to be established in the soul."[12] In writing his devotion to self-surveillance, Thoreau is codifying his attempt to subject himself to reason, to become intellectually stronger. Foucault writes that "what others are to the ascetic in a community, the notebook is to the recluse."[13] Thoreau's *Journal* reflects the desire to make writing an action of the self upon the self, a self-reflexive means of stock-taking that keeps Thoreau responsible to himself.

Reflective simplification becomes Thoreau's way of defending the philosophical life, leading toward a full exposition of simplification in *Walden*. Thoreau's *Journal* offers an ongoing working out of the philosophical work of reflective simplification. In one of Thoreau's early *Journal* entries, he offers a self-reflexive admonition to himself: "I find my life growing slovenly when it does not exercise a constant supervision over itself. Its deeds accumulate."[14] Thoreau's early *Journal* entries often reflect the state of his philosophical education, demonstrating the persistent exercise of developing a philosophical self. In an entry entitled "Discipline," Thoreau writes: "I yet lack discernment to distinguish the whole lesson of to-day; but it is not lost—it will come to me at last. My desire is to know *what* I have lived, that I may know *how* to live henceforth."[15] Thoreau's attention to himself—his "constant supervision" in the first *Journal* entry—invites comparison to the *askesis* of Hellenistic and Roman thought.

The Method of Simplification in Stoic Thought

Thoreau's beginning to his magnum opus, his *Journal* spanning nearly twenty-five years of his life, is a tip of the hat to Ralph Waldo Emerson, his mentor who lends him the idea to begin writing daily. Much has been made of Thoreau's fascinating friendship with Emerson, a union simultaneously beneficial and hindering to Thoreau's literary career and reputation. Thoreau works out his side of the friendship through his journals, where he offers several appraisals and recollections of the friendship gone sour. None of Thoreau's reflections or analyses is more poignant than the one he makes on January 31, 1852, remarking, "Emerson is too grand for me He belongs to the nobility & wears their cloak and manners—is attracted to Plato not to Socrates—I fear partly because the latters life & associates were too humble. I am a commoner."[16]

Thoreau makes the connection between himself and Socrates, as well as connecting Emerson to Plato. Thoreau's argument is not simply that Socrates's status as "commoner" is what separates him from Plato, but that Socratic philosophy is one that is more common—more practical—and less systematic than Plato's. Similarly, scholars will argue that Thoreau's thought is less systematic than Emerson's and that Thoreau's legacy suffers as a result. That Thoreau connects Emerson with Plato also suggests that Thoreau himself does not connect—is not attracted to—Platonic philosophy. Indeed, one finds scant reference to Plato in Thoreau's work. Instead, Thoreau's philosophy carries the spirit of Socratic thinking, particularly practically oriented exercises in simplification and acknowledgment of nature.

Thoreau's identification with Socrates is an identification with the method of philosophy as a way of life. Thoreau's admission to being a "commoner" suggests that he wants little *from* philosophy, and certainly no accolades or school; also, however, it provides a compelling counter to Emerson's famous eulogy of Thoreau, in which he expresses grave disappointment in Thoreau's lack of drive. Thoreau here preemptively responds with the declaration that for himself, the practice on the self that constitutes philosophy is the primary determinant of the value of his life. Emerson moves away from Socrates in the sense that he demands something external to philosophy from philosophy as its fruits, thus carrying him even further from Socratic odes of voluntary poverty, integrity in the face of death, and the education of young students. Thoreau defends the intimate connection between philosophy and life, seeing "the care of the self," to use Foucault's terms, as "a permanent obligation for every individual throughout his life."[17]

Thoreau's simplification echoes themes in Marcus Aurelius, who deals more than other Stoic thinkers with the intransigent world of worldly goods and obligations. When he states in his *Meditations* that "the happy life depends on the fewest possible things,"[18] we know this is a philosophical position earned out of the drudgery of daily struggle with wealth, power, inheritance, self-importance, and the flattery of others. Marcus Aurelius is a philosopher who chooses simplification as method not out of necessity but out of the experience of living the abundant life and finding it wanting. Thoreau, writing of the importance of the newspaper, worries: "Think of admitting the details of a single case of the criminal court into our thoughts, to stalk profanely through their very *sanctum sanctorum* for an hour."[19] Knowledge and wealth are but two of many types of abundance, each demanding the philosopher's attention. Simplification, then, becomes a matter of existential defense.

Thoreau's learning in the Bill Wheeler eulogy resembles the important education Marcus Aurelius acknowledges in the opening pages of his *Meditations*. In particular, Marcus Aurelius notes that his tutor teaches him "to have few wants, and to do my own work, and mind my own concerns; and to turn a deaf ear to slander."[20] He is in this case practicing toward achieving the independence that comes from radically simplifying one's life commitments. What, however, is the purpose behind simplification? It is to "school thyself to live that life only which is thine, namely the present, so shalt thou be able to pass through the remnant of thy days calmly, kindly, and at peace with thine own 'genius.'"[21] Simplification offers one a bare look at one's own life, serving as a ground from which a philosophical investigation into vital values can take place. Marcus Aurelius is keenly aware of the determination of his own existence, its radical contingency, and its incommensurability with the complicating avenues of dreams, regrets, or empty hopes.

Reflective simplification is the philosophical method that reduces life to the classic Stoic concept of one's "own." Marcus Aurelius argues that his philosophical goal is to arrive at the point of saying: "*I have to the full what is my own.*"[22] Identifying the crusade of ownness with the "ruling reason," he articulates: "Never forget that the ruling reason shews itself unconquerable when, concentrated in itself, it is content with itself."[23] Here we see not victimhood but reasonable appropriation of one's own commitments and potentiality. Marcus Aurelius absolves himself of the concerns to which he can offer no action, hoping instead to instill within himself respect for that which appears before him. In this sense, he is reducing his horizon, using philosophy not as a tool for expanding one's purview but for contracting it. Reflective simplification requires a consistent effort, because one's life is always drawn to expansion, to craving more outside of oneself. In one of Thoreau's early essays, "The Service," he states that "bravery deals not so much in resolute action, as healthy and assured rest."[24] Marcus Aurelius develops a similar philosophy, finding philosophy's most difficult work in teaching one not to concern oneself with indifferents, either one's own or those of another.

Reflective simplification offers three avenues of study: "Thou hast three relationships—the first to the vessel thou art contained in; the second to the divine Cause wherefrom issue all things to all; and the third to those that dwell with thee."[25] Later Stoicism is perhaps best known for its articulations of the first two of these three relationships, but Marcus Aurelius, a ruler, is keenly aware of the difficulties in managing the third. He makes, on the one hand, statements such as "That which is not in the interest of the hive cannot be in the interest of the bee,"[26] signifying a dedication to collective norms and pursuits that defies individualist articulation. Marcus Aurelius's existential position is not the radical individualist, but the reticent ruler aiming to apprehend the tools of living the good life: "So keep thyself a simple and good man, uncorrupt, dignified, plain, a friend of justice, god-fearing, gracious, affectionate, manful in doing thy duty."[27] His major attention is not to the duties to which he must pay heed, but the problems those duties provide in terms of evaluating one's life. He supports the fulfillment of duty, but only when performed with full understanding of duty's ability to bind one in an intractable social position. Philosophy invokes the words *purity, divinity, genius, independence*—all terms poisoned by interaction with social values. Political life overtakes one's consciousness, leading to the question "What is my mind now occupied with? Fear? Suspicion? Concupiscence? Some other like thing?"[28]

Marcus Aurelius lives the connections between himself and his environs; as such, he does not imply or think a world separated from his world existentially. Simplification, in this sense, does not mean withdrawal but the virtue of putting things in their proper place. The dangers of political life come not from living amongst others but from allowing the closeness to others to trigger one's passions in an unfit way. Virtue, then, is a matter of keeping oneself on the track to which nature places that self. As Hadot argues, "Living beings experience joy when they fulfill the function for which they are made, and act in accordance with their nature."[29] Finding one's nature requires stripping off functions, whether they are created by the self, institutions, or one's neighbors. Marcus Aurelius's philosophy is persistent and repetitive, digging more deeply into the same basic problems and questions, vexing the reader with its inability to move past a point. However, if we view Marcus Aurelius as a thinker primarily absorbed in processes of reflective simplification, his philosophy comes into focus as exercises in determining the limits of one's commitments and engagements.

Marcus Aurelius uses his method of simplification to enhance the view of the everyday, much in the same way that Thoreau will in the *Journal*. Foucault finds: "All of this—this gaze on the representative object that must reveal it in the naked state, in its totality, and in its elements—is what Marcus Aurelius calls *blepein*. That is to say: looking closely, contemplating well, fixing your eyes on, acting so that nothing escapes you, neither the object in its singularity, freed from its surroundings, naked, [nor] in its totality and its particular elements."[30]

Simplification is a preparatory method that is both tested through the vision of the everyday and buttresses the importance of that vision for the self. Foucault mentions that, for Marcus Aurelius, "his analytical examination will thus have the value of freedom for the soul."[31] Marcus Aurelius develops a method of envisioning that aims to comprehensively study his world, but he must first prepare himself to undertake a radical re-visioning of the landscape. Simplification opens the possibility for us to properly evaluate nature—that is, to place a value upon nature that reflects its vital contributions and its relation to us. Foucault finds that this relates to Epictetus's "stroll-exercise": "We take a walk outside and look at what is going on around us."[32]

The primary focus of simplification for Marcus Aurelius reduces our desires for things to their (undesirable) elements. Our wants are the result of miscategorizing our options, of placing external value upon things: "There are other exercises in Marcus Aurelius that are also analytical exercises, but this time bearing on the decomposition of things into their material elements. . . . Basically, what is a cooked dish that we like to eat with so much pleasure? Remember that it is the carcass of an animal. It is a dead beast. What is this *praetexta* bearing the famous *laticlave* that is so envied? Well, it is wool and dye. What is wool? It is hair, sheep's hair. What is the dye? It is blood, the blood of a shellfish."[33]

Marcus Aurelius repeatedly practices the reduction of things to their material elements as a way of achieving a sense of freedom over them; of course, as we know from Foucault's rendering of Stoic thought, this freedom is always precarious, constantly in harm's way due to the nature of desire and our fastidious attention to the offerings of the environment. Foucault notices that Marcus Aurelius, like Epictetus, fashions a notion of self-writing that creates and recreates maxims of freedom over the domination of externals. Clearly, Marcus Aurelius finds himself unable to permanently conquer the enemies of the free self, and his philosophy becomes the persistent struggle to keep them in check.

Writing and Living Philosophy

Stanley Cavell's *The Senses of Walden* remains the hallmark treatment of Thoreau's text as a piece of philosophy. Cavell, arguing early in the text that Thoreau is the heroic figure of his own book, claims, "For the writer of *Walden*, its task is epitomized in discovering what writing is and, in particular, what writing *Walden* is."[34] Cavell homes in on Thoreau's writing of *Walden*, orienting his phenomenological look into the experience of reading the text as an entry point into the purpose for writing it: "Once in it, there seems no end; as soon as you have one word to cling to, it fractions or expands into others.

This is one reason that he says, 'There are more secrets in my trade than in most men's . . . inseparable from its very nature.' . . . But we do not yet know much else about that trade."[35]

Cavell's choice to make his book about reading *Walden* is clear from the outset, where he quotes first from the "Reading" chapter of *Walden* and makes the early claim that Thoreau is writing a heroic text. Cavell argues that Thoreau is interested in writing "the nation's *first* epic, so it must represent the bringing of language to the nation."[36] Cavell's reading of *Walden* is enormously successful primarily because it makes *Walden* necessary as a literary exercise but, more importantly, as an account of scriptural truth.

Cavell's intersecting interests of writing and scripture transform our understanding of *Walden*, giving the text a unique status in nineteenth-century American literature. Thoreau is, according to Cavell, attempting to bring America to maturity by giving it the scripture it requires to come to a sense of itself and its purpose. The setting alongside Walden Pond is important, given that Thoreau's scripture performs the two necessary baptisms: the baptism of water (via the pond) and the baptism "of the spirit, by the word of words. This is immersion not in the water but in the book of Walden."[37] Cavell makes the case that *Walden* constitutes a modern scripture using the fundamental characteristics of prophecy: "(1) their wild mood swings between lamentation and hope . . . (2) the periodic confusions of their authors' identities with God's . . . (3) their mandate to create wretchedness and nervousness . . . (4) their immense repetitiveness."[38]

The four characteristics of prophecy and the prophet structure the argument that Thoreau is composing a secular scripture, a prophecy of the present, but its primary function is to tie the content of *Walden* to the act of writing the book. Each characteristic of the prophet is contained within the book—but is also (and more importantly) contained within the writing of the book.

Cavell's interesting analysis of "The Bean-Field" suggests that the use of obvious metaphor (Thoreau hoeing beans in order to serve him as a story one day) is in fact a mockery of nineteenth-century parables of nature. What, then, is Thoreau doing in the chapter? "Hoeing serves the writer as a trope— in particular, a metaphor—for writing. In the sentences preceding his little parable of the hoer-hero, the writer has linked these two labors of the hand: 'It will bear some iteration in the account, for there was no little iteration in the labor.'[39]

According to Cavell, Thoreau's major metaphors serve to communicate the necessity of writing *Walden* in order to solidify the prophet's call to heed his generation. Cavell beautifully establishes the mood swings of the "Bean-Field" chapter, locating Thoreau's transition to solemnity and out again toward the end of the chapter. The mood swings of the prophet are also the lamentations and hopes of the writer: "Hoeing is . . . also an emblem of the physical act of writing."[40] Cavell's most important passage from *Walden*—Thoreau's early desire to improve time and "notch it on his stick"—clarifies the purpose of writing the text: "The notching must mark not simply the occurrence of time but the improvement of it . . . the act of marking must itself be the improvement."[41]

Cavell invokes the work of writing to such a degree in his analysis of *Walden* as to refer to Thoreau as "the writer" countless times in the text. Replacing the proper name Thoreau with "the writer" recreates Thoreau's identity and his fundamental purpose in *Walden*. Cavell suggests to us through his renaming that Thoreau becomes *the* writer and the *writer*, each characterization extending the distance between Thoreau's existence and its representation on the page through words. *Walden*, under this strenuous and rewarding reading, is a text about text, a work of philosophy that is consumed in its own manifest destiny, a written prophecy tied to the fortunes of the nation-state and the (impossible) redemption of the worker's quiet desperation. Cavell's extraordinary success with this treatment of *Walden* manages to submerge the metaphors of the text under the root metaphors of writing and the writer. Even those chapters that rebuke reading and writing, such as "Sounds," become the lamentations of the insufficiencies of language; that is, "Sounds" begins to read like a *writer*'s frustration. Look at the final paragraph of *The Senses of Walden:* "The boon of Walden is *Walden*. Its writer cups it in his hand, sees his reflection in it, and holds it out to us. It is his promise, in anticipation of his going, and the nation's, and Walden's. He is bequeathing it to us in his will, the place of the book and the book of the place."[42]

To say that the book is the fulfillment of Thoreau's promise is more than a self-evident truth; Cavell argues that the genesis, work, and outcome of the book are the promise—that the book about the writing of a book is the promise of the book and the writing of it. Thoreau (as the writer) sees his reflection and lets us see it as well. Cavell's *Walden* is the prophetic text of America and the writer.

Cavell's reading of *Walden* remains the standard examination of the text with good reason. No philosopher has taken such a comprehensive examination of the text's meaning or created a rich theoretical work of its own from Thoreau's pages. My reading of *Walden* is heavily influenced by Cavell's, with some important distinctions. My first and most important source of disagreement is with Cavell's major premise, that *Walden's* purpose is to establish Thoreau as "the writer." On my reading, Thoreau's root metaphor is not writing but philosophizing, leading away from the characterization of the prophet and toward that of the sage.

Edward McGushin's analysis of Foucault's late lectures helps to frame the distinction between the prophet and the sage. Foucault characterizes the truth of the prophet in the way "the prophet must constitute his subjectivity in the form of 'mediation.' That is, the prophet does not speak in his own voice but is the voice of the beyond, the voice of the gods."[43] The prophet is bound to speak the truth as a testament to the gods and speaks with the knowledge of the future. The sage, on the other hand, presents truth in a different register: "The sage speaks in her own name and speaks the wisdom that belongs to her, which is her own possession. . . . The sage constitutes her subjectivity through a withdrawal from the everyday world and is characterized by reticence. For this reason the sage does not feel an obligation to speak her wisdom, but chooses instead to remain silent and to live apart from others. When petitioned the sage will speak, but like the prophet, will speak enigmatically."[44]

Thoreau's *Walden* constitutes his fundamental affirmation of his wisdom and ascension to the level of American sage. Though not known himself as the "sage of Concord," Thoreau uses *Walden* to demonstrate the philosophical intensity of his withdrawal and its bearing on his understanding of key philosophical concepts: "so to love wisdom as to live according to its dictates, a life of simplicity, independence, magnanimity, and trust. It is to solve some of the problems of life, not only theoretically, but practically."[45] Thoreau uses *Walden* as the proving ground for the exercises in philosophical training he records in the *Journal*. This element of understanding adds to the complexity of Thoreau's masterpiece and its creative beginnings.

Thoreau's *Journal:* Admonishments of Simplification

Thoreau's *askesis*, reflected particularly in the pre-*Walden Journal* entries, retains the force of Foucault's characterization of self-writing and helps to establish one purpose behind Thoreau's *Journal* as a work of philosophy. Thoreau's admonishments within the *Journal* read as reminders to himself—although the *Journal* is not strictly a private document, Thoreau remains its most persistent and involved reader—to reacquaint himself with the philosophical virtue of reflective simplification. Take, for example, this entry from early August 1850: "It is not easy to make our lives respectable to ourselves by any course of activity—We have repeatedly to withdraw ourselves into our shels of thought like the tortoise—somewhat helplessly—& yet there is even more than philosophy in that. I do not love to entertain doubts and questions."[46]

This entry anticipates Thoreau's desire to live a life that is respected, and not merely respectable, in *Walden*, but it also points to the ambiguities of the work on the self that Thoreau engages. Thoreau enlivens the work on the self by demonstrating his hesitance to its demands, noting that he finds himself withdrawn into thought "somewhat helplessly." We may be quick to assume that Thoreau's philosophical sensibility comes through the force of will, but Thoreau reminds us that the exercise of philosophical life goads and prompts us from our desire to experience the satisfaction of maintaining assumptions. Not many of us "love to entertain doubts and questions," but Thoreau nonetheless continues to entertain them in order to produce a self that reflects his own ambitions.

Thoreau's glorification of the work of selfhood (what I choose to call "ownness," following both Epictetus and Stirner) exists even in the earliest entries of the *Journal*. In an entry on March 5, 1838, Thoreau writes: "Such is man—toiling, heaving, struggling, ant-like—to shoulder some stray unappropriated crumb, and deposit it in his granary. . . . And is he doomed ever to run the same course? Can he not wriggling, screwing, self-exhorting,—self-constraining, wriggle or screw out something that shall live—respected, intact, intangible, not to be sneezed at?"[47]

Thoreau first chastises the social valuation of "busyness," reacting to the common charge that his lifestyle makes him a "Dolittle." Interestingly, Thoreau laments the perpetuity of work and its subterranean psychological correlate but finds himself pining for a similarly perpetual and subterranean work of his own: "Why not live a hard and emphatic life?"[48] Thoreau's charge here is that the self finds itself working for meager rewards, and constrained by the meager rewards to perpetuate the cycle of labor. Are the rewards of a philosophical life greater? For Thoreau, philosophy also offers limited reward, but the reward remains with the self as its own. To follow his remark in *Walden,* the work of philosophy maintains that one's drudgery remains one's own, while labor in the marketplace becomes the perpetuation of *"aes alienum,* another's brass."

Thoreau's clarification of the value of his work reflects a lifelong desire to place philosophy in the service of joy. Thoreau's *Journal* is replete with brief reflections like the following from late 1846: "Think what a mean and wretched place this world is—that half the time we have to light a lamp that we may see to live in't."[49] After this passage, Thoreau writes, "Then we are begotten and our life has its source from what a trivial and sensual pleasure."[50] Thoreau here locates the work of philosophy as a constant overcoming of the mood of emptiness, the ennui that haunts Thoreau's vocationally unsuccessful early years. Thoreau writes the mood in order to memorialize it, but also to remind him of its power; it has, in this case, worked through Thoreau to exhibit a renunciation of nature and of his own life. The two targets in these quotes add solemnity to the quick reflections. Thoreau doubts the majesty of the world and the sanctity of the self. Later in the same passage, he remarks: "It is only your lean men that have a word to say about life & the philosophies— The full orbed belly well encased in fat in no place worn down to the bone rolls through the world without a creak or sound."[51] Philosophical growth requires the overcoming of obstacles, even those that are self-produced. Indeed, we could see Thoreau's decision to spend two years at Walden Pond as the manufacture of a problem that requires the hardening of the self.

Thoreau's laboring toward philosophy comes in the service of joy. Sherman Paul notes in his comprehensive study of Thoreau, *The Shores of America:* "Emerson's doctrines were directed to the end of power, Thoreau's to the end of joy."[52] Paul argues that this accounts for much of the discrepancy between Emerson and Thoreau, but it also explains the rationale behind Thoreau's engagement with simplification. In an entry from January 8, 1842, Thoreau writes: "What offends me most in my compositions is the moral element in them. . . . Strictly speaking morality is not healthy."[53] Thoreau's simplification, exemplified in this case, is reflective and intensive. Reflecting upon his own writings, Thoreau finds an alien morality within them, or an inability to properly place the moral in its context. Thoreau's inward battle with his moralizing tendency carries an overarching lens throughout his work; indeed, as I will demonstrate in a later chapter, Thoreau's reform papers display the difficulties involved in Thoreau's attempt to free himself from the constraints and applications of morality.

Thoreau hangs on to the practices of simplifying his life commitments in order to achieve a fullness of joy. Thoreau mentions in an early *Journal* entry that "simplicity is exuberant."[54] The self enhances life through reducing the affairs to which it attends. Once we insert desire into our inner life and free it from the constraints of approval or historical meaning, simplification becomes a powerful tool in the service of presence and the cultivation of inwardly meaningful private life. Simplification invites individuals to make their own lives: "I take some satisfaction in eating my food, as well as being nourished by it. I feel well at dinner-time as well as after it. The world will never find out why you don't love to have your bed tucked up for you—why you will be so perverse. I enjoy more drinking water at a clear spring than out of a goblet at a gentleman's table. I like best the bread which I have baked, the garment which I have made, the shelter which I have constructed, the fuel which I have gathered."[55]

This important entry finds Thoreau reducing his valuations to simple necessities of life: eating, drinking, clothing, and shelter. These familiar themes from *Walden* allow us to envision Thoreau simplifying his life and philosophy to its four basic elements. But Thoreau is also alerting us to the joyful affirmation of simplifying one's basic choices. Finding joy in food requires a valuation of the growing of the food, preparing of the food, eating of the food, and digestion of the food. By taking ourselves out of one or more of these processes, we complicate our ability to properly evaluate our basic life choices. Thoreau's withdrawal is not one of victimhood, but of strength, power, self-reliance, and determination. Thoreau offers a reflectively simplified view of the hero, one who owns the commitments and engagements of his own private and finite life.

Thoreau believes to have isolated an essential temperament of the philosopher through the practices of simplification and voluntary poverty: "It is always a recommendation to me to know that a man has ever been poor, has been regularly born into this world, knows the language. I require to be assured of certain philosophers that they have once been barefooted, footsore, have eaten a crust because they had nothing better, and know what sweetness resides in it."[56]

Thoreau holds voluntary poverty as a virtue of simplification, feeling that he comes closer to an understanding of himself through the advantages poverty offers. Thoreau formulates poverty as a restriction of choice—which, if we are to understand him correctly, gives advantage to the simplifying practices. Withdrawal from fashionable social or political activity, working on a restricted plane of opportunity, the philosopher exposes himself to a life without distractions, one preparatory to new and exciting endeavors. Simplification in this case turns the social problematic of poverty—which may be the poverty of culture, manners, friends—into a virtue. The horizon of experience prevents individuals from coming to a full understanding of another self; as a result, the boundedness of our experience leads to an opportunity to introspect, come to grips with the variegated moods and mannerisms of individual life, in order to enrich the experience of the self comprehensively.

Thoreau spends a good deal of time working out the individual's relationship to his work and the importance of that work for the cultivation of the self. In a letter to Blake, Thoreau argues that "they who seek honestly and sincerely, with all their hearts and lives and strength, to earn their bread, do earn it, and it is sure to be very sweet to them. A very little bread—a very few crumbs are enough, if it be of the right quality, for it is infinitely nutritious. Let each man, then, earn at least a crumb of bread for his body before he dies, and know the taste of it—that it is identical with the bread of life, and that they both go down at one swallow."[57]

Thoreau's work ties itself to simplification. The self has the opportunity to get his living by simplified means—in Thoreau's life, through surveying or hoeing beans at Walden Pond. The importance is not the work, nor its contribution to society, but the contribution the self makes to its own life. The work of an individual is commensurate with that individual's life. This conclusion leads Thoreau to declare that too much work, either on one's own behalf or on behalf of others, is unhealthy for the self's life. Simplification includes getting one's living, but not transforming one's labor into a project that outstretches the self's natural boundaries. It is up to individual selves to establish and cultivate work habits that facilitate virtue, but we cannot go too far, lest we risk losing that integrity we receive through working for ourselves.

Simplification emphasizes the self's confidence in its ability to follow its own desires and live through withdrawal, refreshment, and return. Once Thoreau manages to simplify his life satisfactorily (for the moment), he feels a vital strength rise within himself: "But whatever we do we must do confidently (if we are timid, let us, then, act timidly), not expecting more light, but having light enough. . . . If one hesitates in his path, let him not proceed. Let him respect his doubts, for doubts, too, may have some divinity in them.

. . . When, in the progress of life, a man swerves, though only by an angle infinitely small, from his proper and allotted path . . . then the drama of his life turns to tragedy, and makes haste to its fifth act."[58]

Our confidence in ourselves comes from dealing with the world and our opportunities as they present themselves to us, and acting on the vital values we establish in order to live with consummate self-reliance. The path we may establish for ourselves is a plot that should be altered only by ourselves; if we cannot affirm a change in our lives, we should not follow that change. This is not, however, an example of Thoreau's moralizing of individual life; much to the contrary, in fact, Thoreau demonstrates that all too often our lives lose their course by gaining a moral sense, and thus we hand our vital strength to the institutions that desire us for our strength. The moral sense reduces to a feeling of duty; as a result, those who would move off their own path, then, "are cursed with *duties,* and the *neglect of their duties.*"[59]

Thoreau's affirmation of life depends on the simplified response to the pleasures of the world. When Harrison Blake asks Thoreau if he knows anything of sorrow, Thoreau responds: "I know comparatively little. My saddest and most genuine sorrows are apt to be but transient regrets. The place of sorrow is supplied, perchance, by a certain hard and proportionally barren indifference. . . . I am too easily contented with a slight and almost animal happiness. My happiness is a good deal like that of the woodchucks."[60]

Importantly, Thoreau does not argue that the hardness of life lies in sorrow, but in the active opposition of forces inimical to the self. Simplification, in its orientation toward the world, provides Thoreau the chance to engage in joyful practices without the need to complicate matters through requirements, manners, or necessary duties. The simplified view of life occupies the space of joyful affirmation in its most comprehensive sense, with the self given the utmost directive through apprehension of presence. Thoreau often compares himself to the animals he sees, at least in part because their happiness is vital, not historically constituted but grounded in pure sensation. The woodchuck, in Thoreau's example, does not carry with it an institutional guilt—it is not motivated by the desire to affix itself to social norms or construct moralities to defend itself against the desires of the flesh.

Our inability to experience joy in affirmative contexts stems from submitting to others in the production of our happiest experiences: "I never in all my walks came across a man engaged in so simple and natural an occupation as building his house. We belong to the community. . . . Where is this division of labor to end? and what object does it finally serve? No doubt another may also think for me; but it is not therefore desirable that he should do so to the exclusion of my thinking for myself."[61]

Thoreau argues that through giving in to the comforts of community, we engage in a trap: we complicate our lives in an attempt to simplify them. Thoreau's philosophy recognizes the fundamental shifts in individual life occurring through increasing externalization in America's advancing industrial economy. Daniel Walker Howe explains Thoreau's relationship to the changing shape of work: "Practicing thrift as a form of spiritual discipline, Thoreau turned his back on the consumer products that his countrymen embraced so eagerly. Yet he did not scorn the industrial revolution; he felt in awe of the railroad trains that passed not far from his cabin."[62] Thoreau is expert at reducing the lens of everyday life to questions of personal identity. For Thoreau, the transformation of the self under market democracy involves shifting from the corporeal, experiencing personal identity to an ideal, imaginary public identification. Thoreau engages this problematic in everyday terms because the quest for identity is not a metaphysical battle, but a sociopolitical one. Thoreau can appreciate the ingenuity of the locomotive while keeping his critical eye on the existential application of the train's meaning. Thoreau's argument that "we belong to the community" means that the community is taking us away—the process of capitalism and democracy, promising to ease our burdens, causes the complication that comes with the loss of personal identity.

Thoreau's method of simplification has to allow the focus on collective understandings of truth to give way to the primacy of perception. "Who shall say what *is*? He can only say *how* he *sees*."[63] Peck argues that one purpose of Thoreau's *Journal* is to "emphasize the primary, defining, phenomenological qualities of the thing in itself."[64] Thoreau's *Journal* presents the fruits of having simplified the demands upon his perception, and the tendency to allow the *how* of his vision to vitalize his senses. Peck further argues that parts of the *Journal* "strive toward an objectivist, presentational view of the world."[65] Take a representative sample of Thoreau's "presentational view":

On the pitch pine plain at first the pines are far apart—with—a wiry grass between & golden rod & hard hack & St Johns-wort & blackberry vines—each tree nearly keeping down the grass for a space about itself—meditating to make a forest floor. & here & there younger pines are springing up. . . .[66]

Saw a maple *in the water* with yellowish flowers. Is it the water brings them forward? But I believe that these are all the barren flowers—& the perfect flowers appear afterward.—When I look closely I perceive the sward beginning to be green under my feet—very slightly. . . .[67]

At first the bare ground showed itself in the middle of the road & rapidly widened giving the birds wider pasture; then the grass in the fields began to peep through & the landscape to acquire a russet hue again.[68]

In each case we find Thoreau at various points of his mature life—late summer 1851, middle spring 1852, middle spring 1854—describing the results of a walk. These representative samples of Thoreau's reporting demonstrate the hold that he keeps on the primacy of perception, not trying to create or recreate a natural fact but to commit to his own memory the way in which he perceives the emergence of the grass in spring or the emergence of new pines in the forest. Thoreau in this case describes not *what* he sees so much as *how* he sees—honing his perception, taking a closer look, accepting first impressions but not giving them authoritative standing, paying close attention to minute changes, stating tentative convictions, attending to the evidence of flowering and its possible causes—in a way that is more than merely presentational. Thoreau is showing the *how* of his world.

More than reporting the conditions of the pines or the possibility of a flowering spring, Thoreau is performing an examination of his perceptive powers. Reflective simplification requires the persistence of challenges to one's perceptions and opportunities to focus on how one sees the surrounding landscape. Thoreau does not record observations of nature *merely* to test his philosophical sensibility, but the requisite training for a life of simplification continually peeks into his observations and perceptions. When Thoreau records a perception in his *Journal*, part of that record is the record of his ability to pare down the world, to be able to employ his senses and take seriously his own mandate to reduce the scope of his life. Thoreau's attention to political matters takes on the same character of the challenge. If Thoreau is prepared well enough through the practice of reflective simplification, he can recuse himself of externals and concentrate on the basic phenomena of his everyday life. Thus, the world becomes for Thoreau a twofold test of his

Socratic hold on himself: can he leave politics alone, and can he manage to perceive his world in its most minute details without rushing to make extravagant claims about it?

The Questions of *Walden*

Epictetus presents a Socratic philosophy that distills the ancient practice of philosophy into a discursive run of *elenctic* and *protreptic* questions and examinations, perpetuating foundational questions about the importance of a philosophical life. Epictetus inherits the Socratic method and enforces it with the young students who attend his lessons. A. A. Long argues: "Epictetus involves his audience continuously. His questions are ways of getting them to interrogate themselves, and his responses or illustrations are equally designed to shatter complacency and effect a transformation of consciousness."[69]

Epictetus employs the Socratic *elenchus*, a method of cross-examination where one's interlocutor is responsible for supplying a definition, only to have that definition undermined as a way of demonstrating the interlocutor's distance from philosophical understanding, but Epictetus also weaves the *protrepsis* as a Socratic method as well. The *protreptic* involves one making one's case by employing a string of exhortations meant to prod one's interlocutors into self-examination. The *elenctic* and the *protreptic* are used by Epictetus throughout his teachings, modified to include numerous rhetorical questions in rapid succession and shorter exhortations. Long convincingly argues that Epictetus's method is primarily an adaptation and updating of the Socratic method.

Of the myriad ways of studying *Walden*, Thoreau's persistent use of rhetorical questions is paid little attention. The book begins with questions, not of Thoreau's but of the recreational curiosity of Concord's townspeople that force the book and its intensely personal focus to come to light. People ask Thoreau about his "mode of life," including his food, loneliness, charity, and other related concerns. Thoreau responds: "I will therefore ask my readers who feel no interest in me to pardon me if I undertake to answer some of these questions in this book."[70] Thoreau is toying with himself and his audience, because those who have no particular interest in him would not care to read a book that is, ostensibly, *only* about him. But the passage also alerts us to the fact that Thoreau's book is in the business of answering questions, and questions continually haunt the text. Thoreau demonstrates, as I will argue, that by asking the questions he also answers them—that is, in nudging his readers toward reflective simplification, he answers the call of the questions continually asked. Thoreau uses the ubiquity of his questions as a sign of the maturity of his philosophical exercises and the material that forces a psychic shift in the student.

Thoreau's method of Socratic questioning in *Walden* is simple: each question is an admonishment, a challenge to one to concern oneself with one's life, to simplify one's commitments and render a natural life. The first questions Thoreau asks in the text refer to those who have the "misfortune" of inheriting farms: "Who made them serfs of the soil? Why should they eat their sixty acres, when man is condemned to eat only his peck of dirt? Why should they begin digging their graves as soon as they are born?"[71]

These questions reinforce Thoreau's claim to the misfortune of acquiring property, and their rapid-fire nature is meant to place the reader in an uncomfortable place of forced acknowledgment of his or her ignorance. Thoreau repeats the exercise three pages later: "Look at the teamster on the highway, wending to market by day or night; does any divinity stir within him? . . . What is his destiny to him compared with the shipping interests? Does he not drive for Squire Make-a-stir? How godlike, how immortal is he?"[72]

Thoreau fulfills the prompts that lead to the construction of the book. He is going about answering questions simply by asking them. The effect on the reader is to promote the reader's contestations of inner life. Thoreau utilizes the rhetorical question in order to reduce the reader, to make reflective simplification the necessary consequence of having read the text.

It is important to note that Thoreau addresses the questions with a certain population in mind: "Perhaps these pages are more particularly addressed to poor students."[73] Although Thoreau does not preclude any reader, his decision to teach young students about the subject of economy and life in the woods is telling.[74] Thoreau's use of persistent questioning is a philosophical device that echoes Epictetus's educational strategy in *Discourses*. Epictetus employs the method in ways like the following: "Do you wish, then, to know whether you have received any good? Produce your judgments, philosopher. What does desire promise? Not to fail in getting. What does aversion? Not to fall into what we are avoiding. Well, do we fulfil their promise?"[75]

Epictetus argues by offering questions to which students already know the answer, and following that question with another question, in a way that reminds us of Socrates's aim at getting toward truth. Epictetus's *Discourses* prods students not to answer the question, but to feel the effect of the question upon their lives. Questioning, for Epictetus, produces an existential crisis in the life of the student. Thoreau mentions, in the first chapter of *Walden*, that "our moulting season, like that of the fowls, must be a crisis in our lives."[76]

Thoreau's questions are particular insofar as they are largely directed at the goal of simplification. The questions prompt the reader to consider the unnecessary complications of his existence, strengthening one's resolve to become like the philosopher, who can "walk out the gate empty-handed without anxiety."[77] Consider the following rush of questions from "Solitude": "How far apart, think you, dwell the two most distant inhabitants of yonder star, the breadth of whose disk cannot be appreciated by our instruments? Why should I feel lonely? is not our planet in the Milky Way? . . . What sort of space is that which separates a man from his fellows and makes him solitary? . . . What do we want most to dwell near to?"[78]

Every question in the string considers a particular rearticulation of Thoreau's place in time and space. The first question forces us toward a universal standpoint of life, while the second personalizes the universal standpoint and goads us to reconsider its consequences. The third question causes us to reconsider the concept of solitude, now loosened from the social problematic caused by our alleged loneliness, and the fourth asks us, finally, to uncomplicate our lives by choosing that to which we will endear ourselves. In the movement of four questions, Thoreau takes the reader from a universal point of view, the unity of all matter across space, to the starkly individual choice of one's dwelling-place. Questions like these seduce the reader into accepting the premise of simplification and reveling in the consequences.

Thoreau's questions often have the force of reducing his attention to externals, philosophically unhinging his conscience. The final paragraph of "The Bean-Field" offers the following: "These beans have results which are not harvested by me. Do they not grow for woodchucks partly? The ear of wheat . . . should not be the only hope of the husbandman; its kernel or grain . . . is not all that it bears. How, then, can our harvest fail? Shall I not rejoice also at the abundance of the weeds whose seeds are the granary of the birds?"[79] Thoreau loosens his hold on his beans, but, more importantly, he loosens his hold on controlling his world. Thoreau's questions goad the reader, but they also demonstrate the way in which one practically loses hold of one's external affections. Thoreau is instructing the young student how he ought to go about losing his affections and attentions to externals in a very Socratic way. Thoreau's attention to the status of his beans—"My enemies are worms, cool days, and most of all woodchucks"[80]—is relieved only through the simplifying process of exercising questions of release. He begins this chapter with a question, "What shall I learn of beans or beans of me?"[81] and responds at the end of the chapter with his dramatic rethinking of the natural and its comprehensive value.

Thoreau uses dramatic questioning in order to facilitate his larger philosophical purposes. In the "Conclusion," Thoreau offers the following string of questions:

> Shall a man go and hang himself because he belongs to the race of pygmies, and not be the biggest pygmy that he can? . . . Why should we be in such desperate haste to succeed, and in such desperate enterprises? . . . It is not important that he should mature as soon as an apple-tree or an oak. Shall he turn his spring into summer? If the condition of things which we were made for is not yet, what were any reality which we can substitute? . . . Shall we with pains erect a heaven of blue glass over ourselves, though when it is done we shall be sure to gaze still at the true ethereal heaven far above, as if the former were not?[82]

Interestingly, Thoreau's questioning method here removes any answer besides the answer implicit in the question from the realm of possibility. Thoreau hits upon an important philosophical tool: by posing simplifying questions in a dizzying string, one can force the only possible answer to these questions to become an inevitability. In this particular instance, this is a useful persuasive trick, as Thoreau prepares the reader to understand the tale of the artist of Kouroo, endowed with "singleness of purpose and resolution," who makes "no compromise with time, [so] Time kept out of his way."[83] Thoreau uses the previous questions to set the pace toward patience and the single pursuit of a lofty and faraway goal, making the artist of Kouroo appear divine in his ability to apply the correct simplifying principles developed through the previous paragraph.

Thoreau composes 193 rhetorical questions in *Walden*, his most prominent method of teaching philosophy to young students. Thoreau's use of the rhetorical question alerts us to one of the distinctions between *Walden* and the *Journal:* Thoreau now writes as a sage, as one who has crossed the valley of his philosophical apprenticeship and is now in the position to teach the way of philosophical learning to Americans. Thoreau's method of simplification in *Walden* bears the fruit of establishing the way out of a life of anxiety, an unfortunate reality of nineteenth-century American life. Thoreau's famous remark that "the mass of men lead lives of quiet desperation" locates the basic problem of an unphilosophical life: we are overtaken by anxiety, uncertain of our interpretive capabilities for the myriad cultural and personal offerings of modern life.[84] Thoreau's statement at the end of the same paragraph—"it is not a characteristic of wisdom to do desperate things"— cements the connection between philosophical practice and the release from anxiety.

Thoreau, acting as the sage of nineteenth-century America, offers his philosophical work as the student's most effective way out of the trenchant anxiety of his time. Thoreau's specific mentions of anxiety include the following:

No man ever stood the lower in my estimation for having a patch in his clothes; yet I am sure that there is greater anxiety, commonly, to have fashionable, or at least clean and unpatched clothes, than to have a sound conscience. . . .[85]

It is desirable that a man be clad so simply that he can lay his hands on himself in the dark, and that he live in all respects so compactly and preparedly, that, if an enemy take the town, he can, like the old philosopher, walk out the gate empty-handed without anxiety. . . .[86]

[The woodchopper Alek Therien] came along early, crossing my bean-field, though without anxiety or haste to get to his work, such as Yankees exhibit. . . .[87]

The true husbandman will cease from anxiety, as the squirrels manifest no concern whether the woods will bear chestnuts this year or not.[88]

Do not seek so anxiously to be developed, to subject yourself to many influences to be played on; it is all dissipation.[89]

Thoreau isolates the feeling of anxiety as the philosophical problem of modernity because it is pervasive and difficult to locate. Anxiety is produced by the unnecessary complication Thoreau decries at the beginning of the text, wherein young Americans purchase and hold land and jobs without reflecting upon their existential value. Here, Thoreau isolates anxiety as the feeling most associated with early capitalism and fashions his philosophical work as a response to (and way of living within) the capitalist framework.

Thoreau carries his own anxieties as well. He remarks: "In any weather, at any hour of the day or night, I have been anxious to improve the nick of time, and notch it on my stick too; to stand on the meeting of two eternities, the past and future, which is precisely the present moment."[90] Thoreau's anxious feelings about his ability to "improve time" constitute the transformation of capitalist anxiety (with its objectless orientation) to the vigilant care of the self that characterizes Thoreauvian philosophical simplification. Thoreau co-opts capitalist language and uses it to augment his philosophical goal: "So many autumn, ay, and winter days, spent outside the town, trying to hear what was in the wind, to hear and carry it express! I well nigh sunk all my capital in it, and lost my own breath into the bargain."[91]

Thoreau speaks of his capital being used to do the unthinkable: listening to the wind, trying to hear the sounds. Thoreau builds philosophical capital in order to spend it attempting to apprehend the sounds of nature. Thoreau is not the only one who employs this goal, either. Writing of a red squirrel in "Winter Animals," Thoreau notes that the squirrel approaches nature similarly, "now thinking of corn, then listening to hear what was in the wind. So the little impudent fellow would waste many an ear in the forenoon."[92]

Looking and listening become the ways in which Thoreau transforms the capitalist domination of time into a celebration of poverty and aimlessness. Time, interpreted under the lens of capitalism, is a thing that is saved, borrowed, spent, or wasted. Thoreau's anxiety about "improving time" completes his desire to be closer to nature—one of the key purposes of existential simplification. Thoreau finds children around the woods who "looked in the pond and at the flowers, and improved their time."[93] Seeing and hearing become the ways in which Thoreau makes a virtue of "wasting" or "killing" time altogether. "Sometimes, in a summer morning, having taken my accustomed bath, I sat in my sunny doorway from sunrise till noon, rapt in a revery, amidst the pines and hickories and sumachs, in undisturbed solitude and stillness, while the birds sang around or flitted noiseless through the house, until by the sun falling in at my west window, or the noise of some traveller's wagon on the distant highway, I was reminded of the lapse of time. I grew in those seasons like corn in the night."[94]

The existential payoff of reflective simplification is the improvement of time through which we gain the opportunity to carry "a strange liberty in Nature, a part of herself."[95] Thoreau's occupation of the concept of time reveals the completion of his life philosophy in the presence of nature and its sensuous communication.

Cautious Simplification

Walden is, of course, a book primarily about Thoreau's status as philosopher, but there are two important interactions in the text that demand explanation. Thoreau's portrait of Alek Therien, the (unnamed) Canadian woodchopper, seems to idealize Therien's life of simplicity as a model for the American student. Thoreau writes, "He interested me because he was so quiet and solitary and so happy withal; a well of good humor and contentment which overflowed at his eyes."[96] Therien strikes Thoreau as a man who bypasses the anxiety common to those who unnecessarily complicate their lives. His irrepressible satisfaction with his life seems to beckon a Stoic interpretation: "He was so simply and naturally humble—if he can be called humble who never aspires—that humility was no distinct quality in him, nor could he conceive of it."[97] Therien seems to have solved the practical problems of life, one of the prerequisites for philosophy introduced by Thoreau early in the text.

But Thoreau does not quite understand Therien: "I did not know whether he was as wise as Shakespeare or as simply ignorant as a child."[98] Though Thoreau finds high value in Therien's life, he finally admits that "his thinking was so primitive and immersed in his animal life, that, though more promising than a merely learned man's, it rarely ripened to anything which can be reported."[99] Thoreau finds the limit of Therien's appeal and stumbles upon a fundamental check on the simplifying mode of philosophy: Thoreau's celebrated idea of "half-cultivation" in which one plunders the advantages of civilized life while maintaining an eye on the cycle of nature and its affirmations. Therien exists as a philosophical cautionary tale for Thoreau, a limit case that shows how far his simplification can take him if not accompanied by philosophical purpose. Thoreau writes a good deal about Therien to remind himself and his readers of the necessity of maintaining a philosophical orientation to life.

In addition to Therien, the other "others" who figure prominently in the text are the John Field family, an unfortunate group of Irish immigrants whose desire for prosperity blinds them to philosophy. Thoreau describes them in desperate terms: "But therein, as I found, dwelt now John Field, an Irishman, and his wife, and several children, from the broad-faced boy who assisted his father at his work, and now came running by his side from the bog to escape the rain, to the wrinkled, sibyl-like, cone-headed infant that sat upon its father's knee as in the palaces of nobles, and looked out from its home in the midst of wet and hunger inquisitively upon the stranger."[100]

The Field family represents the cautionary tale of one of Thoreau's major means of simplification: the philosophical vow of voluntary poverty. Just as Therien represents the limitations of simplification, the Fields allow the reader to distinguish the poverty Thoreau cherishes and strives toward from the involuntary poverty of the blindly optimistic. Thoreau attempts to convert Field to the affirmation of his mean life: "I purposely talked to him as if he were a philosopher, or desired to be one."[101] After Thoreau laid out his theory of voluntary poverty to the family, "his wife stared with arms a-kimbo, and both appeared to be wondering if they had capital enough to begin such a course with."[102] Of course, in this case, Thoreau is returning to his early inversion of the notion of capital, arguing that what the Field family needs is not money, but the courage to suspend one's desire for money. Living in simple circumstances and experiencing the bonds of poverty are not sufficient to make an American philosopher. One must embrace the opportunity to affirm meanness while also recognizing the vital power of suspending care.

2

Poverty Eternal

What shall I do with this hour so like time and yet so fit for eternity?
—Thoreau, *Journal*, February 7, 1841[1]

Thoreau's interest in history frames *A Week on the Concord and Merrimack Rivers*, manifests itself in natural history essays, and makes its presence felt in the pond chapters of *Walden*. Thoreau's *Journal* is, however, the primary source for gauging his view of his own personal history. In a poignant journal entry from July 16, 1851, we find Thoreau pining for childhood:

> Methinks my present experience is nothing my past experience is all in all. I think that no experience which I have today comes up to or is comparable with the experiences of my boyhood—And not only this is true—but as far back as I can remember I have unconsciously referred to the experience of a previous state of existence. 'Our life is forgetting' &c . . . Formerly methought nature developed as I developed and grew up with me. My life was extacy. In youth before I lost any of my senses— I can remember that I was all alive—and inhabited my body with inexpressible satisfaction, both its weariness & its refreshment were sweet to me.[2]

In this rare moment, Thoreau allows the sense of time to wash over his self-analysis, and the generally tight hold he keeps on his journal unwraps. The vitalization of his senses is an enormously important topic for Thoreau, and here we feel its loss in his daily life. The source of Thoreau's melancholy is perhaps the most interesting part of the entry. Thoreau's lament comes from a remembering—or, perhaps, an acknowledgment—of the distance between himself and nature. For Thoreau, the loss of one's senses comes about from the realization or the theorization that nature and the self do not coordinate their respective growth; that nature, perhaps, does not appeal to the soul as a common friend.

Thoreau invites an important philosophical question in this passage—the question of possible expression of vitalism within temporality. I refer to Thoreau's expressive philosophy as "vitalist" for the purpose of clarifying an important part of his persistent philosophical questioning. For Thoreau, vitalism refers to the enlivening of the senses in the service of life, holding life as a principal valuative measure of one's existence.[3] Thoreau's *Journal* presents the difficulty of apprehending an appreciation of the fullness of life, and these difficulties are most often related to the experience of time. As Thoreau writes on July 6, 1845 (two days after moving to the cabin at Walden Pond): "Stop—Avast—Why so fast? In all studies we go not forward but rather backward with redoubled pauses, we always study *antiques*—with silence and reflection. Even time has a depth, and below its surface the waves do not lapse and roar."[4] This entry gains an added measure of depth when read in light of Thoreau's desire to develop a livable philosophy of time. When Thoreau laments that we study antiques, he refers not only to the study of the past and its relics, but to the study of his own past, and of the effect of the past on him. Simply put, Thoreau's desire to transcend time is rooted in a lived experience that is familiar to the reader: the loss of youth and the stubborn desire not to miss its passing. Thoreau maintains hope that time does not live him, but that he may be able to find a way of expressing life through a lens that is beyond (or besides) time.

Thoreau's lament is strengthened by the finality of the first passage. Feeling the pain of the arrow of time, Thoreau is at the mercy of his memory, which simultaneously preserves a sense of happiness and alienates him from that happiness. While this passage seems out of character for Thoreau, it provides an important context for his broad philosophical goals. Thoreau problematizes time in a way that is not at all unique—the lament over lost youth is, after all, a well-established literary trope—but for Thoreau the corrective becomes an expression of the meaning of philosophy itself. Thomas Allen argues, "Thoreau invests his temporal capital in self-development, cultivating his inner, imaginative life."[5] Thoreau's project of rethinking time goes beyond ways of spending it, however. What Thoreau attempts to accomplish through *Walden* and the journals that inform the period is an overcoming of time itself in the service of maintaining exuberance in life. This chapter argues that *Walden* demonstrates the apex of a long-standing goal for Thoreau's thought: to merge the ancient philosophical principles of the universal vision, apprehension of nature, and voluntary poverty into a means of overcoming the problems and pitfalls of bounded time.

Thoreau on the Universal Vision

Thoreau's own interest in his growth references constant change—indeed, as the above entry demonstrates, Thoreau tends to place his own experience into generational epochs and concern himself with the changes and transformations of aging. Thoreau nicely juxtaposes this concern with his understanding of nature's continuity in an entry from 1847 to 1848: "What means this *tragical* change which has no counterpart in nature—but is confined to the life of man—from infancy to youth—from youth to manhood—from manhood to age—while nature changes not and is never more than one year old."[6]

This curious entry requires a thorough analysis, as it appears an uncharacteristically shallow reading of nature's changes. Thoreau, more than perhaps any other American in the nineteenth century, was keenly aware of nature's constant transformation—so aware, in fact, that he spends a great deal of the last third of his life cataloging nature's various transformations. If we read this journal entry in the context of Thoreau's understanding of nature in his late essay "Autumnal Tints," we understand the meaning behind his argument: "I think that the change to some higher color in a leaf is an evidence that it has arrived at a late and perfect maturity."[7] Thoreau's introduction to the essay presents the argument that the autumn presentation of the leaf's changing color and subsequent shedding is a sign of growth and maturity, not a death or decaying of the tree. This in itself is important, but what is more important for Thoreau is what is suggested by the autumnal presentation (and, indeed, other manifestations of seasonal life): the tree, as part of nature itself, experiences a sort of eternal recurrence of its growth and decay each and every year.

It is extremely important here that Thoreau claims nature is "never more than one year old." Thoreau connects us to the myriad ways in which the concept of the year takes on philosophical importance for him. Thoreau's encompassing project in his late years involved chronicling nature's changes in each month as recorded in his journal entries, to culminate in the planned *Kalendar*, an exhaustive work of natural history that details Concord's yearly birth, life, death, and rebirth.[8] Of course, Thoreau's masterwork, *Walden*, also presents itself as the result of a year's stay in a border life. Thoreau's interest in the concept of the year attends to a temporal puzzle that Thoreau's philosophy aims to conquer: how does one internalize nature's lesson of consistent rebirthing, without succumbing to the all-too-human problem of remorse, decay, and nostalgia? This question animates Thoreau's *Journal* and his experiments with time and eternity in *Walden*. In an entry from August 21, 1851, Thoreau instructs himself in the method of apprehending nature's sense of time: "You must walk sometimes perfectly free—not prying nor inquisitive—not bent upon seeing things—Throw away a whole day for a single expansion, a single inspiration of air."[9] Transcending time carries the cost of losing the productive capacity of one's hours and days.

In an entry from March 14, 1852, Thoreau demonstrates the desperation he feels for moving away from the contemporary concern with productive temporality.

> I go forth to make new demands on life. I wish to begin this summer well—to do something in it worthy of it & of me—To transcend my daily routine—& that of my townsmen to have immortality now—that it be in the *quality* of my daily life, . . . May I purify myself anew as with fire & water—soul & body. . . . May I attain to a youth never attained. I am eager to report the glory of the universe.—May I be worthy to do it—To have got through with regarding human values so as not to be distracted from regarding divine values.[10]

The yearning in this entry strains Thoreau's sense of the possible and complicates his expectations for a summer renewal. The disposition of the self who constantly desires renewal suggests disappointment or delusion, but perhaps neither is in operation in the quotation above. Thoreau begins with a familiar charge to "make new demands on life." This suggests a sense of power over the direction of the future, which is arrived at through an acceptance of the inability of the present to satisfy itself. The quote gets interesting when Thoreau desires to "have immortality now," desiring to push an uncertain but wished-for future into the present through an act of will, or a demand upon life. Thoreau's demand for immortality in the present, witnessed here, suggests the philosophical and existential necessity of overcoming the ontological facts of time prior to experiencing a more intense enjoyment and satisfaction with his daily life. From early in his mature thought, Thoreau categorizes his most basic existential problems as problems of time.

Throughout his *Journal*, Thoreau responds to the problem of time by amplifying the traditional Stoic doctrines of the universal view and the standpoint of nature. In an entry from December 28, 1852, Thoreau applies a universal view to the buzz of life: "It is worth the while to apply what wisdom one has to the conduct of his life surely. . . . A broad margin of leisure is as beautiful in a man's life as in a book. Haste makes waste no less in life than in housekeeping. Keep the time—observe the hours of the universe—not of the cars. What are 3 score years & ten huriedly & coarsely lived to moments of divine leisure, in which your life is coincident with the life of the Universe."[11]

Thoreau's counsel to himself is to "keep the time," that is, to cultivate awareness of a certain type of time, to maintain a hold on time as he lives. He qualifies by assuring himself that he will watch the hours of the universe, take long patterns and developments as his model, and use this example as a way of keeping himself from too busily rushing into a life calling or observational opportunity. Thoreau consistently instructs himself to adopt a standpoint of the universe in order to keep himself from keeping the time of the railroad cars—the encroaching problem of clock-time so well described in *Walden*.

Thoreau also settles on another advantage of the universal view of life that is more troubling. In his construction, the existential value of a universal view of time contends that a few precious moments of apprehension of the universal is more vital than the rest of one's life spent living coarsely. In order to clarify his meaning, Thoreau continues: "One moment of life cost many hours.—hours not of business but of preparation & invitation. . . . That aim in life is highest which requires the highest & finest discipline."[12] Philosophically, Thoreau is again sounding the call to equate the practice of philosophy (which he will later call the "improvement of time") with discipline and preparation. Thoreau's temporal pull is itself an enormous existential gamble: as a philosopher who values life from the standpoint of life, Thoreau posits that a lifetime of preparation followed by one or two moments of encased universal experience justifies itself vitally. Thoreau concludes: "How much—What infinite leisure it requires—as of a lifetime, to appreciate a single phenomenon!"[13] In a formulation that works its way into *Walden*, Thoreau offers his life as a preparation point for the apprehension and knowledge of one universal viewpoint.

Thoreau's understanding of the vital enjoyment of these experiences of the universal—the experiences that abandon clock-time—is developed in an exuberant entry from July 11, 1852:

> What is called genius is the abundance of life or health so that whatever addresses the senses—as the flavor of these berries—or the lowing of that cow—which sounds as if it echoed along a cool *mt* side just before night—where odoriferous dews perfume the air and there is everlasting vigor serenity—& expectation of perpetual untarnished morning—each sight & sound & scent & flavor—intoxicates with a healthy intoxication—The shrunken stream of life overflows its banks makes & fertilizes broad intervals from which generations derive their sustenances. This is the true overflowing of the Nile. . . . If we have not dissipated the vital the divine fluids—there is there a circulation of vitality beyond our bodies.[14]

This entry overflows with the energy of suspended or overcome time. Thoreau's mood is ecstatic, and the writing delivers us through its cadence to a sense of momentary suspension. Thoreau's description carries extra weight through its careful word choice, which pits incommensurable states and feelings next to each other. The most interesting pairing is of *serenity* and *vigor,* two terms that describe one's satisfaction in the overcoming of time and also the vitality that is lent to one only through the long acts of preparation and self-control necessary to experience eternity through the dews, the taste of the berries, or the sound of the cow. Thoreau writes this passage as the culmination of a long period of suffering within time—practically through his professional "failures" and the stigma attached to them, as well as the more abstract struggles against his own past and its reminiscences. When Thoreau refers, in "Life without Principle," to business as a "negation of life," he equates life with precisely this feeling described in the entry above. The "circulation of vitality beyond our bodies" referred to here is nothing more than one's connection to a universal sense of boundlessness, flooding the stream of time (here the Nile) with momentary exuberance.

A significant portion of Thoreau's interest in nature lies in its ability to gauge his comportment toward the universal vision. He writes in June 1852: "With our senses applied to the surrounding world we are reading our own physical & corresponding moral revolutions. Nature was so shallow all at once I did not know what had attracted me all my life. . . . The

perception of beauty is a moral test."[15] A walk or a long look at the full summer color around him examines Thoreau's preoccupations and allows him
the opportunity to take stock of himself and his apprehensions. We can see,
through these *Journal* entries, how Thoreau applies the sense of *askesis* previously articulated into the overcoming of time. Thoreau's philosophical training is buttressed through constant feedback from walks, visions, and sounds.
Thoreau writes in the same passage, "When in bathing I rush hastily into
the river the clam-shells cut my feet."[16] The conclusion to Thoreau's train of
thought suggests an intimate awareness of the moral consequences of his
physical actions. The cutting of the clam-shells is not an accident, but an
event prepared for by Thoreau's preoccupation with the concerns of clock-
time. In this case, hurrying toward the river signifies a disengagement from
the time that is not calculated in seconds and minutes, an ontological dislocation that manifests itself physically through the gentle but insisting teachings of nature.

Thoreau's universal vision leads him to a new way of seeing the objects
in his environment. Thoreau deliberately slows the movement of time not
only in his own mind, but in attending to the phenomena of the world that
facilitate a universal register of consciousness. In an early entry from 1842
to 1844, Thoreau supplies a glance at his purposive watching: "Many a time
had I stood on the bank of the stream watching the lapse of the current—an
apt emblem of all progress—following the same law with the system, with
time—with all that is made. The weeds at the bottom gently bending down
the stream, shaken by the watery wind, though still firmly planted where
their seeds had sunk—but anon to die and go down the stream. The shining
pebbles at the bottom not anxious to better their condition."[17]

The stream is the most common metaphor for time in Thoreau's work,
particularly in *Walden,* and here it supplies an avenue through which Thoreau accepts the necessary flow of time's movement. Perhaps the most compelling use of words in the passage is Thoreau's description of the "lapse of
the current," where he makes a direct connection between the flow of the
water and the flow of time. Outside of a metaphorical meaning, the passage
does not make sense—the current is not lapsing in the sense of a decline, but
in the sense of marking a period of time. The water represents the concept of
time, which Thoreau notes is a useful signal of "all progress." If we look at the
objects in the stream, we see distinctive reactions to time and their impact on
Thoreau's understanding of himself.

The first objects Thoreau recognizes are the weeds, fated to grow from the bottom by a deposit from above. The weeds stand their ground, maintain themselves firmly footed in the place of their birth, but the current affects them nonetheless, as they are "shaken" by the "watery wind." The movement of time affects one's ability to plant oneself in a single place, as the current pushes one alongside it until, ultimately, one loses one's place and the current takes the remains down the stream. This is a poignant description of the will to withstand time and time's ultimate victory over the self. Thoreau's second object of interest, however, is more relevant to his own relation to time. The "shining pebbles" at the bottom of the stream earn the interpretation of being "not anxious to better their condition." Thoreau presents the weeds and the pebbles as two possible responses to the stream of time and, without fanfare, demonstrates the philosophical value of slowness, of patience, of dedicated work upon oneself *within* one's place (the pebbles are, after all, shining). The pebbles do not move—or, at least, Thoreau does not write of their movement, because there is no movement to be made. The stream is the example of "all progress," and Thoreau offers his subtle counsel on the concept of progress: suspend one's temporal location and the interpretation of time as progress, and hold close to oneself.

Time and Poverty: *Walden*'s Philosophy of Time

Thoreau's work on time leads through the *Journal* to *Walden*, in which we find Thoreau engaged in a rethinking and re-visioning of the ancient relationship between time and eternity. Thoreau's most novel accomplishment with respect to *Walden*'s philosophy of time is to distill time's solution into a merger of presence and eternity. Thoreau writes often of the improvement of time and, in the second chapter of the book, refers to "the present" as his next experiment. Cavell's penetrating insight into Thoreau's purpose in the text stands: "Of course he means that the building of his habitation (which is to say, the writing of his book) is his present experiment. He also means what his words say: that the present is his experiment, the discovery of the present, the meeting of two eternities."[18] Cavell does not settle on this passage but instead connects the passage to the meaning of America in Thoreau's text. While his argument is the most perceptive argument ever delivered about *Walden*, Cavell misses an opportunity to explore more clearly the concept of time in the book. I argue here that *Walden* delivers upon the promise of the *Journal,* and Thoreau develops a philosophy of time that responds favorably to his desire to overcome the particular strictures of temporality.

Thoreau punctuates the centrality of time to *Walden* with the last paragraph: "Such is the character of that morrow which mere lapse of time can never make to dawn. The light which puts out our eyes is darkness to us. Only that day dawns to which we are awake."[19] The lapse of time is an insufficient means toward self-improvement; here, as elsewhere, Thoreau implicitly critiques the notion of time as inevitable progress. Instead, he asks the reader to reorient the relationship of time to the self, and to think about the concept of "improving" time. For Thoreau, the notion of improving time replaces the early capitalist takeover of time's chief metaphors: that we *spend, save, borrow,* and *waste* time suggests the strong connection between time and capital. Sarah Allan argues, "Even those of us who would only use the term Time is Money in a jocular manner speak—and conceive—of time as something that we can save or spend; invest, budget, borrow, share or spare; win or lose."[20] Thoreau not only shifts his focus to the concept of "improving time" but uses that very concept to eliminate the domination of time over the self: "That time which we really improve, or which is improvable, is neither past, present, nor future."[21] One of the chief functions of *Walden,* then, is to disturb and reconstruct the self's relation to lived time. Thoreau negates the existence of time while, at the next break, admonishing us for forgetting its necessity and vital import.

Walden undertakes to explore a concept of existence reminiscent of Marcus Aurelius's meditation on death: "It is but the present that a man can be deprived of, if, as is the fact, it is this alone that he has, and what he has not a man cannot part with."[22] Thoreau's ownness pushes him toward taking control of the present moment in order to bleed it dry; indeed, while Thoreau's *Walden* is full of examples of his dismissal of ownership, it is perhaps the ownership of the twin horizons of temporality—the past and the future—that Thoreau is mostly endeavoring to relieve. The retreat of *Walden* is Thoreau's opportunity to experiment with himself. Marcus Aurelius explains: "Men seek out retreats for themselves in the country, by the seaside, on the mountains, and thou too art wont to long above all for such things. But all this is unphilosophical to the last degree, when thou canst at a moment's notice retire into thyself."[23] Thoreau's retirement into himself does not present itself as a vacation from himself, but as a work in himself and through himself.

That time is a concern central to *Walden* is a claim best articulated by
Tauber's *Henry David Thoreau and the Moral Agency of Knowing,* wherein he
masterfully establishes the centrality of time to Thoreau's overall moral project. Tauber finds that Thoreau uncovers three key insights into the nature of
temporality: first, Thoreau "was the first to recognize the ultimate subjectivity of time."[24] Time is an ultimately distorting tool when applied to our lives,
and its employment engenders the "trivialization of our lives." Second, Tauber finds that Thoreau places his quandary of time within the experience of
the outward, arguing that "nature's flux . . . must be appreciated constantly
in the present."[25] Tauber finds that Thoreau's belief in the constant becoming of nature makes necessary the deep, detailed knowledge of (and experience with) the outside. Finally, Tauber suggests that Thoreau, particularly
in *Walden,* harps on our "slavery to temporality."[26] Tauber artfully constructs
a view of Thoreauvian temporality that catapults concerns with time to the
forefront of Thoreau's thought.

Perhaps Tauber's most impressive insight is his distillation of Thoreau's
relationship between time and eternity: "For Thoreau, nature's deepest
ontology is the present, which is pulled out of time to be perceived as a
part of eternity."[27] By "toeing the line" between past and future, as Thoreau notes in *Walden,* he expresses the desire to both intensify his sense
of presentness and simultaneously situate himself within the infinite. The
present, for Thoreau, allows for the only experience of time that is not subject to the domination of time pastness or futurity. As Tauber notes, Thoreau earnestly cultivates self-awareness in order to carve out "a niche in
the infinite."[28] This notion of the present as the temporal eternal clarifies
Thoreau's philosophical project of a "life in the woods." The experience of
presence in nature is Thoreau's gateway to self-consciousness and the universal vision, providing both platforms of experience through the sensual
intake of natural phenomena and the exalting effect of his release into his
senses. Tauber recognizes this fact of *Walden* but chooses to transform
his argument about time and eternity into a case for Thoreau's morality of
self-identification. While the argument has merit, Tauber misses the way
in which the higher and the lower merge in the creation of an eternally
present self.

This is nowhere clearer than in the important last paragraph of "Where
I Lived and What I Lived For": "Time is but the stream I go a-fishing in. I
drink at it; but while I drink I see the sandy bottom and detect how shallow

it is. Its thin current slides away, but eternity remains. I would drink deeper; fish in the sky, whose bottom is pebbly with stars."[29]

Thoreau uses the notions of digging and looking downward to develop his sense of how a natural orientation and investigation develop. While Thoreau fishes, that is, engages with time, he mines the bottom of time's impact through the entanglement with nature's own processes. While Thoreau finds himself in time, he finds himself becoming aware of its shallowness. It is no mistake that Thoreau presents a natural scene to describe the critique and overcoming of temporal barriers. The interesting portion of the text comes next, when Thoreau appears delirious with the notion of "fish in the sky, whose bottom is pebbly with stars." Thoreau offers a representation of the way in which digging deeper—that is, digging into one's own table of values and existential practices—is a preparation for an eternal viewpoint. The fish and pebbles—that which was *below* the water of temporal flow, arrived at through the work of digging and seeing below time—upend themselves and become the signals of the higher or eternal point of view. Thoreau's metaphor of cultivation, especially in "The Bean-Field," is not a trope, as Cavell believes, but a signal of the ways in which the depth of self portends the breadth of time.

Thoreau upends the feeling of eternity and its spatial location by using the visual signal of "burrowing" to explicate his philosophical process of overcoming bounded time. The process of this temporal extraction of the self is violent, as Thoreau notes: "The intellect is a cleaver; it discerns and rifts its way into the secret of things."[30] He pulls us in further to the method, arguing: "My head is hands and feet. I feel all my best faculties concentrated in it. My instinct tells me that my head is an organ for burrowing, as some creatures use their snout and fore-paws, and with it I would mine and burrow my way through these hills. I think the richest vein is somewhere hereabouts; so by the divining rod and thin rising vapors I judge; and here I will begin to mine."[31]

The merger of the lower and the higher in this passage anticipates Thoreau's dance with animal and spiritual in "Higher Laws": "I found in myself, and still find, an instinct toward a higher, or, as it is named, spiritual life, as do most men, and another toward a primitive rank and savage one, and I reverence them both."[32] Thoreau constantly plays with our sense of space and value, arguing not that the head can act in the same way as the hands and feet (that is, as an organ of digging and discovery), but that *his* head in fact *is* hands and feet. Thoreau does not give this quality to all, but to himself—but he also allows us further proof that he is discussing time, as a clock is the machine whose face is attached with hands and feet. Once the head situates itself as the property of the higher law, he then uses it to dig or burrow, and tells us that his head performs this function as an animal would use its nose or paws. Thoreau confounds our understanding of the animal process of discovery by identifying with it, particularly the searching qualities of looking for the "richest vein." Then, in one final act of disorientation, Thoreau gives us his base of judgment: he tells us that he begins to mine where he is told by the "divining rod." The divining rod, of course, was used to discover water. Why would Thoreau, whose purpose in *Walden* is, perhaps above all, to discover and produce a means of overcoming bounded time, burrow for water/time? As we will discover, Thoreau merges time and eternity in such a way that the self locates the pure experience of eternity only within time itself.

Thoreau repeats the lesson later, in "The Ponds." In this case, he reflects upon midnight fishing in the pond and the ways in which his consciousness is altered by the dark and the absorption of his senses in the scene around him: "It was very queer, especially in dark nights, when your thoughts had wandered to vast and cosmogonal themes in other spheres, to feel this faint jerk, which came to interrupt your dreams and link you to Nature again. It seemed as if I might next cast my line upward into the air, as well as downward into this element which was scarcely more dense. Thus I caught two fishes as it were with one hook."[33]

In this case Thoreau's mind moves to eternal thoughts and principles, only to find himself brought back to presence through the jerking of his line. It is clear, however, that he is on the border of time and eternity in the passage, as he is connected with nature but also within the dust of the eternal's afterglow. So he moves upward and downward at the same time, simultaneously engaging in nature (which, to Thoreau, means that he experiences lived presence) and partaking of eternal lessons that presence has to offer. This rare experience of catching two fishes resonates throughout *Walden* and constitutes a major portion of Thoreau's interest in merging himself with his natural surroundings.

Thoreau carries the water metaphor for time in order to release time from its early capitalist master metaphor. In the conclusion, he reminds us: "Let us not play at kittlybenders. There is a solid bottom everywhere."[34] Thoreau cautions us not to run on the thin ice—that is the game of kittlybenders—but to search out the solid bottom beneath the water. Thoreau's assurance that there is "solid bottom everywhere" recognizes the reach of eternity but also reassures the philosophical student who undertakes a life of voluntary poverty on its behalf. Thoreau wants himself and the reader to seek out eternity while also recognizing the necessity of remaining in time. Later in the conclusion, he writes: "The life in us is like the water in the river."[35] In other words, the life in us *is* time, and the vitalizing practices of private life, those which Thoreau loves so dearly, have to be discovered within a precarious grasp upon absolute presence. As Thoreau writes in "The Pond in Winter," "Ice is an interesting subject for contemplation."[36] Time needs to be mastered, but it also needs to be employed and respected as a source of subjectivity and consciousness.

One overlooked portion of the "Where I Lived and What I Lived For" paragraph introduces us to Thoreau's neat merger of time and eternity: "I do not wish to be any more busy with my hands than is necessary."[37] This line complicates Thoreau's construction of temporality and enriches his response, because it makes concrete the connection between time and work. Thoreau's desire to avoid busyness is his primary response to the problem of time in *Walden:* Thoreau wishes not to be "any more busy with [his] hands than necessary" because, for him, "loafing," as Walt Whitman would call it, solves the problem of living within bounded time. The experience of non-directedness, of responsive living, is Thoreau's method of transcending time through acquiescence to the present-ness of temporality. Here, Thoreau's celebration of a loafing life inherits the merits of *wuwei:* "The sage 'wanders' in the wilderness of 'doing nothing'; and having planted a useless tree in the realm of Nothing Whatever, 'vaguely, does nothing (*wuwei*) beside it; [his mind] wandering.'"[38] Reflective poverty provides the ethical impetus to revel in the freedom of time that compels Thoreau throughout *Walden.* Thoreau's first chapter, a guidebook in the ethico-philosophical purpose of economy, reveals its purpose in the overcoming of time and the revelatory freedom of momentary experiences of eternity.

Thoreau persuasively makes the case for doing nothing and applies this virtue to the passing of his historical time as well. In the conclusion, Thoreau writes: "—not to live in this restless, nervous, bustling, trivial Nineteenth Century, but stand or sit thoughtfully while it goes by."[39] We read here the ethical justification of Thoreau's life, his response to the lifelong criticisms he faced for his unwillingness to fulfill his potential. Thoreau claims to have created a philosophical personality that can opt in and out of its own histori-cal period—and the claim is, above all, a claim to have quelled the domina-tion of historical time on the self's ambitions, desires, and horizon. Thoreau has given his readers the rationale for overcoming bounded time and pro-vides the way in which it can be accomplished. The thought of "doing noth-ing" critiques the Protestant ethics' means and ends. Thoreau's celebration of the "artist of Kouroo" attests to this purpose. The artist of Kouroo solves the relationship between time and labor: "Having considered that in an imper-fect work time is an ingredient, but into a perfect work time does not enter."[40] The artist of Kouroo strives after one object, the making of a staff, in the way that Thoreau strives after the making of a self. The singleness of purpose could be confused for misguidedness, impractical activity, or inefficiency, but the artist is celebrated for his constant work on himself. The artist's major accomplishment, finds Thoreau, was that since "he made no compromise with Time, Time kept out of his way, and only sighed at a distance because he could not overcome him."[41] Singleness of purpose, residing in the shell of "doing nothing," conquers the problem of time's constant movement within and over individual life.

Walden's conversation between the hermit and the poet finds Thoreau articulating two complementary visions of the sage, having conquered time in compelling ways. The hermit, once alone, asks himself: "Let me see; where was I? Methinks I was nearly in this frame of mind; the world lay about at this angle. Shall I go to heaven or a-fishing?"[42] The poet and the hermit's work is fishing, and they find that they require some of this work in order to nourish themselves. The hermit's choice of going to heaven or fishing is a false choice, because it is only through fishing that one apprehends heaven. The disorienting experience is represented as a disorientation of space (the higher and the lower, once again) but is in fact a disorientation of time. The hermit fears he will lose his thoughts forever—and then finds himself losing his thoughts and chasing them away. He then aims to recreate his thoughts but finds that they are lost to time—or lost in time—and he cannot have them back. The final lesson: "There never is but one opportunity of a kind."[43] We learn that even the sage, the thinker who can suspend time's domination, cannot recreate the past once it achieves its character of pastness.

Thus far I have argued that Thoreau contributes two primary philo-sophical virtues to his audience in *Walden:* simplification and poverty. I add the terms "reflective" and "voluntary" to these two virtues, because Thoreau

wants the reader to be aware of the necessity of using these virtues philosophically. The two other principal human characters in the text are Alek
Therien and John Field (alongside his family), both of whom I mention in
the previous chapter. Therien is a cautionary tale in *un*reflective simplification, and the John Field family cautions the reader against an unreflective
or involuntary poverty as a virtue. Thoreau supplies these two characters to
stress the importance of his own virtues—they are, after all, the only two
interlocutors in the text with whom Thoreau carries on long conversations—
and to distance himself from an unprincipled condition of involuntary poverty or bare simplicity. Thoreau counsels Field to understand the meaning of
America as "that country where you are at liberty to pursue such a mode of
life as may enable you to do without" coffee, tea, and meat.[44] Thoreau mentions that he "purposely talked to him as if he were a philosopher, or desired
to be one."[45] For Thoreau, the philosopher would be known by a commitment to voluntary poverty. The final remarks on the interaction with Field
find Thoreau counseling his reader, "Let not to get a living be thy trade, but
thy sport."[46]

Thoreau's sense of life in *Walden* in many ways reflects the differentia-
tion he composes in a March 1858 journal entry: "It is surprising that men
can be divided into those who lead an indoor and those who lead an outdoor
life. . . . He lives an outdoor life; *i.e.* he is not squatted behind the shield of
a door, he does not keep himself *tubbed*."[47] Thoreau defends the outdoor life
not because it is outdoors, but because it is where he locates his sense of *vitality* and presence. Sensing the move toward an indoor life, a domestication
that is at the same time, paradoxically, a loss of provincialism, sacrifices the
vitality of natural life (located in the self-awareness of the senses) for ease,
comfort, and the false necessities of town life. Thoreau's realization of the
modern philosophical model of withdrawal and return, dramatized throughout *Walden*, represents a literal awakening of philosophy in the service of
maintaining experimental life. The life we choose for ourselves, insofar as
it is possible for us, must follow an inward pull in order to "crack the nut of
happiness."[48] Thoreau lives outdoors because to understand our natural life,
we must "get our living in it."[49]

In an entry from May 1857, Thoreau writes that "the Americans are very
busy and adventurous sailors, but all in someone else's employ."[50] The early
pages of *Walden* harden the diagnosis of American disharmony. The value
of a philosophical account of time is evident: "I see young men, my towns-

men, whose misfortune it is to have inherited farms, houses, barns, cattle, and farming tools; for these are more easily acquired than got rid of."[51] In the face of the American dream of home ownership and self-sufficiency, Thoreau uncovers the costs related to tethering oneself to property, particularly inherited property. To have property thrust upon oneself, to live a life one does not choose but which has been chosen for oneself, to labor without end toward fulfilling the necessities of modern life, is a "fool's life."[52] The consequences are existential: "Most men, even in this comparatively free country, through mere ignorance and mistake, are so occupied with factitious cares and superfluously coarse labors of life that its finer fruits cannot be plucked by them."[53] Thoreau is a keen observer of the growing tendency to occupy one's time with a series of vacuous pursuits. Labor in the service of superfluities distracts the self from its mission toward fulfilling the fullness of its personal, private existence. The "finer fruits" of life, as we will see, keep Thoreau aware of the costs of labor.

Thoreau's theory of labor takes the vitalist position against the modern labor machine on the grounds that the impossibility of enjoyment in machine labor minimizes individual worth and the proper use of the body. In October 1858 Thoreau writes in his journal, "You come away from the great factory saddened, as if the chief end of man were to make pails; but, in the case of the countryman who makes a few by hand, rainy days, the relative importance of human life and of pails is preserved . . . when labor is reduced to turning a crank it is no longer amusing or truly profitable."[54]

Labor becomes a starting point for a discussion of the value of life because labor, while providing much of the meaning within life, is often discounted for its relation to individual value. Factory life turns human beings into tools, into the producers of pails; but an individual who constructs a pail when the time suits dominates the object with his body, never allowing the object to invert the relationship with the maker. The individual remains the primary source of value, and the self values itself for its ability to create for itself, not for its ability to assist a device efficiently toward a needless end.

Thoreau's experimental vitalism responds to the existential problem he poses in the book: modern life leaves individuals with insufficient means of finding out what they enjoy and experimenting with disparate avenues of pleasure and meaning. The alienation of labor forces individuals into driving themselves toward unchosen ends; as a result, individuals become obsessed with meeting goals they do not care about. Thoreau argues that the slavery individuals place themselves under takes precedence over "Negro slavery," and that the attention paid to matters outside of one's personal field is "frivolous."[55] Suggesting that one's inner torment is more vexing than the public problem of slavery is a privatist declaration of independence for Thoreau and for those who heed his invitation to experiment with their own lives. Individuals subject themselves to scrutiny and ridicule without having seen the advantages of living in accordance with the rules to which they bind themselves. Thoreau states, "No way of thinking or doing, however ancient, can be trusted without proof."[56] But the lives of most around Thoreau are trusted without the proof that they enhance the immanent feelings of life for those living them. There is an assumption made about the evils of slavery that is easy for many to see, because it remains at a distance existentially; however, for one to account for one's own life, to experiment with and seek proof for one's own valuations is much more difficult to grasp, because it is so much closer to us.

The result, for Thoreau, is "tedium and ennui which presume to have exhausted the variety and the joys of life."[57] Pushing further, Thoreau reports on families in Concord who desire to sell their homes but find themselves unable, and "only death will set them free."[58] In addition to being tethered to homes and farms, individuals operate under the mistake that home and farm sustain them personally. Modern America is able to construct distinguished homes, but "it has not equally improved the men who are to inhabit them."[59] The propertied portion of the American dream is a dead letter for Thoreau, as he utilizes the chapter "Where I Lived, and What I Lived For" to demonstrate. Thoreau does not deny the seduction of purchasing a home but keeps it within his imagination rather than in practice. "In imagination I have bought all the farms in succession."[60] Thoreau's second chapter is ripe with imaginings, lending the imagination its own avenue of experimentation. After spending the opening chapter on the hard facts of his border life, Thoreau experiments without the tether of commitment, arguing that individuals need to avoid the commitments that entrap experimental possibilities.[61]

Thoreau's commitment to voluntary poverty is explored throughout *Walden*, becoming one of the major themes of the text. Thoreau replaces the labor of the hands with "Reading," a chapter that explores the philosophical benefits of suspending historical considerations of classical texts. Thoreau is searching here for a way to force beloved literature toward a vital purpose— to make it worth one's while, or for reading to improve one's time. Thoreau treats reading as a labor, writing that "we must laboriously seek the meaning of each word and line, conjecturing a larger sense than common use permits out of what wisdom and valor and generosity we have."[62] Thoreau reduces the distance between himself and the author of an enduring text, which is the first step in using reading to unbound time. Replacing the labor of the hands with the labor of the mind, Thoreau stresses the importance of having one's time unburdened by trivial work in order to prepare oneself for the interludes of eternal understanding that come through what I call *receptive nothingness*.

Receptive nothingness characterizes the sensual experiences Thoreau describes intermittently in *Walden*. None is better than the second paragraph of "Sounds," which finds Thoreau presenting a phenomenology of receptive nothingness:

> There were times when I could not afford to sacrifice the bloom of the present moment to any work, whether of the head or hands. I love a broad margin to my life. Sometimes, in a summer morning, having taken my accustomed bath, I sat in my sunny doorway from sunrise till noon, rapt in a revery, amidst the pines and hickories and sumachs, in undisturbed solitude and stillness, while the birds sang around or flitted noiseless through the house, until by the sun falling in at my west window, or the noise of some traveller's wagon on the distant highway, I was reminded of the lapse of time.[63]

This paragraph is a high point of Thoreau's work. The description of the experience begins with the "bloom" of the present, a plant given the opportunity to demonstrate itself through the hard work of cultivation. Thoreau notes that he could not "afford" to sacrifice the moment (again inverting the capitalist interpretation of temporality) to hand-work or head-work, recalling the second chapter's merging of the head and the hands through burrowing. The description of the experience itself, however, is demonstrative of Thoreau's belief in the payoff of a life of voluntary poverty. Thoreau's first three chapters, read in this way, prepare the reader for the experience of understanding and committing to the *importance* of a morning spent receiving, through the senses, an exhilarating connection between the self and its environs. Thoreau's wager with time here is dramatic—his purpose, or one of his purposes, is to convince the reader of the value of giving up on the productive capacity of time in order to prepare oneself existentially to appreciate the finite perfection of a moment of merged presence and eternity.

Thoreau is quick to isolate time as the primary purpose for his morning reverie. "My days were not days of the week, bearing the stamp of any heathen deity, nor were they minced into hours and fretted by the ticking of a clock; for I lived like the Puri Indians, of whom it is said that 'for yesterday, to-day, and to-morrow they have only one word, and they express the variety of meaning by pointing backward for yesterday, forward for to-morrow, and overhead for the passing day.'"[64] Thoreau's days retain their fullness, expressed through the inability to distort them into a clock or a calendar. Thoreau's time, here, is lived time, and it is important to note how unbounded it is. Thoreau is not practicing escapism but is merging himself creatively with the eternal properties of nature. In the beginning of this chapter, we found Thoreau lamenting his youth in the *Journal*. Here, however, he is able to express, "My life itself was become my amusement and never ceased to be novel."[65] The novelty of Thoreau's life stems from his ability to transform his understanding of nature and the self through moments like the morning reverie. Voluntary poverty teaches Thoreau to want, or will, few things. The strongest advantage of this philosophical position is not that Thoreau then has fewer items to care for, but that he finds himself contorted existentially toward a mood of receptiveness, rather than a mood of frustrating willing.

The first paragraph of "Sounds" solidifies Thoreau's receptiveness. In a passage quoted earlier, we add to our previous understanding of the text by attending to Thoreau's receptiveness: "What is a course of history, or philosophy . . . compared with the discipline of always looking at what is to be seen?"[66] Thoreau presents the case of receptive nothingness in several registers throughout *Walden,* and in this passage he attempts to reorient our thinking about perception by merging its power and authority with reception. Looking at "what is to be seen" is a discipline; that is, it requires sustained attention and constant thought. The thought, here, is turned toward taking pleasure in whatever nature provides to the senses. This is Thoreau's hedonism, located in nature's realm of offerings primarily to his senses. The "discipline" required in this particular passage particularly concerns the work of avoiding demands upon one's time that create or affirm the oppression of clock-time. It is not surprising that Thoreau laments the railroad not primarily for its sound, but for its ability to amalgamate all Massachusetts life to the regularity of clock-time: "They go and come with such regularity and precision, and their whistle can be heard so far, that the farmers set their clocks by them, and thus one well conducted institution regulates a whole country."[67]

Thoreau's voluntary poverty allows him the opportunity to make experiments with nature. He uses the first paragraph of "Solitude" to describe another such encounter: "This is a delicious evening, when the whole body is one sense, and imbibes delight through every pore. I go and come with a strange liberty in Nature, a part of herself. As I walk along the stony shore of the pond in my shirt sleeves, though it is cool as well as cloudy and windy, and I see nothing special to attract me, all the elements are unusually congenial to me."[68]

Thoreau uses the beginning of "Solitude" to describe his release from the anxieties of unforced labor outlined in the first chapter of *Walden*. The reader of the text must recognize the connections in place between the preparatory experience of simplification, the vow of voluntary poverty, and the fruits of these types of revelatory experiences. Perhaps the most educational portion of the passage is Thoreau's recognition "I see nothing special to attract me." The philosopher who takes upon himself a life of voluntary poverty trains the body and the mind to widen the field of perception and reception, to the point of his inability to make his consciousness selective. Voluntary poverty allows Thoreau this opportunity, because he releases himself from basic wants. He is left, here, with the possibility of imbibing everything, but without the desire to codify his options.

In a letter to H. G. O. Blake from August 10, 1849, Thoreau connects time and poverty in his counsel: "I might say . . . be not anxious to avoid poverty. . . . What a pity if we do not live this short time according to the laws of the long time,—the eternal laws!"[69] Thoreau teaches Blake the essential connection between poverty and temporality. Thoreau isolates poverty as the way to live "the laws of the long time." In the conclusion to *Walden*, Thoreau makes another interesting connection: "Cultivate poverty like a garden herb, like sage."[70] Thoreau's metaphor of cultivation is familiar throughout the text, but here the key item is his choice of herb. Thoreau's subtle connection between poverty and the sage is telling, as it identifies the sage with the cultivation of poverty. This, of course, is different from the *acceptance* of poverty—Thoreau, in this case, turns poverty into a strived-for goal and a key virtue of the philosophical life. The sage aims for poverty. Thoreau revisits the point a page later: "The shadows of poverty and meanness gather around us, 'and lo! creation widens to our view.'"[71] The apex of Thoreau's conclusion is spent giving the reader admonitions about the relation between time and poverty, suggesting its high place among lessons learned from the text. Poverty and meanness, in this case, administer the work of preparing the self for a wider view of creation. It is *only* through the condition of poverty that the self prepares itself to experience the fullness of life.

Thoreau poses the problem in the form of an existential question: "Why do you stay here and live this mean moiling life, when a glorious existence is possible for you? Those same stars twinkle over other fields than these.— But how to come out of this condition and actually migrate thither? All that he could think of was to practice some new austerity, to let his mind descend into his body and redeem it, and treat himself with ever increasing respect."[72]

The way out of the average everydayness of modern life is found in the practice of a "new austerity," a way of denying oneself the desire for a particular pleasure. Thoreau's *Walden* is full of his own accounts of this austere measure, and they do not need recounting here. It is not as important that Thoreau argue for self-denial as that Thoreau articulate austerity and voluntary poverty as purposeful preparatory philosophical work. Reflective simplification and voluntary poverty join here in the creation of a philosophical self suited to mind its own business. Thoreau's strategic imperative of poverty allows for universal vision, but it also insulates the self against its own passing desires to change the state of things, and not "accept the case that is."

3

Life near the Bone

But one might say, in another paradox, that *Walden*'s triumphant success
is precisely what constitutes its defeat. For underlying that triumph is a
forsaking of civic aspirations for an exclusive concern with "the art of living
well."
   —Michael T. Gilmore, *American Romanticism and the Marketplace* [1]

It is rather derogatory that your dwelling-place should be only a
neighborhood to a great city—to live on an inclined plane. I do not like their
cities and forts, with their morning and evening guns, and sails flapping in
one's eye. I want a whole continent to breathe in, and a good deal of solitude
and silence, such as all Wall Street cannot buy.
   —Thoreau, *Familiar Letters* [2]

In the letter quoted above, a young Thoreau dismisses his time in Staten
Island, finding himself longing for his provincial home. That Thoreau spends
a period of mere months living outside of Massachusetts is not altogether
remarkable, but the way he phrases his desire is. Thoreau writes his desire
in an ironic way, first positing that the expanse of the city abhors him but
that he wishes to have a "whole continent" to breathe in. The whole continent, for Thoreau, is mentioned in the conclusion to *Walden*: "Be a Colum-
bus to whole new continents and worlds within you, opening new channels,
not of trade, but of thought." [3] Thoreau further clarifies his advice, admonishing the reader to "explore the private sea, the Atlantic and Pacific Ocean
of one's being alone." [4] Sherman Paul refers to these quotations representing
Thoreau's "inward exploration," and we see the importance Thoreau places on
exploration when he makes the following remark: "Obey the precept of the
old philosopher, and Explore thyself." [5] Thoreau amends the famous Socratic

dictum that one *know* thyself and instead suggests the action of exploration, without claiming to supersede Socrates's advice. Thoreau is merely arguing that exploration is the means to knowledge, and that the only type of knowledge worth having is that which concerns the self. Thoreau concludes *Walden* with the push to explore oneself in order to know oneself comprehensively, to avoid only a partial knowledge of the self.

Thoreau asks us to "be / Expert in home-cosmography," advice that he believes constitutes the central message of *Walden*.[6] Thoreau's provincialism is strategically placed within an argument that one take a wider view of the universe. Thoreau alerts us, in the conclusion to *Walden*, to what he has shown us throughout the text: that the universe and the self are one—or, to make the point more explicitly, that the self is a universe.[7] Thus, Thoreau couches his provincialism not as a contraction of the self but as an expansion of the self to the point of connection with (and as) the universe. One strong message of *Walden*, then, is to expand oneself by contracting the space in which one operates ethically.

Walden's provincial philosophy cements Thoreau as one of the foremost philosophers of the village in modern thought. *Walden* is in many ways a testament to the border life, the immersion in the sights, sounds, and visions of the small town and its natural surroundings. Another provincial philosopher of modernity, Martin Heidegger, also consistently defends his village life, arguing that the whole of his philosophy is constructed out of a border life in a remote village. In a remarkable article from 1934, Heidegger explains his living choices in "Why Do I Stay in the Provinces?" The language and description in the brief piece compare favorably with Thoreau's in *Walden*, and we receive a picture of a provincial life that defends itself from its absorption in the work of philosophy and the work of ecology:

> This is my work-world. . . . Strictly speaking myself I never observe the landscape. I experience its hourly changes, day and night, in the great comings and goings of the seasons. The gravity of the mountains and the hardness of their primeval rock, the slow and deliberate growth of the fir-trees, the brilliant, simple splendor of the meadows in bloom, the rush of the mountain brook in the long autumn night . . . all of this moves and flows through and penetrates daily existence up there, and not in forced moments of "aesthetic" immersion or artificial empathy, but only when one's own existence stands in its work.[8]

Identifying the Black Forest as his "work-world," Heidegger dissolves the subject/object relationship between himself and the world by dichotomizing his experience with the pitifully minimal aesthetic experience of the "observer." Heidegger's major focus here is on creating a new understanding of his surroundings, arguing that he never "observes" the landscape but instead experiences "its hourly changes." Heidegger defends provincial life as a place of settling, pushing its advantages beyond the picture postcard toward a reoriented consciousness of the self within its place. Heidegger argues not that he becomes his landscape, but that the landscape's transformations are experienced by him.

Heidegger continues: "On a deep winter's night when a wild, pounding snowstorm rages around the cabin and veils and covers everything, that is the perfect time for philosophy. Then its questions become simple and essential."[9] Thoreau performs a similar arc in *Walden,* maintaining that his credentials as one who belongs near the pond, immersed in the woods, establish the ground on which he can construct a workable philosophy. He notes in the conclusion, "We need the tonic of wildness—to wade sometimes in marshes where the bittern and the meadowhen lurk, and hear the booming of the snipe. . . . At the same time that we are earnest to explore and learn all things we require that all things be mysterious and unexplorable, that land and sea be infinitely wild. . . . We can never have enough of nature."[10] Heidegger and Thoreau alert us to the necessity of nonhuman space to the practice of philosophy; we must first encounter life as a problem, a genuine (dare we say "natural") problem of existence, prior to philosophizing. The Heideggerian snow-storm presents a problem situation from which philosophy must dig out an answer; the Thoreauvian marsh exhibits the reorienting sense of wonder in which we wade with questions of being.

Heidegger's preference for his provincial cabin allows for a kind of work that strips off the partiality of urban life commitments: "People in the city often wonder whether one gets lonely up in the mountains among the peasants for such long and monotonous periods of time. But it isn't loneliness, it is solitude. In large cities one can easily be as lonely as almost nowhere else. But one can never be in solitude there. Solitude has the peculiar and original power not of isolating us but of projecting our whole existence out into the vast nearness of the presence of all things."[11]

Heidegger's rethinking of solitude establishes the village as a space for encouraging a wider understanding of things. It is only in the mountains (or in the woods, or near the pond) that one can answer the question, as Thoreau's hermit does in the first section of "Brute Neighbors," "I wonder what the world is doing now."[12] The hermit finds himself in solitude, "as near being resolved into the essence of things as ever I was in my life."[13] In fact, if we glance at the "Brute Neighbors" chapter, we see Thoreau, in solitude, describing encounters with (wild) mice, a phoebe, a robin, a partridge, an otter, a raccoon, a woodcock, ants (in battle), cats, a loon (cunning in its hiding), and ducks. Thoreau describes these "neighbors" as part of the essence of things, answering the question at the beginning of the chapter: "Why do precisely these objects which we behold make a world?"[14]

On first reading, Heidegger's essay presents itself as the self-defensive compensations of a village malcontent, a judgment often thrown at Thoreau for *Walden* as well. Instead, what we find upon further reading is the yearning to justify village life *not* to the city, but to the projects that construct a valuable life: simplicity, independence, work: "Let us stop all this condescending familiarity and sham concern for 'folk-character' and let us learn to take seriously that simple, rough existence up there."[15] Thoreau's *Walden* can be read the same way, as the laboring of an individual attempting to reintegrate himself into a series of values exclusive to border life, identifying the work, freedom, and completeness offered through village life. One of *Walden*'s major purposes, then, is to establish the value of provincialism. Thoreau accomplishes this particular task by identifying a core concern of philosophy since Plato: completion or wholeness in the soul. *Walden* defends Thoreau's choice of using his environment to develop a sense of wholeness of the soul. Identifying the problem of indebtedness as a constraint on wholeness, Thoreau connects his philosophy with Stoic concerns and presents *Walden* as a philosophical defense of wholeness updated to the nineteenth century.

Thoreau's Incidental Stoicism

In a journal entry from July 6, 1840, Thoreau offers an evaluative criterion for his daily writing exercises: "Let the daily tide leave some deposit on these pages, as it leaves sand and shells on the shore. So much increase of *terra firma*. This may be a calendar of the ebbs and flows of the soul; and on these sheets as a beach, the waves may cast up pearls and seaweed."[16] There are several interesting movements in the reflection, beginning with the mixture of sea metaphors (the daily tide) and writing metaphors (using "leave" as a verb but reminding us of its employment as page). When we examine the passage, we find that Thoreau is describing the process of journaling. The daily tide— that is, the day's events in their ebbing and flowing—is effectively writing the journal itself. Thoreau's engagement in early journaling, developed here through the understanding that the tide itself *leaves*—that is, creates pages— suggests a phenomenological approach to the apprehension of daily inter- course. Thoreau recognizes that his journal is a remnant of a "casting up" of both pearls and seaweed, and his consciousness of its mixed quality rein- forces its phenomenological character. Thoreau refuses to compromise the contents of the journal, according to this early entry, because his goal is to report on the wholeness of his life by attending to its particulars.

On the previous day Thoreau writes of a desire to "go where we will discover infinite change in particulars only—not in generals."[17] Thoreau is directing us to understand the purpose behind his journal entries, partic- ularly those that suggest mere reporting. Look at three examples from the July/August 1840 *Journal:* "As I picked blackberries this morning by star- light, the distant yelping of a dog fell on my inward ear, as the cool breeze on my cheek."[18] "Any melodious sound apprises me of the infinite wealth of God."[19] "It behooves us to make our life a steady progression and not be defeated by its opportunities."[20]

I do not choose these passages for their remarkable nature or for their representation of Thoreau's *Journal* (each written within a period of one month), but because they supply us with a key to interpreting the movement of Thoreau's journal writing. The first entry appears to fall into the category of reporting, but a deeper reading demonstrates that Thoreau is experiencing a lesson he will incorporate into his understanding of doing philosophy. If we pay attention to Thoreau's surroundings, we find that he is picking blackber- ries by sunlight, making the Concord woods his "work-world" in Heidegger's sense, and preparing himself for the hearing that will take place. Thoreau's reward for his philosophical preparation is the faint sound of a yelping dog, which may appear to us a poor reward, indeed.

If we turn to Thoreau's *Walden*, however, we find that the purpose of philosophical education is to prepare ourselves to listen to our surround- ings: "So many autumn, ay, and winter days, spent outside the town, trying to hear what was in the wind, to hear and carry it express! I well-nigh sunk all my capital in it."[21] Thoreau spends his days trying to hear what is in the wind (in this case, the yelping dog), so that he can carry it express (both a jab at letter-carrying services and a reminder of his hope to proclaim what he hears to others). The passage gains importance when we see that already, in 1840, Thoreau is trying to hear what is in the wind (the yelping falls on his ear like the breeze upon his cheek). To clarify the meaning of the short passage, Thoreau offers contextualization in the latter two passages. In the second passage, we find that any "melodious sound" triggers a representation of God's bounty—that is, of the abundance, creative capacity, and sufficiency of nature. In the third quote, Thoreau applies the first two to the project of the *Journal* itself—a philosophical search for wholeness that settles on unearthing particulars and amplifying the educational and existential potential of everyday life.

Thoreau's journal entries alert us to the understanding that hearing is an important way of doing philosophy: "When the accents of wisdom and eloquence have died away—I discover that the chirp of the crickets is still clear in advance."[22] Thoreau's philosophizing is met with a profound skepticism toward philosophy's traditional mannerisms, recognizing the infinite supply of nature's sounds as sure to outlast the temporary fashion of schools of understanding. Borrowing from a quote attributed to Thales, Thoreau writes in the *Journal:* "To Thales is attributed the saying—'It is hard, but good, to know oneself; virtue consists in leading a life conformable to nature.'"[23] Four days later Thoreau writes, "Social yearnings unsatisfied are the temporalness of time."[24] Thoreau's satisfaction with nature's conformity opposes itself to the idea of one's social desires, which, when unsatisfied, make one *feel* time in a unique way. In fact, Thoreau suggests that social desires are the manifestation of time's dominion over the self. This interesting way of opposing nature and society supplies Thoreau with one of the major philosophical purposes of the Walden Pond excursion and the subsequent book: to discover the ways in which the self overemphasizes partial components of its life at the expense of the soul. Thoreau's desire to make nature manifest in himself, in this sense, reads like Epictetus's effort to take nature seriously as a concept and principle that allows one to remain one's own.

In the opening paragraphs of the *Discourses,* Epictetus offers this very interesting counsel: "Only consider at what price you sell your freedom of will. If nothing else, man, at least don't sell it cheap."[25] Epictetus's constant concern with the freedom of the will grounds his Stoic philosophy, offering a terminus for his practices of rooting unnecessary desire and attention from individual life. What Epictetus does in this specific passage, however, is introduce indebtedness as an important philosophical concept. How does one "sell" one's freedom of will? In this case one makes oneself indebted to projects, hopes, pursuits, or desires beyond one's capacity to realize. Epictetus, as philosopher of freedom, alerts individuals to the constraints—artificial and natural—on their desire to accomplish their nature. The concern with debts moves beyond philosophy to the practice of life, as Epictetus critiques those who indebt themselves economically to a variety of doomed projects (large homes, fine clothes, expensive habits). These individuals indebt themselves to their own desires, but, more importantly, their desires indebt them to serve another at the expense of their own freedom. This space between indebtedness and freedom in both Epictetus and Thoreau's *Walden* is the topic of this chapter.

Epictetus's counsel seems familiar to those who follow Thoreau's critique of work in the opening pages of *Walden*. The Roman Stoic position of identifying the boundaries of personal freedom via a series of practical exercises in evaluating life echoes in Thoreau's *Walden*, as we can see from a very similar passage: "The cost of a thing is the amount of what I will call life which is required to be exchanged for it, immediately or in the long run."[26] Thoreau's perpetual consideration of the *costs* of life is what originally leads him to move to Walden Pond from 1845 to 1847; at this point the young Thoreau has lived his life either with his parents or with Emerson and, having few prospects for venturing out on his own, aims to build his own home through means he can afford.[27] But the cost of, as Epictetus terms them, "externals" is what truly animates Thoreau's philosophy in *Walden*. Thoreau's taxonomy of life, in which he places under the name of false necessities fashion, elegant food, news, politics, base friendships, and so forth, carries a strong ethos of practicing the privatist politics of authentic selfhood in nineteenth-century America.

Epictetus's Socratic philosophy draws primarily from Socrates's invulnerability, which Epictetus forms into a theory of freedom.[28] Epictetus threads Socratic invulnerability into a theory of what Christopher Gill calls "psychophysical holism" that promotes a structured self that orients its freedom on its capacity to withstand temptation: "He is free who lives as he wills, who is subject neither to compulsion, nor hindrance, nor force, whose choices are unhampered, whose desires attain their end, whose aversions do not fall into what they would avoid."[29]

Epictetus envisions every psychic or physical act of commitment to a project outside the scope of one's own well-reasoned life as a clipping of the self, detaching part of the self's originary wholeness to an external ideal. For Epictetus, one's life commitments are tested in everyday existence, primarily through the luxuries that facilitate civilized life: "Is it not true that the more softly the lion lives the more slavishly he lives?"[30] Epictetus's practice of philosophy as a constant watch over the self's commitments reminds us of Thoreau's counsel toward the beginning of "Where I Lived, and What I Lived For": "As long as possible live free and uncommitted."[31]

Both Thoreau and Epictetus develop a Socratic philosophy of freedom that privileges the wholeness of soul. Epictetus asks, "Your farm, is it under your control to have it when you want, and as long as you want, and in the condition that you want?"[32] Similarly, Thoreau writes that "a man is rich in proportion to the number of things which he can afford to let alone."[33] In this sense, Thoreau and Epictetus mimic what Socrates develops as essential to the existential practice of philosophical principles: invulnerability, loose commitments, and voluntary poverty. Each of these measures is undertaken to insulate the soul against the enchanting offers of external ideals. Epictetus rails against compulsion, while Thoreau aims his sword at desperation; in each case, to be sure, we see the recounting of the Socratic character.

Experiments in Wholeness

Thoreau's *Walden* traverses a number of disparate themes, each providing entrée into the comprehensive philosophy of life developed within the pages of his masterwork. In this chapter, I choose to concentrate on a theme prevalent throughout the work: Thoreau's existential investigation of what constitutes a *non-desperate life*. Thoreau's search for an alternative value structure for personal conduct is not unique in his time; indeed, Thoreau occupies an important space within the first genuine American reform movements of the early to mid-nineteenth century. Thoreau's type of reform—which is, more often than not, *not* reform at all—provides later commentators with considerable moral trouble. His desire to build a cabin near Walden Pond and spend two years hoeing beans and writing *A Week on the Concord and Merrimack Rivers* is the more troubling because of its contemporary counterparts: the utopian small communities of the 1840s, with high aims and complex reorganizations of social institutions. Thoreau was more than familiar with the communitarian utopian movements: two of the most famous, George and Sophia Ripley's Brook Farm and Bronson Alcott and Charles Lane's Fruitlands were transcendentalist reform ideals placed into practice. Thoreau's sojourn occupies a similar space.

Thoreau's Walden experiment shares more in common with Brook Farm and Fruitlands than mere historical interest. *Walden* and the Brook Farm and Fruitlands experiments aim toward recreating an agrarian ideal that is fading from fashion, being replaced by the young cosmopolitanism of easier travel and frequent newspapers. Thoreau's *Walden*, with its persistent reference to the railroad, its interspersed conversations with those trying to make a living out of the new rules of alienated labor, and its forceful opening chapter, "Economy," aims to recover a self-sufficient ideal that is vanishing due to the thrust of business and the individual's misplaced sense of necessity. Similarly, Brook Farm aims to restore the dignity of individual life by reconnecting the complete individual through labor of the body and the mind, and Fruitlands reorganizes social life around the stripped-down ideals of necessity in food, drink, clothing, and shelter. Thoreau's experiment in personal purification aims to shun the new realities of economic modernization and mass democracy, and Brook Farm and Fruitlands build themselves on similar principles.

Brook Farm and Fruitlands: The Problem of Partiality in Transcendentalism

A recent renaissance in the scholarly treatment of the utopian community movement in the nineteenth century has, unfortunately, not been accompanied by an analysis of these movements' political ideas. The communitarian movement was not an offspring of any political party, as Whigs and Democrats alike partook of the movement without much difficulty or infighting.[34] But there is much in these movements that speaks of a theory of politics, a particularly American theme of the *limitations* of politics as a means of social change. Carl Guarneri's richly detailed history of the utopian socialist movement, *The Utopian Alternative*, argues that communitarian movements and the transcendentalist spirit of Emerson provide competing social theories of the United States: "As a system of ideas, American Fourierism stood near the very center of the antebellum debate over the future of the Republic. . . . In the North, Emerson and other writers developed the concepts of 'self-reliance,' 'individualism,' and 'free labor' in explicit opposition to the utopian socialist challenge."[35]

Guarneri's focus is on the adaptation of Fourierism from France to the United States, where, as a totalizing system of knowledge and social organization, it becomes a social-scientific community, expressly defined and minutely organized to optimize the tendencies of individual character types and social expectations. Though Brook Farm transitions to Fourierism in 1844, as a sort of last-ditch effort to gain funding, and Fruitlands never makes the transition, being wholly opposed to the specifics of Fourierism, the opposition between communitarian living and self-reliance remains vivid and fitting. Thoreau, alongside Emerson, finds himself at odds with *how* the new America—sovereign, powerful, and expanding—will reconcile itself with its lofty expectations.

Brook Farm

Although not the first utopian community in the United States, Brook Farm is perhaps the most famous. Founded in West Roxbury, Massachusetts, in the spring of 1841 by George Ripley, a former Unitarian minister and member of the Hedge Club of early American transcendentalists, and Sophia Ripley, educator and early transcendentalist, Brook Farm holds the loftiest of aims. Noting a split between the work of the hands and the work of the mind, Ripley and others attempt to suture the intellectual and manual labors of human beings into a new vision of wholeness via a self-sustaining community. Regaining completion amidst the fracturing of oncoming capitalism and the literal fracturing of the northern and southern United States is a major theme in transcendentalist thought. In a letter to Emerson during the autumn of 1840, Ripley argues that Brook Farm aims to "insure a more natural union between intellectual and manual labor than now exists; to combine the thinker and the worker, as far as possible, in the same individual; to guarantee the highest mental freedom, by providing all with labor . . . to do away with the necessity of menial services, by opening the benefits of education and the profits of labor to all."[36]

Many of Ripley's themes—completion of the self, relations between self and nature, the honesty of pure labor, freedom from necessity—are highlights of Thoreau's sojourn at Walden Pond as well. The transcendentalist ethos of the time—to remake the world—focuses on the aspects of individual life undergoing dramatic change at the time, particularly hired labor. One could argue convincingly (as Richard Francis does) that *the* purpose of the transcendental utopias is simply to solve the question of early capitalism's transformation of the laborer to the worker.[37]

Suturing the disparate parts of the individual into a complete self is buttressed by the fixation across transcendentalist thought that the universal exists within the particular, though our emphasis on particulars sometimes eclipses the universal from our purview.[38] The most striking passage of Emerson's "The American Scholar," for instance, captures the fracturing of individual life perfectly: "The state of society is one in which the members have suffered amputation from the trunk, and strut about so many walking monsters—a good finger, a neck, a stomach, an elbow, but never a man."[39] Emerson's visual impact—the self as a part amputated from the whole, doing the work of the particular without the aid of the universal, a *walking monster*—crystallizes the horror and the seriousness of the question at hand. Individuals find themselves split from the originary wholeness that composes them—but what precisely is to blame for the split?

Guarneri argues that the utopian socialist movements respond primarily to the crisis of early capitalism: "Associationists sincerely believed their society to be at a critical turningpoint, when new competitive industrial and commercial forms had to be reshaped before they became permanently entrenched."[40] Clearly, Brook Farm organizers hold similar views, arguing that the time is ripe for reform in the United States, while the genesis of a new social and economic order is in its earliest stages. Brook Farm begins not with the Fourierist embrace of the material progress of nations, but with reorganization by reinventing an agrarian past of the unified self. Contrary to the Fourierists, transcendental American reform projects look consistently to the past—real or imagined—for inspiration in transforming the material conditions of present life. While Brook Farm relays the critique of early capitalism, it does so with joy—at least at first: "The farm offered a simple and basically comfortable life where members could pursue intellectual and spiritual growth, through either private studies or group activities such as reading circles, musical performances, and dramatic presentations. In contrast to many residents of Puritan Boston, members delighted in spontaneity and fun."[41]

Brook Farm offers a solution to the fracturing of self by privileging labor of individual discretion. One can hardly underestimate the degree to which Brook Farm's early popularity hinges on its free-spirited answer to the question of how one is to get a living. One can now, through the organization of the farm, do the work one desires when one desires to do it. One must not amputate a part of oneself to dedicate to labor at the expense of the rest of the body and mind.

Of course, Brook Farm's labor by discretion is not all smooth sailing. Nathaniel Hawthorne's *The Blithedale Romance*, a novel recounting the time he spends at Brook Farm in 1841 and 1842, contains a series of curious passages from a group of young women, each of whom carries the excitement of the new venture but finds herself asking: "Have we our various parts assigned?"[42] The question of labor is still open, even in Brook Farm's utopia. Zenobia, a major figure in Hawthorne's novel, quickly takes the mantle of defending the household labor of women, mirroring the reality of Brook Farm's de facto sexual division of labor. While Sophia Ripley, cofounder of the farm, spends time as a teacher, this is hardly a novel form of labor for bright young women in the mid-nineteenth century; and, when Brook Farm makes the transition to a Fourierist "phalanx" in 1844, Sophia Ripley is named head of the "Domestic Series."[43] Hawthorne continually returns to the (lack of) intellectual or moral fruit yielded by his physical labor: shoveling manure. George Ripley, particularly in the later years, spends precious little time doing labor of any sort at the farm.[44]

Given the philosophical goal of suturing the self together with intellectual and manual labor, Brook Farm necessitates an ethos of equality in order to function along its aims. While the Ripleys heartily endeavor to make this so, the stubborn necessities of farm life bring forward a healthy crop of workers with no desire for the higher labor of intellectual exertion. What occurs can easily be foreseen, as the young Brook Farmer Sophia Eastman notes. "'There is an aristocracy prevailing here,' the seventeen- or eighteen-year old told her family right away, 'and many complain of being neglected.'"[45] By the summer of 1842, just a year into the Brook Farm experiment, the needs for skilled farm labor and for an influx of money create a class system: those who come for intellectual labor minus the headaches of traditional town life, and those who search the still-shaky economic landscape of the northern United States in search of physical labor opportunities. Brook Farm, more quickly than most would imagine, transitions from a lofty ideal of self-completion into a class system barely hanging on to its ideals.

Sterling Delano, whose *Brook Farm: The Dark Side of Utopia* remains the best treatment of the community, writes this history as a tragedy, and rightly so. Brook Farm's short history is one of always being on the brink, scrambling for members and money. Brook Farm's fateful decision to transition from anti-political agrarian utopia to Fourierist productive phalanx in 1844 is the death knell of the transcendental portion of the experiment.[46] The quiet farm life becomes a desperate struggle to produce, sell, and ship. The phalanx mercifully meets its end in 1846, when the expensive and massive main building, still under construction, catches fire and burns to the ground.[47] The question the tragedy of Brook Farm brings to the fore, however, is what precisely went wrong? Richard Francis makes the argument that "perhaps this verdict is just a cumbersome way of saying that, in the end, the Transcendentalist-Fourierist view was simply wrong. Nature was not organized in the way it was claimed."[48] Brook Farm represents a movement away from the burdens of early capitalism, crystallized as a splitting of the individual into its most productive parts—but are we correct to assume that the failure of Brook Farm signals the failure of structural reorganization of life along transcendentalist lines?

Fruitlands

Brook Farm's six-year existence stands up well in comparison with the life of Bronson Alcott and Charles Lane's Fruitlands community. Fruitlands lasts only seven months, due to a mixture of infighting, money problems, little food, and Abigail Alcott's decision to bring the community to a close via her brother, an important investor in the project.[49] Fruitlands tells a story of an idealist stubbornly driven by his vision of the world, and the friends and relatives he can convince to share (and pay for) his dream. The inimitable Bronson Alcott, whose complex philosophy of vegetarian asceticism brings precious few followers, nonetheless represents another attempt to achieve transcendental completeness through a reorganization of social institutions. Alcott's idiosyncrasies—wearing only homemade linen clothing, and refusing to use oxen to manage a ninety-acre farm, eating only vegetables that grow above ground—thereby "aiming toward heaven"—animate an extraordinary tragedy in the quest for completion of the self.

Fruitlands gets its start in the summer of 1843, when Alcott, freshly returned from a rejuvenating trip to England, and Charles Lane, an English admirer who makes the return trip to Massachusetts, search for a fit piece of land to begin a new utopian community. They settle on a ninety-acre farm near Concord, which they oddly christen "Fruitlands" (though it contains only a half dozen poorly bearing fruit trees). Despite his repudiation of the concept of property, Lane purchases the farm for $1,800, using all of his money and a great deal more in loan. Alcott, penniless from an unsuccessful turn as a schoolteacher (his conversations with children, published in book format, cause a minor scandal) and farmer, nonetheless takes charge of the community, which consists of Alcott and his family; Lane and his ten-year-old son; Joseph Gardiner Wright (briefly); and a series of short-term visitors. Fruitlands is more openly political than Brook Farm, as Alcott is an avowed anarchist, and Lane offers an early and dense defense of libertarianism.[50] In an early effort to attract members to the community, Alcott delivers a lecture on the philosophy of completion. "We, therefore, ignore human governments, creeds, and institutions . . . we deny the right of any man to dictate laws for our regulation, or duties for our performance; and declare our allegiance only to Universal love, the all-embracing Justice."[51]

Fruitlands embraces the concept of a totalizing reorganization of human life and conduct. The degree to which this reorganization takes place would fracture the community—Lane, a single man, desires to transcend the family, while Abigail Alcott (and to a lesser extent, Bronson Alcott) understandably bristle at the notion. Alcott, like Thoreau, attempts to ground life in principles higher than those of politics—in this case, the principle is an appeal to a universal (love or justice) that transcends time and place.

Fruitlands' major philosophical push is for what Abigail Alcott terms "diffusive illimitable benevolence," a theory of a particular, small organization having the effect of transforming the whole of society through its shining example.[52] Alcott and Lane plan Fruitlands as an experiment in living, one that they (particularly Lane) feel will transform the burgeoning American social and economic world toward a more complete and divine end. Diffusive illimitable benevolence grasps the transcendental combination of the universal and the particular but also works as a theory of truth in disclosure. Alcott's vision of Fruitlands is a vision of truth—truth in social life—that must be disclosed in order to be dispersed and lived in other contexts. The particular life of Fruitlands is agrarian and local, but its impact, echoing the utopian socialist movement at large, intends to be global.

Money Problems

It is fitting to conclude the discussion of Brook Farm and Fruitlands with a discussion of their money problems. Both Brook Farm and Fruitlands are enormous farms, far beyond what is needed to sustain the number of individuals within; of course, this leaves the Ripleys, Alcotts, and Lane in terrible debt. Thoreau's famous quote from *Walden* "It is difficult to begin without borrowing" is not related directly to the utopian communities but represents his explanation for borrowing an axe to begin building his own cabin.[53] Thoreau's meticulous accounting of his intakes and expenditures reveals a thoroughly different understanding of the problems of money and labor in the early nineteenth century. Money problems, in fact, give us one of the starkest differences between Thoreau and early communitarianism: communitarians locate the sense of freedom, of completion of the self, within the collective value of labor and the freedom to choose forms of labor. For Thoreau, one is free to the degree that he or she is not *committed* to something, whether it is a house or a prison.[54] Thoreau is at pains to point out exactly the degree to which he remains free, which offers an implicit critique of the motivations and methods of Brook Farm and Fruitlands. Indebtedness spawns desperation.

Brook Farm and Fruitlands aim to recreate the individual by offering the completions fractured by the fates of early modern capitalism. This agrarian dream, upset in Brook Farm by the transition to Fourierism, and in Fruitlands by the inabilities of its members as farmers, suffers ultimately at the hands of the market. Brook Farmers cannot make anything that will sell, they cannot get their own members to pay their dues or membership fees, and the wells of easy borrowing run dry. Fruitlands is doomed from the start, having few laborers, little understanding of agriculture, and poor land for performing the types of work they wish to perform. These idealistic movements are brought down ultimately by the stubborn realities of the nineteenth century. Thoreau, offered to camp in Brook Farm in 1841, notes famously, "I think I had rather keep bachelor's hall in hell than go to board in heaven."[55] Thoreau negates the specifics of the movement, but this does not suggest that his own sojourn does not share the principles and hopes of the movement.

The connection between *Walden* and the Brook Farm/Fruitlands experiments often neglects the crucial issue of money and debt. In a key article on Thoreau's politics in *Walden*, Brian Walker offers this summary: "Thoreau's central theme is that working conditions in a market democracy can easily undermine liberty and erode autonomy."[56] Walker's brilliant essay connects *Walden* to the problem of work but stops at the inhumanity of the practice of labor without deconstructing the cause of market labor—the problem of debt. While we can read *Walden* as an argument for the reworking of the practice of labor, it is more fruitful for us to examine the problem Thoreau examines himself: that the act of indebtedness, of becoming indebted through commitments—whether social, filial, intellectual, or economic—creates the conditions through which labor becomes necessary. Thoreau is not so much trying to reform labor as he is attempting to ground the self in its ability to bypass commitment, to refuse to take on the debts that one does not or should not choose. Walker is correct to argue that *Walden* attempts to "render poverty livable."[57] But Thoreau's major philosophical push in *Walden* is to challenge and reshape the notion of indebtedness and the subsequent problem of fate.

In another way we see Thoreau's quotation "It is difficult to begin without borrowing" explaining the difficulties not only of work but of philosophy. In a 1928 letter, Heidegger offers the following: "Perhaps philosophy shows most forcibly and persistently how much man is a beginner. Philosophizing ultimately means nothing other than being a beginner."[58] Thoreau makes a point of mentioning the lack of books at his cabin during his two-year stay and declares with verve, "There are nowadays professors of philosophy, but not philosophers."[59] As explored above, one of Thoreau's motivations in *Walden* is to recreate the practice of philosophy, returning philosophy to its concerns with "voluntary poverty" and away from the borrowings of the wisdom of others. Again, as a means of freedom, Thoreau is attempting to locate his own philosophical abilities without indebting himself to a fresh tradition; of course, this is the popular justification of Thoreau's American newness (borrowed from Emerson), which subjects all history, all nature, and all purpose to the whim of the ever-present American individual. If philosophy is about being a beginner (in Heidegger's phrase), Thoreau is attempting to find something more raw in the connection between philosophy and practical life. Removing the debts one incurs in attempting to become something or someone else is the crucial first step in this mission.

In dealing with questions of debt, fate, freedom, and work, Thoreau connects himself to ancient philosophy, particularly its Stoic variant. Walker argues rightly that the "key to *Walden* is the way it combines ancient philosophical practices and modern economic calculations to set out a strategy by which citizens can realize their liberty."[60] This argument is made clear through the comparison of Thoreau's concerns with partiality, wholeness, and debt alongside those of Epictetus, whose *Discourses* offers a pre-Thoreauvian analysis of the promises and pitfalls involved in describing the boundaries of individual freedom amid the promises of commitment, esteem, and public evaluation.

Problems of the Self in Epictetus: Stoic Themes and *Walden*'s Philosophical Force

The question of partiality and wholeness not only abounds in nineteenth-century American philosophy but was an important concern of the Roman Stoics as well. Epictetus's powerful endorsement of Socratic philosophy in Book 1 of the *Discourses* alerts us to the context of the problem: "We . . . think of ourselves as though we were mere bellies, entrails, and genitals, just because we have fear, because we have appetite, and we flatter those who have power to help us in these matters."[61] Our split within ourselves is the doing of our desires, which prompts us to value matters—emotions, circumstances, and individuals—the effect of which is not under our control. "Well, what about my brother's life?—That again is the subject of his own art of living, but with respect to *your* art of living it comes under the category of externals, like a farm, like health, like good repute."[62] Epictetus's method of prodding and thrusting individuals into a state of contentedness with their present state anticipates Thoreau's own method, and the ultimate goal of this philosophical exercise is the same practical end: "Stop admiring your clothes . . . stop admiring your wife's beauty."[63] Each philosopher wrestles with the conditions under which individuals make themselves partial through their existential dedication to matters outside their control.

Epictetus's concentration on eradicating one's partial commitments to others—what Ortega y Gasset will term *alteraction*—leads to a philosophy of ownness that demands one pay attention to oneself first and foremost: "No one is dearer to me than myself."[64] Epictetus attends to himself because he believes it is his nature as a situated self to act as a free man, to practice his freedom in such a way that this freedom is maintained or expanded.[65] Ridding oneself of one's partial commitments is not a matter of luxury for the Stoic philosopher; indeed, it is an important precondition for coming to philosophical thinking: "You have to submit to discipline, follow a strict diet, give up sweet-cakes, train under compulsion."[66] The philosopher becomes so through preparing himself to unify the desires of his body with the demands of nature and the mind, "so to love wisdom as to live according to its dictates, a life of simplicity, independence, magnanimity, and trust."[67]

Concerns that lead the self outward situate the self as the servant of an external cause or individual. "But if you gape open-mouthed at externals, you must needs be tossed up and down according to the will of your master. And who is your master? He who has authority over any of the things upon which you set your heart or which you wish to avoid."[68] Epictetus later counsels, "Never lay claim to anything that is not your own."[69] Epictetus's claim that another can master the self through dictating the self's fulfillment of desire rests on the argument that commitment to an external cause creates a false or faulty indebtedness to another, pushing us beyond our own toward what is unnatural for us. Epictetus seals the philosophical power of ownness by attributing it to God: "And what is the law of God? To guard what is his own, not to lay claim to what is not his own."[70] The consequence of living outside oneself may include public esteem and outward success, but the internally demanding force of outwardness perpetuates one's distance from one's own accounts of control.

Thoreau says in an 1849 letter to Harrison Blake, "Let us live a *thread* of life."[71] Thoreau's consistent return to the actions of reducing, simplifying, and moving backward echo in Epictetus's philosophy as well. The practice of unifying oneself underneath the umbrella of one's own *will*able actions necessitates that one's hopes and yearnings significantly reduce in favor of more measured expectations from one's life and the world. Living a thread of life may be all that there is for the whole self, because it is one's own thread. Epictetus argues, "You did not come into the world to select unusually fine places, but to live and go about your business in the place where you were born and enrolled as a citizen."[72] This argument echoes Thoreau's in "Resistance to Civil Government": "I came into this world, not chiefly to make this a good place to live in, but to live in it, be it good or bad."[73] Understanding the proper boundaries of the self's effects on its life and the lives around it is the paramount objective of both Stoic and Thoreauvian philosophy. Epictetus asks, "And how shall I free myself?" and he answers: "Direct your aversion towards the things that lie within the sphere of the moral purpose."[74] Thoreau, in an early letter to Blake, laments that some "are cursed with duties."[75] Duties are a curse insofar as they arise unnecessarily out of mistake; one binds oneself to the assumed duties of his or her parents, the community, friends, social mores, or other externalizing devices.

The Story of Partiality in Thoreau's *Walden*

As mentioned above, there are an extraordinary number of topics, themes, and interpretations of Thoreau's *Walden,* but one of the more underrepresented areas of focus is Thoreau's motivation for writing the book (and for having the experience). Thoreau's ethos in *Walden* is a non-desperate life, and the bulk of the first chapter of the book, "Economy," will diagnose the problem of desperation in nineteenth-century New England. The question of what causes desperation, and what a desperate life entails, leads Thoreau back to the communitarian movements mentioned. Similarly to Brook Farm and Fruitlands, Thoreau employs the transcendentalist goal of reconstructing the self by creating the mythological wholeness with nature through labor. Emerson's desire to redeem history through its marriage to presence, echoed in Thoreau's *A Week on the Concord and Merrimack Rivers,* receives a more radicalized treatment in *Walden.* Thoreau is reconstituting the conditions of private life—what Thoreau calls "necessity"—as a means of transporting the self out of the puzzles of one's own historical time and into the safe space of a self-reliant, unhistorical mind: "Every man is tasked to make his life, even in its details, worthy of the contemplation of his most elevated and critical hour."[76]

The problems of partiality and completion haunt *Walden:* the first aim of his book, to critique the concept of property as necessity, contains an explicit critique of partiality: "I see young men, my townsmen, whose misfortune it is to have inherited farms, houses, barns, cattle, and farming tools. . . . Why should they begin digging their graves as soon as they are born?"[77] Thoreau maintains this critique throughout the first chapter and into the second, where he uses his imagination to "buy" several farms in his mind, only to cede ownership in reality. Property represents partiality in a twofold sense: first, one is literally taking a part of the world for one's own, at the expense of the rest of the world (or, in Thoreau's mind, the rest of the village). One finds oneself focusing work, joy, and trial on the partiality of one's "own" property, forsaking that which is not owned, the wild, new, expansive provincial world Thoreau inhabits. Second, property represents partiality in a social sense: it is through the acquisition of property that individuals become workers, having "no time to be anything but a machine."[78] Emerson's criticism of partiality as becoming monster and Thoreau's criticism of the individual as a machine display the grotesque imagery of partiality, transforming the self into something other—*monsters* and *machines* are, after all, other terms for incomplete human beings.

Individuals are made partial through a desperate attempt to hang on to the things they do not know they do not need. As Thoreau notes famously, "men labor under a mistake."[79] The mistake of necessity contains vital consequences. Some of Thoreau's strongest language in *Walden* comes from his critique of the everyday life of the new worker. "It is very evident what mean and sneaking lives many of you live," Thoreau argues, "always on the limits, trying to get into business and trying to get out of debt, a very ancient slough, called by the Latins, *aes alienum*, another's brass."[80] Thoreau describes the details of this desperate life, wherein individuals are always committed to the projects of another. This privatist concern with those the self serves reminds the reader of Max Stirner's preface to *The Ego and Its Own*, in which Stirner attempts to recover a sense of freedom as self-enjoyment. Thoreau similarly locates the necessities of market life as a loss of freedom, a dissipation of the self's conception of itself. Interestingly, Thoreau could be describing life at Brook Farm, where the desperate search for money quickly outweighs the virtues of collective life. Thoreau's diagnosis of the desperate life remains strictly on the consequences of social life for the individual and does not carry with it the "disease" of collective reform.

Thoreau writes *Walden* as an individual, for individuals, so it is no surprise that he is so attentive to the conditions of the individual psyche. Perhaps the most striking passage of the famous first chapter is Thoreau's concern for personal affirmation:

> I sometimes wonder that we can be so frivolous, I may almost say, as to attend to the gross but somewhat foreign form of servitude called Negro Slavery, there are so many keen and subtle masters that enslave both north and south. It is hard to have a southern overseer; it is worse to have a northern one; but worst of all when you are the slave-driver of yourself. Talk of divinity in man! Look at the teamster on the highway, wending to market by day or night; does any divinity stir within him? His highest duty to fodder and water his horses! What is his destiny to him compared to the shipping interests? . . . How godlike, how immortal is he?[81]

Thoreau's evaluation of the importance of a cause to oneself may escape us on first reading. It is important to note, however, that Thoreau critiques our attention to chattel slavery not because it is somehow less gross than we feel, but that it remains at a distance from our personal lives. Highlighting vital distance and not severity is a foundational source of personal value for Thoreau. To argue that one's private opinion of oneself is somehow worse than slavery is a nonsensical argument unless we understand that Thoreau argues *that it is worse for that particular self,* because it is one's own life. As Thoreau argues, our lives are in some way irretrievably partial.

Thoreau's diagnosis of desperation reaches an apex with his discussion of private opinion and public opinion. There are several important takeaways from this passage, but the most important is that Thoreau will somehow measure a non-desperate life by the self's ability to find the things that are closest to it. The communitarian move to remake society in order to remake the individual is far from Thoreau's mind—as is Emerson's individualist move to remake society by first remaking the self. Thoreau's aim is to bypass desperation personally, and to let the world be as it is. "Our opinion of ourselves is our fate," Thoreau notes, and he aims to allow individuals sufficient room for completing themselves via a hard-wrought investigation into individual wants and desires.[82] Thoreau's privatist vision of escaping desperation will be intimately connected to his bedrock concept of "faithfully minding my business."[83] Thoreau does not offer a program of personal reform, but only an invitation to make one's life one's own and to work toward self-completion: "The life which men praise and regard as successful is but one kind. Why should we exaggerate any one kind at the expense of others?"[84]

Thoreau's odd discussion of youth and old age in the opening pages of *Walden* comes to an apex with the notion of partiality: "Practically, the old have no very important advice to give the young, their own experience has been so partial."[85] Later, Thoreau writes, "You may say the wisest thing you can, old man. . . . I hear an irresistible voice which invites me away from all that."[86] Of course, Thoreau himself admits the partiality of his own experiment and its value four pages earlier, arguing that his book is best suited for poor students, but that anyone may plunder the rest for its vital value. Thoreau is quick to dismiss the "partial" experience of the old having an influence on the young, but he is also involved in defending partiality as a way of living a non-desperate life. Partiality, in fact, and the uniqueness of individual experience, is what will set Thoreau's agrarian experiment apart from the agrarian experiments of his transcendentalist acquaintances. Moral teachers of the ages (here Thoreau notes Solomon and Hippocrates) attempt to discover the minute, or particular, laws of human conduct—including the proper length of fingernails and the ethics of the distances of trees.[87] This sort of partiality—partial legislation—receives a good critique from Thoreau. There remains an impossible—or seemingly impossible—relation of partiality and universality in Thoreau's text. Later in the introduction, Thoreau offers this counsel: "Who shall say what prospect life offers to another? Could a greater miracle take place than for us to look through each other's eyes for an instant?"[88]

Our social lives are undeniably partial, and Thoreau envisions no way of reconciling individual lives toward a universal goal. "The only cooperation which is commonly possible is exceedingly partial and superficial."[89] If Brook Farm and Fruitlands aim at reducing partiality, Thoreau argues that they are wrong in their diagnosis of the problem. The problem of living a partial life has more to do with the everydayness of alienation, which can be solved only through a thorough reconciling of one's true necessities. Thoreau's concentrations throughout "Economy" on food, shelter, clothing, and fuel—the basic necessities of human life—mimic the reorganization of these necessities within the communitarian reform movement. Thoreau, however, argues that his community of one, with its lack of capital, privatist personal ethic, and "voluntary poverty," represents the truly philosophical way of coming out of the desperate circumstances of collective life.[90]

Partiality represents the limit of political life: we are always attempting to understand another, to reform another, without the proper means of knowing what that person needs. This is the locus of Thoreau's critique of reform. Thoreau argues that he would stay away from reformers, "for fear that I should get some of his good done to me—some of its virus mingled with my blood."[91] The reformer works not primarily out of a desire to change the world, but to shake off a part of itself that it cannot handle: "I believe what so saddens the reformer is not his sympathy with his fellows in distress, but . . . his private ail."[92] A vital shortage in individual life—an individual severed from himself, experiencing the horror of another kind of doubleness—accounts for the desire to reform others. But, as Thoreau mentions, we live so far distant from another: "Often the poor man is not so cold and hungry as he is dirty and ragged and gross. It is partly his taste, and not merely his misfortune. If you give him money, he will perhaps buy more rags with it."[93] Reformers desire to "fix" others out of a sense of personal embarrassment on their behalf, but this is as close as we get to another person. Politics, the means by which we negotiate the distributions of rights and responsibilities, always plays at a remove from the actual lives of individual participants.

If the everyday world of participatory politics provides no way beyond a desperate life, and the social organization of life offers little, Thoreau gives breath to amending the concept of self-completeness within an individual. By the time of *Walden*'s publication in 1854, Thoreau is well on his way to becoming absorbed in the particulars of Concord's natural life, and the influence of nineteenth-century natural science will push the romanticism of Thoreau's early theories of completion toward a more empirical holism.[94] As such, *Walden*'s "hero" will be the individual who can find completeness within the confines of a private life.

The Canadian woodchopper, Alek Therien, certainly qualifies as the most heroic figure in *Walden*. Thoreau is unreservedly celebratory of Therien, partially because he represents something Thoreau so desires to cultivate: "In him the animal man chiefly was developed."[95] Thoreau's interest in wild figures, such as the woodchopper and Maine woods guide Joseph Polis, augments his frequent appeals to wildness on his own behalf: "I caught a glimpse of a woodchuck stealing across my path, and felt a strange thrill of savage delight, and was strongly tempted to seize and devour him raw; not that I was hungry then, except for that wildness which he represented."[96] Thoreau mentions later in the same paragraph: "I found in myself . . . an instinct toward a higher, or as it is named, spiritual life . . . and another toward a primitive rank and savage one, and I reverence them both."[97] While Thoreau reverences the spiritual and the animal, it is clear from his description of Therien that the project of self-completion involves coming to grips with the animal inside. In many ways Thoreau's *Walden* deals with the concept of savagery similarly to Rousseau's *Second Discourse;* we get the sense, with this description of the hero, that regaining the virtues of savagery is a more difficult task than achieving the virtues of a civilized life.[98]

Therien "interested me because he was so quiet and solitary and so happy withal," a sense of completion achieved through a lack of self-doubt, introspection, and guilt.[99] The woodchopper's self-assurance compels Thoreau because it is so innocent, so provincial, and so antiquated. When Thoreau asks him if he is a reformer who would like the world to be changed, Therien, shocked, replies, "No, I like it well enough."[100] His simple philosophy of life internalizes the functions of institutions without moralizing them and offers Thoreau a glimpse of his philosophy in action. Thoreau finds him so interesting that he "would any day walk ten miles to observe it, and it amounted to the re-origination of many of the institutions of society."[101] The split of the individual, in this case, is bandaged through the reacquaintance of the self with the animal within. Of course, Therien is limited, as Thoreau notes: "His thinking was so primitive and immersed in his animal life, that, though more promising than a merely learned man's, it rarely ripened into anything which can be reported."[102]

As a result of Therien's intellectual deficiency, Thoreau stops short of declaring him the ideal man. Indeed, Thoreau's celebration of his "half-cultivated field" in "The Bean-Field" chapter alerts us to the necessity of intellectual and instinctual cultivation in the composition of the complete soul. In the process of hoeing beans, Thoreau transcends the practice—"It was no longer beans that I hoed, nor that I hoed beans"[103]—and the bean field achieves its primary purpose, "to serve as a parable-maker one day."[104] We find that Therien offers the promise of a simplified existence, but it is one that falls short of realizing the complete soul.

Therien represents a portion of completion of the self, for Thoreau a boon to the mood of *Walden*. Contrasting the woodchopper with the John Field family, Irish immigrants renting the Baker Farm, yields an understanding of Thoreau's context. Thoreau visits the family and attempts to educate them on his own simple existence. The Field family, a brutal example of the desperation of the times, settles in the United States with a hope of becoming self-sufficient and having the luxuries and trappings of successful life. However, Thoreau argues, "the only true America is that country where you are at liberty to pursue such a mode of life as may enable you to do without these [things]."[105] His words to the Field family fall flat, as they concern themselves primarily with making a decent life out of the partial successes of small material advantages. Thoreau cannot and will not take them seriously, and they provide a useful counter-example to the woodchopper. Thoreau's "only true America" again places the emphasis of freedom on one's freedom from encumbrances of the modern world.

The emphasis on partiality and completion in Thoreau's *Walden* represents an amendment of the transcendentalist philosophy of unity between the particulars and the universal. For Thoreau, partiality is the necessary condition of social life—as such, we cannot hope to transcend it. Inward partiality, however, is in our power to change. To become inwardly complete, and thus to achieve an active and meaningful sense of freedom, individuals must plumb their own lives for the partialities, the alienations, that take their time and stretch their commitments. For Thoreau, this is his path to a non-desperate life.

A Non-Desperate Life: *Walden* and the Completion of the Self

Thoreau's diagnosis of the modern problem of partiality relies on his overarching critique of social means of reforming society. The search for a non-desperate life, a fulfilling life within the confines of an ever-changing society, brings Thoreau to the connections that dominate his later thought. In the opening paragraph of "Solitude," Thoreau writes: "This is a delicious evening, when the whole body is one sense, and imbibes delight through every pore. I go and come with a strange liberty in Nature, a part of herself. . . . I see nothing special to attract me, all the elements are unusually congenial to me."[106] Thoreau describes the feelings that many echo upon experiencing truly great moments; here, however, the importance lies in Thoreau's refusal (or inability) to locate the centrality of that feeling on one particular object. Therien's ease and acquiescence to the world pale in comparison with Thoreau's uncontested affirmation that "all the elements are unusually congenial" to him. The natural life—the serene, confident, non-desperate life—shuns the partiality of selective attention and finds itself affirming all that surrounds. What appears a mystical experience for Thoreau effectively demonstrates the requirements for escaping the problem of partiality.

Thoreau's sense of completeness also demonstrates itself in the opening paragraph of "Sounds": "What is a course of history, or philosophy, or poetry, no matter how well selected, or the best society, or the most admirable routine of life, compared with the discipline of looking always at what is to be seen?"[107] Demonstrating that he indeed looks at what is to be seen, Thoreau describes himself "in undisturbed solitude and stillness, while the birds sang around or flitted noiseless through the house."[108] The moments of quiet presence, which decorate the opening lines of several middle paragraphs in *Walden*, act as evidence of the possibilities and consequences of existential completeness: in these moments Thoreau is perfectly content, not desperate, a part of nature itself, having achieved the completeness desired by transcendentalists. "Be rather the Mungo Park, the Lewis and Clarke and Frobisher, of your own streams and oceans; explore your own higher latitudes."[109] Thoreau refurbishes the classical dictum to "explore thyself," offering it in the context of traveling within oneself to know—and then live—the various parts of the self.[110]

Thoreau's dictum that one become "expert in home-cosmography" suggests a self-satisfaction that does not seek the substitute satisfactions of travel. Thoreau's response to the railroad, the newspaper, and the telegraph, often viewed as stubborn ramblings, offers the grounds for a cogent defense of provincialism. One of Thoreau's goals in *Walden*, according to David Robinson, is to reignite the Jeffersonian agrarian myth.[111] But Thoreau goes further—his goal, in this particular case, is to defend the type of life in which one is not always searching for something beyond the self. Thoreau lives outside of Concord for six months out of his life and speaks of Concord as his definitive place: "My feet forever stand / On Concord fields / And I must live the life / Which this soil yields."[112] Yet around him, the speed of interstate communication is on everyone's mind: "We are in great haste to construct a magnetic telegraph from Maine to Texas; but Maine and Texas, it may be, have nothing important to communicate."[113]

Thoreau's definition of the philosopher—one who lives according to "simplicity, independence, magnanimity, and trust"—eschews the desperation of the early market through a continual practical investigation into the principles of its life. Thoreau's *Walden*, like the *Meditations* of Marcus Aurelius or the *Discourses* of Epictetus, is repetitive, because the non-desperate life is perpetually involved in overcoming the same problems—the extravagances of feeding necessities, the problem of others, and the question of how to spend one's time. Thoreau's primary paradox in *Walden* is that simplification, honed through solitude, provides the enduring richness of life. Thoreau's emphasis on solitude is, among other things, a solidification of the method of experiencing exhilaration in life: "There can be no black melancholy to him who lives in the midst of Nature and has his senses still. . . . I trust that nothing can make life a burden to me."[114] The unburdened life, another term for the non-desperate life, connects Thoreau's philosophy of getting a living to his broader privatist philosophy.

In a journal entry from the summer of 1845, Thoreau writes: "To live to a good old age such as the ancients reached—serene and contented—dignifying the life of man—Leading a simple epic country life—in these days of confusion and turmoil."[115] This quote, which turns from the goals of Wordsworth to Thoreau's own goal, connects the agrarian ideal of the "simple epic country life" and the serenity of the non-desperate ideal to the imminent confusion of contemporary social life. Thoreau offers *Walden* as an invitation to a radical individualism because the problems he diagnoses cannot be solved through a mediated or transcendentalized reconfiguration of society. The quotation that opens this essay, taken from Michael Gilmore's fine book *American Romanticism and the Marketplace*, is chosen not because it presents a unique view of Thoreau's time at Walden Pond; indeed, one could argue that Gilmore's quote is representative of the majority opinion of Thoreau scholars. The interpretation of Thoreau's experiment as a failure obfuscates Thoreau's purpose in writing the book: simply put, political life offers few avenues through which individuals can meaningfully improve their lives, given the breadth and depth of trenchant social changes. Thoreau's alternative to Brook Farm and Fruitlands stems from the same purpose—to reconfigure or suture the individual's disparate parts—but Thoreau recognizes, or theorizes, that the self cannot transfer its social allegiances to another group without paying significant costs of life.

Thoreau's nexus of freedom is, as he mentions in a poem from his time at Walden Pond, "freedom from care."[116] Once Thoreau reaches the point of articulating his philosophy of freedom, he opens eyes to the rationale behind his temporary relocation to Walden Pond. Thoreau's particular brand of freedom—a release from concern with externals—renders mass democratic politics unable to solve the philosophical problems of individual life. Politics is, first and foremost, about externals; it rarely contains vital value but is generally dissipated as a spectator sport through the mediation of the newspaper. Thoreau's Walden experiment cannot be interpreted as a failure for its inability to found a society or even a civic moral; indeed, Thoreau's experiment could not be conducted under conditions of abstract sociality. For Thoreau to free himself from care—and to offer this existential freedom as an invitation to readers—he rejects the communitarian social cure in favor of an individual experiment that provides a cure by removing the symptoms.

Thoreau's non-desperate life is finally achieved as the individual suspends care from the types of concerns plaguing the average individual. The modern disease of improving oneself operates as a sort of lived servitude to ideals that do not respond to the demands of life. Thoreau offers instead: "However mean your life is, meet it and live it; do not shun it and call it hard names. . . . Love your life, poor as it is."[117] Later in the conclusion he offers this solace to the voluntary poor: "If you are restricted in your range by poverty, if you cannot buy books and newspapers, for instance, you are but confined to the most significant and vital experiences. . . . It is life near the bone where it is sweetest."[118] When one finds oneself within the bonds of poverty—and feeling desperate from its tightening grip—Thoreau offers that one merely suspend care. The wholeness offered through a simple acceptance of ownness supplied by attending to one's cares at the expense of the public absolves the self of the trifles of that which is not one's own.

4

Wildness

The Phenomenology of Freedom

America is said to be the arena on which the battle of freedom is to be
fought; but surely it cannot be freedom in a merely political sense that is
meant. . . . Now that the republic—the *res-publica*—has been settled, it is
time to look after the *res-privata*—the private state—to see . . . that the
private state receive no detriment.
—Thoreau, *Reform Papers*[1]

Beyond constituting a central portion of his political thought, Thoreau's sense
of wildness provides the phenomenological foundation of his philosophy. To
make this argument suggests that for Thoreau *wildness* most often refers to
the *philosophical disposition* of one who is prepared for the visceral description
of phenomena within the sphere of consciousness. As such, Thoreau's wildness morphs from its characterization as "that which disturbs and confounds
settled projects" into the positive valuation of freedom experienced in a body
in space and time, coexistent with the others who facilitate and preempt
wildness.[2] Wildness is not only a phenomenological disposition but, importantly, one that unfolds the experience of existential freedom within place.
Take, for instance, Thoreau's description of the horse's condition: "What is a
horse but an animal that has lost its liberty."[3] Thoreau's description of the life
cycle of the horse is one of wildness interrupted by the slavery of servitude to
human beings, psychologically reduced to an employee of the human interest. For Thoreau, the change in the horse is deadening—it loses its liberty by
losing its grip on the visceral parts of its nature. For the horse, the visceral
self constitutes its being, suggesting that the loss of wildness signals the loss
of its entire life. The horse becomes a thing, an appendage to a cart, a means

107

of transporting goods or people, but no longer a thing that moves with the instincts of its freedom. In losing its liberty it loses the ability—the potential—to express its liberty through its instinctive actions.

Thoreau's notion of wildness, located in his preference for the wild—particularly as opposed to the politics—provides a curious case for liberal interpretations of his thought. For the most part, Thoreau's wildness remains unaddressed within political interpretations of his work, despite its centrality in his comprehensive philosophy. Two notable exceptions, Jane Bennett's *Thoreau's Nature* and George Kateb's "Wildness and Conscience," aim to interpret the concept of wildness as a precursor to the traditional Thoreauvian theme of "civil disobedience." Thoreau's wildness, as a phenomenological disposition, expresses the experience of freedom as it is found within the complex spatial and temporal relations of climbing, studying trees, watching toads, or scaring woodchucks. Wildness is not only a precursor to a political philosophy, not a way of disrupting common political life to inspire a new political life—it represents nothing less than Thoreau's wholesale reconfiguration of the life of freedom, one of our most treasured political concepts. Wildness is the disposition capable of carrying out a lived experience of existential freedom, without reducing that freedom to its correlates within the public sphere. If Thoreau is a philosopher of freedom (and I believe that he is, perhaps above all else), it is through wildness that this freedom is disclosed in its complexity and corporeality.

This chapter interrogates the formation and changing shape of Thoreau's concept of wildness. Wildness serves several functions in Thoreau's thought, and I resist the urge to compartmentalize or simplify the concept. I will follow the trajectory of wildness from Thoreau's early essay "A Natural History of Massachusetts" through his mature essay "Walking."

Ways of Wildness: Political Interpretations

Sherman Paul's comprehensive evaluation of Thoreau's thought offers many insights, perhaps none more poignant than his clarification of Thoreau's concept of wildness: "Thoreau didn't say *wilderness*, he said *wildness* because . . . more than the actual wilderness itself he valued its psychic correlative: *wildness*, the instinctual, *wildness* as *willed-ness*, the expression of will, in the interest of keeping open one's vital, instinctual life."[4]

Paul highlights the uniqueness of Thoreau's contribution to our understanding of nature and politics. Thoreau's concept of wildness relates not only to nature itself but to nature's relationship with the will as means of earning individual attention, desire, commitment, and evaluation. Wildness is not wilderness but the remnant of a natural process inside of us that still responds to what is vital after the social lays claim to our time and our evaluation of life. Wildness is in some way a grasping for maintaining a self that is becoming less and less possible in democratic and early industrial America. Wildness relates to the psyche, and the psyche's survival of its most trenchant time and surroundings.

Uses of wildness in contemporary political reflections on Thoreau tend to make positive connections between the concept of wildness itself and Thoreau's political theory, particularly Thoreau's civil disobedience. Jane Bennett's excellent *Thoreau's Nature* provides a nice summation of this approach: "My Thoreau, however, takes one down a somewhat different path—to reflection into the type of self capable of an act of conscientious dissent and into the processes through which that individual may come into being. . . . What is required is a periodic withdrawal from social intercourse, episodes of self-induced aphasia . . . an awareness of the Wildness or genius within, the investment of one's highest hopes and ideals into the person of another."[5]

I quote Bennett at length because her approach is nuanced and persuasive but ultimately retreats into a standard interpretation of Thoreau's comprehensive philosophy. Bennett's final argument is that wildness exists as a prerequisite for political action, and that Thoreau's overall project of "self-fashioning" moves Thoreau toward subjectivity capable of performing civil disobedience. While Bennett understands Thoreau's lifelong project of self-cultivation, she places it within the *telos* of responsibility to the other, discounting Thoreau's use of wildness as a way out into the freedom from care. Thoreau is consistently dissatisfied with his forays into politics and erects wildness as a way of describing his trepidation toward political commitments. Thoreau is not constructing a "self capable of an act of conscientious dissent" but instead strives to construct a self that does not rely on political interpretations of freedom in which to ground life.

Bennett's shortcoming in this respect surfaces with her preference for using "the Wild," a term that refers to environment itself, instead of *wildness*. Thoreau's concept of wildness is a response to political life, cemented in essays such as "Slavery in Massachusetts" when he states, referring to the governor of Massachusetts, "he did not govern me."[6] To deny that one is governed by the governor is a rejection—a getting past—of bounded political liberty, grounded in the more robust confidence of wildness as absolute freedom. Those who constitute their freedom according to state allowance are bound to be governed by the governor; the individual who cultivates a sense of wildness, on the other hand, leaves the state behind and acts as arbiter over individual life.

Like Bennett, George Kateb attempts to reconcile the concept of wildness with the democratic practice of Thoreau's conscientious politics. Kateb is largely responsible for introducing democratic individuality as the keynote contribution of Thoreau's philosophy, and his "Wildness and Conscience" establishes Thoreau's wildness as a subset of his moral conscience. Kateb defines wildness as "excess and extremism" and claims that the wildness of American individuality is most prominently a counterforce to the wildness of uninhibited government growth and domination.[7] Thoreau (alongside Emerson) utilizes wildness in newly democratic contexts, espousing a sort of minimally political democratic individuality that relies on its own moral sense to ground political commitments. Kateb argues that Thoreau and Emerson "tend in an anarchist direction, but do so for new moral purposes."[8]

Kateb's connection between moral conscience and wildness is uncovered through the anarchism (or rigid libertarianism) Emerson and Thoreau share: "But where is the wildness? If not already found in the elements I have isolated so far, it is seen in the most distinctive aspect of their teaching, especially that of Thoreau, in the doctrine of moral conscience as resistance to government."[9]

This important passage serves not only as a centerpiece of Kateb's argument but as a reflection of the contemporary consensus on Thoreau's contribution to American political thought. Kateb submerges the concept of wildness under the familiar concept of conscience, placing wildness as the disposition that makes moral resistance to government possible for an individual. The consequences of this move are extraordinary: Kateb is forced to deny Thoreau's manifest indifference in favor of a reliance on Thoreau's on-again, off-again moral conscience. Far from Paul's declaration that wildness serves the interests of the instincts, Kateb holds that wildness follows the concerns of the higher law—an ultracivilized response to a problem of civilization.

Having thus situated Thoreauvian wildness within the context of moral conscience, Kateb amends Thoreau's own explanation of his wildness by placing "conscientious" before the term, making the term more moral than Thoreau intends. Moral conscience, for Kateb, is Thoreau's overarching theme, to which all other themes must report: "Conscience is taking with the utmost seriousness what everyone professes, and many fail to take seriously. This is the core of moral conscience as Thoreau conceives it. It is conscience because one must think about the obvious when it is overgrown by indifference, comfort, and self-serving rationalization."[10]

The source of the wildness within this framework of moral conscience is never entirely clear. Kateb's argument is grounded in a reading of Thoreau's "Resistance to Civil Government" (although Kateb uses the title "Civil Disobedience"), particularly in the moral obligation to conscientiously object to a slave-owning government. What Kateb fails to do is connect the reading back to wildness or to supply a rationale for the inclusion of wildness in what is otherwise a standard contemporary reading of "Resistance to Civil Government." Kateb simply assumes that wildness serves the public.

Kateb's Thoreau is a theorist who pines for anarchism but finds himself morally committed to fighting wrongs when he finds them: "Thoreau's orientation to life is intensely moral: he must recurrently see political affiliation as a major moral issue with which every conscientious person must take a personal stand."[11] On this view, Thoreau's wildness domesticates itself in the very thing it tries to escape: the politics of slavery, the Mexican–American War, and the various impingements on natural liberty. Although individuals cannot win battles against the state, the moral conscience requires them to fight: "Good democratic wildness must face up to bad democratic wildness, one anarchism against another, despite the awful unevenness of the struggle. That is the lesson of Emerson and Thoreau."[12]

What connects Bennett and Kateb is the sense that Thoreau's wildness situates itself against the state in order to use its disposition as a means of affecting politics. Thoreau is domesticated by his return to the mass political realm from which wildness is a dispositional retreat. Through the inability to see beyond Thoreau's moral conscience, Kateb reduces wildness to a disposition that enhances moral sensitivity and manifests itself through conscientious resistance to the state. The nuance of Thoreau's concept is largely lost in this reading, substantiated by the fact that Kateb mentions Thoreau's essay "Walking" only once and does not mention *The Maine Woods* or Thoreau's journals. Bennett and Kateb miss that Thoreau replaces political action by setting limits on the political not for moral but for vital reasons. Thoreau cultivates wildness because he is not satisfied with civil freedom's ability to enhance his private life. It is a move motivated by privatism, not by anarchism.

Wildness and the Nature of Freedom: Thoreau's Journals

Thoreau's references to wildness in his *Journal* consistently juxtapose the term with politics, particularly with the value of political participation vis-à-vis internally fought wild experiences. In an entry from July 1852, Thoreau writes: "The grandest picture in the world is the sunset sky. In your higher moods what man is there to meet? You are of necessity isolated. The mind that perceives clearly any natural beauty is in that instant withdrawn from human society."[13]

The isolation associated with a pure experience of nature precludes any type of meaningful political experience. Thoreau withdraws to nature not to complicate his political or moral aspirations but to allow the vitality of natural life—that is, the satisfaction in the experience of nature—to wash him clean of political affiliations and social cares. In a *Journal* entry from winter 1851, Thoreau writes: "Ah, dear nature, the mere remembrance, after a short forgetfulness, of the pine woods! I come to it as a hungry man to a crust of bread."[14] Nature offers Thoreau the opportunity to set his own table of values around the broadened concept of life, to escape the mass of "natural mummies" he believes America to be.[15]

To be sure, Thoreau's journals also exhibit the limits of a life of wildness. An entry from January 12, 1852, yields the following caution: "Go not so far out of your way for a truer life—keep strictly onward in that path alone which your genius points out. Do the things which lie nearest to you but which are difficult to do. Live a purer a more thoughtful and laborious life—more true to your friends & neighbors, more noble and magnanimous—and that will be better than a wild walk. To live in relations of truth and sincerity with men is to dwell in a frontier country. What a wild and unfrequented wilderness that would be!"[16]

Thoreau's journals exhibit the push and pull of his privatist ethos, often representing the strain involved in his elective withdrawal within a single passage. In this case Thoreau finds himself at the limit—at least temporarily—of his affective wildness, noting that relating to one's friends and neighbors with truth is better than a wild walk. This entry seems to validate what Kateb suggests about the moral potential of wildness, but what is striking about the entry is the paucity of similar statements in Thoreau's published writings. There is no corollary qualification of wildness in "Walking," nor is there in Thoreau's reform papers. While it would be disingenuous to claim that Thoreau has no misgivings about the costs involved in more fully realizing existential freedom, it is similarly disingenuous to claim that Thoreau's work does not display a strong tendency toward affirming its possibilities.

One of the most intriguing conceptualizations of wildness in Thoreau's journals stems from his reorganization of the political virtue of community around a patch of stately elm trees, which to him demonstrates the type of collectivity possible under the constraints and possibilities of natural life: "I find that into my idea of the village has entered more of the elm than of the human being. They are worth many a political borough. . . . A fragment of their bark is worth the backs of all the politicians in the union. . . . They attend no caucus, they make no compromise, they use no policy. Their one principle is growth."[17]

The elms are "worth" many political boroughs precisely because they stick to the principle of their life: growth. Thoreau makes an odd formulation toward the end of the passage, decrying the most positively democratic elements of political life. Thoreau's choice to aim his vitriol at caucusing, compromising, using policy—instead of at corruption, deception, or the abuse of power—suggests that democratic politics holds no aesthetic value for Thoreau. He is not convinced with the process or the results and, as a result, pushes for a political valuation of a group of trees that could scarcely be considered agents in any meaningful sense but nonetheless evince the vital values Thoreau expects from private and political life. The elms live a life with principle, and that principle is a vital one; importantly, Thoreau does not choose a moral principle through which to uphold the elm tree but instead concentrates on growth, the vital principle necessary to the maintenance and expansion of life in any form. The burgeoning democratic politics of the nineteenth century, it seems, actually inhibit the vital value of growth—at least the natural growth that is our own potentiality as human beings.

If wildness promises growth, it must allow individuals (and other things) to grow in ways conducive to the will. There is an intimate relationship between the wildness of Thoreau's philosophy and the concept of the will, one of the central contributions of modernity. Thoreau utilizes the will to explicate the freedom required for one to practice wildness. In an entry from January 1853, Thoreau constructs the depth of wildness's vital value:

"Trench says a wild man is a *willed* man. Well, then, a man of will who does what he wills or wishes, a man of hope and of the future tense, for not only the obstinate is willed, but far more the constant and persevering. . . . The perseverance of the saints is positive willedness, not a mere passive willingness. The fates are wild, for they *will*."[18]

The elms grow because that is their natural principle. In this passage, Thoreau works out the etymology of wildness, using John Trench's famous thesaurus to locate wildness as the place of the freedom of the will. To be wild is to "do what he wills or wishes," to construct an individual world that is free because it entrusts individuals with their own choices. This all-too-individualist notion of freedom explains Thoreau's disdain for participatory politics, where virtues are made of compromise, of reaching agreements, of taking oneself away from what one will toward what is possible to be done. Thoreau critiques the value of political participation—not the product of policy, necessarily—as a detriment to the more expansive freedom of cultivating the will. For the person who would be wild, the burning question "is whether you can bear freedom."[19] In this case, Thoreau reorients the concept of freedom—which is tied to the will for moderns—into its primal psychic basis, replacing the political freedom of speech and institutions with the psychic freedom of instinctual life.

Recent research has called into question the extent to which Thoreau's embrace of wildness constitutes an escape from politics. Mariotti argues that "Thoreau is trying to carve out a new space for his own variety of politics *within* nature. He may go into nature to reject the alienating village and mainstream politics ("what is called politics"), but he goes there with a mission, a crusade to carve out a new space for a new type of democratic politics, to create a new type of citizen."[20]

Mariotti's persuasive case depends upon the reorientation of the concept of politics to fit Thoreau's practices of distancing. Mariotti argues that "Walking" demonstrates "*how* Thoreau will wage his war against the State,"[21] that is to say, that Thoreau prepares himself and others to be citizens within the contested space of agonic politics with and against the state itself. Viewed in this light, wildness is a reorienting move, a change in method that distances one from the state to take a more critical stance toward it.[22] The new type of citizen Mariotti takes from Thoreau's wildness is not antipolitical but engaged in a lifelong battle with the state for "refashioning a new, less alienated citizenry."[23]

To make the case, Mariotti has to demonstrate how Thoreau integrates wildness into a theory of politics. While the argument is novel, important, and in large parts correct, Mariotti seems to "stretch the seams" of the political in order to place Thoreau comfortably within an understood rubric. To argue, however, that one's space of withdrawal is political merely because it may lead toward a private reorientation of one's disagreements with the state is not a sufficient case for rethinking Thoreau's wildness. After all, Mariotti mentions that Thoreau "declares war with the state" but leaves out the all-important prior word: *quietly*. Thoreau's wildness rethinks politics, but in a way that aims to arrive at Thoreau's own goal: to be governed less and less, and to spend less time thinking about being governed: "However, the government does not concern me much, and I shall bestow the fewest possible thoughts on it. It is not many moments that I live under a government, even in this world."[24]

Thoreau's disposition toward wildness in his journals often betrays a sense of longing, a wished-for world in which people embraced the instinctual portions of their character. Thoreau longs for the connections that wildness makes possible: "I wish my neighbors were wilder. A Wildness whose glance no civilization could endure. . . . Wild as if we lived on the marrow of antelopes devoured raw. . . . The man for whom law exists—the man of forms, the conservative—is a tame man."[25]

This passage reveals Thoreau struggling to make his way with the world as-it-is. A common criticism of Thoreau's social philosophy is that he expects too much of the world around him, and we see clear evidence of this here. One of the extremes of Thoreau's wildness is that he finds the satisfaction of raw experience so comforting and vital that he desires it for the community as well. Perhaps the journals demonstrate that Thoreau's wildness carries its own limitations—that, after a time, the wish for wildness as a means of navigating a social and political landscape pushes one toward emptily desiring the universality of one's own admittedly local norms. Thoreau's yearning for a collective wildness buttresses his arguments against political participation and community norms; because the world outside is so tame, so conservative, Thoreau cannot risk the vital expense of living within its boundaries.

Freedom as Carelessness: "A Natural History of Massachusetts"

"A Natural History of Massachusetts" constitutes one of Thoreau's earliest efforts to produce his own distinctive contribution to the philosophical and literary world of New England. Written at Emerson's behest, the essay attempts to review several early works on New England's flora and fauna. Characteristically, the work reveals more about Thoreau's own distinctive taste than it does about the characteristics of Massachusetts. Its most stirring contribution is a theory of freedom that denies the supremacy of liberal freedom, allowing us to see Thoreau's escape from practical politics behind a comprehensive view of liberty.

Given that the text portends an examination of New England's natural history, it is strange that Thoreau begins with an excursion into New England's political present. Thoreau notes that the "merely political aspect of the land is never very cheering; men are degraded when considered as the members of a political organization."[26] Thoreau's intent with the swift critique of politics is to create an axiology of nature and natural history that uses politics and social life as a foil. Two critiques unveil themselves early: first, that politics is not "cheery"—that is, that politics is not vitalizing, nor does it produce or sustain joy; and, second, that politics degrades human beings. This critique alerts us to the centrality of the concept of value in Thoreau's essay. The value of politics to life is countered with the value of nature to life. Thoreau is not making the attempt to deny the necessity of politics, as his critique is not one of utility but of "cheeriness." Thoreau's juxtaposition of nature with politics is going to take place on the level of nature's ability to give value to individual life.

It is not only the decay of political life that triggers Thoreau's juxtaposition with nature. Thoreau's interesting oscillation between politics and nature hinges on a comparison that leads us into the source of nature's freedom and the sickness of politics. Continuing with his argument, Thoreau states that "society is always diseased, and the best is the most so."[27] At first glance this appears as one of Thoreau's famous rhetorical oppositions; upon closer reading, however, we find that Thoreau attempts to ground the relationship between nature and politics—the reason for the juxtaposition in the first place: "To the sick, indeed, nature is sick, but to the well, a fountain of health."[28] Thoreau's comparison of politics and nature allows us to see how the early works reflect an explicit trust in nature and in the self's response to being ensconced in nature. Nature is as it appears to the consciousness of the individual—its value reflects the constitutive values of individuals. Nature is indeed as we are—sick if we are sick, but a boon to our health if we are already healthy. Nature has a recuperative function, as Thoreau makes clear, but one has to prepare oneself mentally and physically to receive the treatment offered by the wild apprehensions of natural phenomena.

On this reading, politics is deceptive and not worthy of trust. The "best" society is the sickest; that is, when individuals are led to believe they inhabit a useful working society, they are indeed within the bounds of the most profound pathology. This is more than just rhetorical flight of fancy; the purpose of turning to politics when explaining nature is to offer individuals two concrete means of articulating value for themselves, one that promotes vitality and one that leaves them confused, deceived, sick. For the early Thoreau, politics dissolves the self's trust in itself and represents the inability to allow truth to dictate life's commitments. The most prominent example of this move is Thoreau's treatment of freedom, in which he offers the example of the fox rather than the example of the human defender of liberty. Thoreau's use of nature in this essay reappropriates freedom using largely nonhuman examples. The many animals in the text recreate noble virtues—the nobility of the muskrat, the inspiration of the osprey, and the liberty of the fox. Thoreau does more than make a passing ode to the fox; he characterizes the fox's freedom as carelessness. Carelessness is, of course, the freedom of wildness; in this sense the fox's freedom is determined by its absolute unconcern with human beings and their various problems: slavery, war, work, respect, and the dalliances of civilized life. The fox exemplifies the move away from a social conception of the value of freedom.

Thoreau grounds this comparison of politics and nature within the understanding that nature is itself a type of society. As Thoreau notes late in the essay, "When I walk in the woods, I am reminded that a wise purveyor has been there before me. . . . I am struck with the pleasing friendships and unanimities of nature."[29] Similarly, Thoreau asks early in the essay, "What is any man's discourse to me, if I am not sensible of something in it as steady and cheery as the creak of crickets?"[30] Comparison of politics and nature as ways of navigating social life allows Thoreau to invert the notion of nature as space for withdrawal, suggesting instead that one burden political society with the duty of giving one a reason to leave nature. While Thoreau inhabits the early liberal society that expounds freedom within the political boundaries of the state, Thoreau's freedom constitutes the elective withdrawal from the existential constraints of that form of liberty.

Thoreau introduces the notion that nature can be trusted and that politics cannot. The question then arises: In what do we place this trust? The

answer to that question is unambiguous: Thoreau entrusts nature with preserving the wildness inside of him, thereby affirming his natural life: "It
has a salute and a response to all your enthusiasm and heroism."[31] Nature
affirms what is inside of us, corresponding to our natural life with an unend-
ing supply of what Alan Hodder calls "inspiration and euphoria in the natural world," or, as Thoreau terms it, "ecstasy."[32] Thoreau reflectively simplifies
his world to include only the things closest to him, expanding his sense of
what surrounds him. For Thoreau, this type of life replaces the moral life:
"What a foul subject is this of doing good! instead of minding one's life,
which should be his business; doing good as a dead carcass, which is only
fit for manure, instead of as a living man—instead of taking care to flour-
ish, and smell and taste sweet, and refresh all mankind to the extent of our
capacity and quality."[33]

The regeneration of the senses amidst nature is more important to Thoreau than the reform movements for which he is known. Nature is trusted
with our business, our own vital economy, because it is close to us and behaves
by its own laws. We trust nature with our vitality because it is in nature that
we receive the recognition of that vitality.

Conceptualizing Freedom and Savagery: Thoreau's Correspondence

A twenty-year-old Thoreau writes in a letter to his sister Helen, "For a man
to act himself, he must be perfectly free; otherwise, he is in danger of losing all sense of responsibility or of self-respect."[34] Freedom as a prerequisite
for action grounds Thoreau's notion of wildness as that which allows selves
to express the freedom that is their nature. In the same year, writing about
a teaching career to Orestes Brownson, Thoreau argues for "Freedom—not
a paltry Republican freedom, with a *posse comitatus* at his heels to administer it in doses as to a sick child—but a freedom proportionate to the dignity
of his nature—a freedom that shall make him feel that he is a man among
men."[35] Thoreau's early concern with articulating freedom alerts the reader to
his careful reorganization of political terms.[36] Being unsatisfied with "freedom and culture merely civil," Thoreau aims to connect the ability to perform acts of one's own nature with the feeling of freedom as the absence of
care, as the absence of restraint, but also as the feeling of absorption in the
wonderment of the constantly new natural aesthetic. A freedom "proportion-

ate to the dignity of his nature" refers not only to the status of one's freedom, but also to the method of locating and practicing that freedom. Political life, for Thoreau, is anti-nature; as such, it follows that Thoreau considers the (merely) political characterization of freedom to be one bereft of a natural origin or correlate. Civil freedom is "paltry" because it takes only a part of one's nature—or, even worse, subsumes that nature under an avalanche of civilized mannerisms—and constructs a view of a free life that is in fact not responsive to the natural needs and desires of the human animal.

The horizon of the freedom of wildness is savagery, Thoreau's limit case for his corporeal, embedded liberty. In a letter to Lucy Brown from July 1841, Thoreau notes, "I grow savager and savager every day, as if fed on raw meat, and my tameness is only the repose of untamableness. I dream of looking abroad summer and winter, with free gaze, from some mountainside, while my eyes revolve in an Egyptian slime of health,—I to be nature looking into nature with such easy sympathy as the blue-eyed grass in the meadow looks in the face of the sky. . . . But I forget that you think more of this human nature than of this nature I praise."[37]

Thoreau's reference to his own savagery compares favorably with the famous opening to the "Higher Laws" chapter of *Walden*, in which Thoreau writes of his desire to devour a woodchuck. The sense of wildness as a sort of "untamableness" represents an important strain in American romanticism, echoed in Whitman's famous words in the first edition of *Leaves of Grass* (1855): "I too am not a bit tamed. I too am untranslatable, / I sound my barbaric yawp over the roofs of the world."[38] Perhaps this sense of being not only wild but untamable represents naive self-assertion of the dying relationship between the human being and the truly wild space, but Thoreau utilizes untamableness as the ground for his re-entry into the social world. His argument that "tameness is only the repose of untamableness" justifies his return to Concord after two years at Walden Pond, and his continual trips to the woods, rivers, and mountains of New England. David Robinson argues that Thoreau's 1851 lecture, "Walking, or the Wild," signals Thoreau's apprehension of the "border life" that fully explicates his sense of freedom, a life lived toeing the line between civilized life and the benefits of savage experience.[39]

Thoreau argues that he is primarily concerned not with circumstance but with "*intra*-stances, or how it stands within me," and reflects this in the internal position of savagery regardless of circumstance.[40] The test of wildness is one's willingness to give in to the newness of space and the corresponding feeling of enraptured dislocation or to return to the city and face the slowly deadening effects of civilized life. Thoreau toes the line, most famously in the "Bean-Field" chapter of *Walden:* "Mine was, as it were, the connecting link between wild and cultivated fields; as some states are civilized, and others half-civilized, and others savage or barbarous, so my field was, though not in a bad sense, a half-cultivated field."[41]

Thoreau ventures to nature, to the vast and inhuman, to remind himself of the corresponding rawness within his psyche. Later in the chapter, Thoreau argues that he no longer desires to plant crops but seeds such as "sincerity, truth, simplicity, faith, innocence, and the like."[42] Nature as retreat for wildness does not signify that nature is the place where wildness is bound; indeed, Thoreau often finds himself searching various means of imbibing wildness, of taking that wildness with him. Ultimately, Thoreau is not committed to a life in the wild, because he retains the untamable savage sense within himself. He plants sincerity, truth, and simplicity in the ground because these virtues, like Thoreau's limbs and bones, need to be honed with the carefree attitude adapted outside of pervasive social contact. These virtues, however, are planted internally and are not dependent upon the nature in which they are grown. In constructing an edifice of half-cultivation through which we view Thoreau's enterprise of wildness, we are led to recognize that sincerity, truth, and simplicity are virtues that are themselves cultivated through wildness. In a classic reversal, Thoreau renders trademark virtues of civilized society the effect of losing one's attachment to civilizing mechanisms and allowing one to become more visceral and more provincial. "Higher Laws" performs a similar reversal, arguing that becoming half-cultivated leads one toward more responsible eating practices. Wildness represents a connection with things outside of human interactions; as such, the civilizing mechanisms societies utilize defame and alienate the wider world, leaving one with a locally robust but ecologically bankrupt sense of civilized life.

The Flesh of Wildness: Men and Mountains in Myth and Reality

In July 1857 Thoreau embarks upon his third expedition through the Maine woods, accompanied by local Indian guide Joseph Polis. The literary upshot of the trip, Thoreau's essay "The Allegash and East Branch," is a long meditation on the concept of wildness—both Polis's and Thoreau's own—and the limits of the instinctual self in Thoreau's personal philosophy. Polis provides one of wildness's two limit cases; he, along with *Walden*'s unassuming hero Alek Therien, pushes Thoreau into consideration of the recesses and possibilities of the visceral self. This challenge to Thoreau's concept of wildness leads to modifications in his celebratory attitude toward instinctual selfhood via his critique of Polis and his theory of half-cultivation in *Walden*. Polis, a guide raised in Maine and as knowledgeable of the Maine woods as anyone of his time, exhibits behaviors and holds beliefs that Thoreau finds *too* uncivilized; further, Polis complicates his uncivilized outlook with ultramodern opinions that leave him teetering unsustainably between wildness and civilization. At one point, an exasperated Thoreau writes of Polis's attempt to verbally persuade a muskrat to the group of men: "I was greatly surprised—thought that I had at last got into the wilderness, and that he was a wild man indeed, to be talking to a musquash!"[43] Thoreau is drawn to Polis's unrefined style but also finds himself disgruntled with Polis's meager attempts at civilization (via his cardboard Christianity and his desire to kill a moose for sport) mixed with his unrepentant wildness in conduct.[44]

Thoreau's wildness not only animates *The Maine Woods* but is a foundational aspect of his privatist philosophy. The primary function of wildness is to open a wider field of reference to what it means to have, employ, and handle freedom in an emergent market society. Through this interrogation of wildness, we find that Thoreau's major target is not resistance or forming new practices of democratic critique, but vitalizing individual life by placing an existential emphasis on freedom as a sort of wildness. *The Maine Woods* is Thoreau's attempt to complicate and amplify nature as myth and reality, using the twin goals of seeing nature as reality and uncovering the complicated life of the Native American, both in myth and in the realities that reinforce myth.

Thoreau's *The Maine Woods* offers a précis for his never-completed (and perhaps never seriously contemplated) book on American Indians. Thoreau equates the fate of American Indians with the fate of wildness, arguing that as American Indians adjust to cultural norms of European settlers, the city replaces the wilderness in geographic space and in the psyche. When Thoreau writes of Polis's concerns, he finds that Polis bothers himself primarily with collegiate education and city life and boasts loudly of having a brief exchange with Daniel Webster.[45] Later, when Polis reflects on the lost tools of American Indian youth, he argues that "the present generation of Indians 'had lost a great deal.'"[46] Thoreau could ask specifically what American Indians lose and how—but the answers appear obvious. American Indian children lose their connection to spaces of surprise, challenge, and difficulty. These have been lost through the largely unconscious series of accidents involved in becoming civilized. Thoreau's efforts in *The Maine Woods* to characterize the lives of American Indians offer a tragedy long in the making; while the American Indian may keep, somewhere in the recesses of his mind, a streak of wildness unequaled, he remains always teetering on losing that wildness for the sake of a normalizing civilized life. The American Indian sits in the uncomfortable space between untenable pastness and uneasy acquiescence to a life the white American will never share. Joe Polis argues, "Great difference between me and white man."[47] Thoreau agrees, but the white man gauges the difference, and, offering a one-way ticket to a disembodied and never-quite-fitting cultural acquiescence, Polis's civilizing tendencies offer a bleak future for significant cultural difference.

The Maine Woods plays with the notion of the American Indian as myth and reality, supplying the reader with a dislocating sense of the existence of the other beyond its characterization in myth. Thoreau notes that the "Indian asked the meaning of *reality*," indicating that the Indian is not altogether beyond the realm of myth for white Americans in the nineteenth century. It is compelling that Polis asks after the meaning of reality, as this appears to be Thoreau's historical and personal inquiry as well: what, after all, is the meaning of the reality of the American Indian and, by extension, the nature that is part of its being? "The Indian," as Thoreau calls Polis throughout the text, is not real but a myth, and the wildness that is inside the Indian is also, at least to Thoreau's argument, a myth disrupted through exposure to wild places and the corollary psychic change they effect inside him. "Ktaadn" begins with a search for American Indian guide Louis Neptune, who haunts the essay until after Thoreau's encounter with the starkness of the mountain (the "vast, Titanic, inhuman nature"): "The last proved to be Louis Neptune and his companion . . . but they were so disguised that we hardly knew them."[48] The wildness of the mountain throws Thoreau into a stark and uncomfort-able—perhaps frantic—knowledge of its reality. Unfortunately, the wildness of the American Indian is on the way to a myth ensconced as history: "There is, in fact, a remarkable and unexpected resemblance between the degraded savage and the lowest classes in a great city. The one is no more a child of nature than the other. In the progress of degradation, the distinction of races is soon lost."[49] Louis Neptune was not disguised as a nonhuman, but as a non-Indian—that is, as a degraded white man bent on pursuing the empty dreams of a burgeoning but bankrupt culture.

Thoreau is playing with the myth/reality distinction in *The Maine Woods* as a way of highlighting the mythological problems, constructs, and values of town culture. Thoreau ventures into the woods in order to discover reality, to shake off myth; to do so, Thoreau must locate himself within a series of situations that promise a self-transformative experience. He must be outside of science and in the realm of personal experience. "How much more respectable also is the life of the solitary pioneer or settler in these, or any woods,—having real difficulties, not of his own creation, drawing his subsistence directly from nature,—than that of the helpless multitudes in the towns who depend on gratifying the extremely artificial wants of society."[50]

Thoreau notes the reality of the settler's difficulty in the woods, suggesting that town life offers false or mythical problems. Living and dealing with mythical problems clouds the mind and the body, contorting the self into a series of difficulties and trials for which it has no natural capabilities. The woods become the opposite of their characterization: instead of a mythical place we attend to escape the (all too real) problems of community life, the woods become the place of actual, real problems, and the town becomes the locus of mythical problems. What types of mythical problems do the townsfolk encounter? Earlier in "The Allegash and East Branch," Thoreau offers this exuberant defense of life in the woods: "What a glorious time they must have in that wilderness, far from mankind and election day!"[51]

The Maine Woods offers Thoreau an opportunity to revel in the otherness of nature, its surprising disposition toward enchanting one through its novelty, danger, and wildness. In his magnificent book *Thoreau's Morning Work*, Daniel Peck argues that Thoreau was a "man who depended utterly on the variety and otherness of the world to feed his imagination," and this is nowhere clearer than in Thoreau's meditations on the theme of wildness.[52] "In the middle of the night, as indeed each time that we lay on the shore of a lake, we hear the voice of the loon, loud and distinct, from far over the lake. It is a very wild sound, quite in keeping with the place and circumstances of the traveler . . . I could lie awake for hours listening to it, it is so thrilling. When camping in such a wilderness as this, you are prepared to hear sounds from some of its inhabitants which will give voice to its wildness."[53]

Thoreau's reflection calls into question the primary purpose of engaging the wild. There is little doubt that wildness plays a distinct therapeutic function in Thoreau's thought. In this case, however, we get the sense that wildness is more than metaphysical therapy and more than a reprieve for a civilized sojourner; instead, wildness offers Thoreau a spatial and temporal structure for the workings of memory and imagination on the otherness that alerts him to a robust conceptualization of freedom. The loon disrupts Thoreau's understanding of the call of the bird, which temporarily dislocates his consciousness, but he rallies, taking in the thrilling aspect of the otherness of the situation within its conscious experience. This is vitality, the self-enclosure of a thrilling experience bearing its existential fruits. The self-enclosed experience is affirmative, shedding critical potentiality in sensory experience. As Thoreau matures in *The Maine Woods*, his appreciation of nature's power internalizes itself, becoming consummatory. Thoreau notes importantly that when camping in such a wilderness, "you are prepared" for the disruptions and thrills of the voices of otherness. In a sense, then, these are "soft" disruptions, things that one is prepared for through the act of going camping. Wildness, at this point, is not yet *so* other that it refuses categorization. Thoreau notes later in the paragraph that the sound of "wild beasts" "runs in your head naturally," and that he reproduces the sound of the loon "through [his] own nostrils."[54] This experience of the freedom that assists natural life comes with, but not from, the setting of the woods, in which one who is not predisposed to interpret phenomena through the lens of civilization can encounter the facts of life and play them alongside unimpaired imagination.

Wild situations and wild locations allow the self to practice its freedom from the constraints of common perception born of life spent in rapidly industrializing antebellum New England. Thoreau is quick to attend to the difficulty in achieving wildness, even amidst the phenomenal world that promises its orientation: "Wild as it was, it was hard for me to get rid of the associations of the settlements. Any steady and monotonous sound, to which I did not distinctly attend, passed for a sound of human history. . . . Our minds anywhere, when left to themselves, are always thus busily drawing conclusions from false premises."[55]

Even in the woods, Thoreau feels the effects of monotony, of the familiarity of sounds with which we are never entirely familiar. Thoreau notes that our minds tend toward false premises "when left to themselves," which is to say when not pronounced and alerted by the perception of novelty and dislocation in the mind itself. The wild provides the ground through which wildness makes its appearance, but the Wild itself, as something other, does not guarantee a psychic corollary within the individual. Our minds seek the patterns that make sense of the world we are in; indeed, wildness could be described as the freedom that comes from unleashing one's desire and ability to make sense of the world one perceives and inhabits.

Jane Bennett makes the argument that "the Wild must be treated at a distance, else it ceases to be an object of fascination and becomes something to devour."[56] This point is emphasized with Thoreau's distancing from the character of Joseph Polis: "As we drew near to Oldtown I asked Polis if he was not glad to get home again; but there was no relenting to his wildness, and he said, 'It makes no difference to me where I am.' Such is the Indian's pretence always."[57]

Much of *The Maine Woods* is devoted to Thoreau's burgeoning interest in American Indians and the development and erosion of Native American culture in the United States; this passage, however, alerts us to the inward purpose of *The Maine Woods:* Thoreau's existential separation from the Indians who provide for him the model of wildness. Polis's possession of the wild is not the only distinction between him and Thoreau; Polis, Thoreau argues, also devours wildness, unable to extricate himself from the hunger for the dead moose. This is odd, considering that Polis is as "civilized" as Thoreau himself, and Thoreau is often as uncomfortable with the overcivilization of Polis's behaviors. Behind Thoreau's dismissal of Polis's civilized Christianity, however, is not a critique of Christianity as such, but a critique of Polis's employment of Christianity as someone who is constituted as outside Christian mechanisms of civilization. Thoreau sentences Polis to the fate of the category "Indian" because Polis, unlike Thoreau, is strangely incapable of extricating himself from the pitfalls of a consumptive wildness. For Thoreau, this stands as a cautionary tale to the freedom-reducing power of a wildness that can envelop the body and the soul. One can, indeed, become possessed by wildness in the same way that one can become possessed by politics, or shopping, or gossip. The wild's capacity to encourage freedom consists in its infrequent usage—not so infrequent as to disorient consciousness, but not so frequent as to establish patterns of behavior.

Describing the final ascent to Mount Katahdin in the first essay of *The Maine Woods,* Thoreau notes simply: "There was a skeleton of a moose here, whose bones some Indian hunters had picked on this very spot."[58] Thoreau's exploration of the lives and deaths of moose and American Indians in *The Maine Woods* exists partially as foil for the life and death of wildness—not of the wild, but of the possibility of direct phenomenological inquiry into the life of freedom. When the living American Indian, Joe Polis, whose fame is largely a result of having accepted white norms, meets with the moose, the reader witnesses the collapsing of an avenue of wildness. Thoreau's "Kta-adn" recreates the moose as the great unknown, the living myth of the wild woods: "It is said that they can step over a five-foot gate in their ordinary walk."[59] Thoreau recreates the Indian and the moose—two figures so intriguing in Thoreau's biography because they constitute his final words—as a sort of mythology, but one that is grounded in phenomenological inquiry into his own avenues of wildness.[60] Thoreau uses *The Maine Woods* to mine the personal and national past, the terrain of wildness recreated through the excursion, in order to confront "natural, not political limits."[61]

Trekking toward the natural limits evokes the connection between Thoreau's *Maine Woods* and the Stoic vision of *Walden*'s critical first chapters. Locating wildness in myth and lamenting its loss in the present animates Thoreau's journey in "Ktaadn," but he finds himself, on that last push toward the summit, encountering the actual, not mythological, limits of wildness as a category of human experience. "It was matter, vast, terrific,—not his Mother Earth that we have heard of, not for him to tread on, or be buried in—no, it were being too familiar even to let his bones lie there—the home this of Necessity and Fate."[62]

Nature as resistance, as that which overcomes the self and places it within its existential limits, is the overarching march of "Ktaadn." Leaving the world of myth and facing the limits of the natural world, Thoreau finds himself face-to-face with himself as a corporeal *thing*—himself as matter—thus providing the limit case to wildness as a concept that frees Thoreau to experience wildness within its understood boundaries. Thoreau notes in the famous apex of the essay, "I fear not spirits . . . but I fear bodies, I tremble to meet them."[63] The world of nature is one of *matter:* "daily to be shown matter, to come in contact with it . . . the *actual* world."[64] Reaching the summit of the argument, Thoreau alerts himself to the reality that apprehending the freedom of wildness is a matter of, as he puts it, "*Contact! Contact!*" and not the apprehension that comes through the education of books or mythological stories.[65] Thoreau finds himself a spirit in the world of matter, confronting the limits of his own experience of wildness in a way that is freeing—supplying the boundaries upon which freedom is brought to consciousness.

Thoreau's final pages of "Ktaadn" establish the ground upon which the self apprehends existential freedom. Thoreau continually refers to the woods as "striking" in its "savage" and "stern" qualities.[66] The abruptness with which Thoreau presents the woods as something challenging, difficult, and unknowable to him establishes the freedom he seeks within the walking, boating, and sleeping necessary to confront the basic facts of the mountain. Merleau-Ponty describes this move of establishing freedom through apprehending boundaries in *Phenomenology of Perception:*

> Even what are called obstacles to freedom are in reality deployed by it. An unclimbable rock face, a large or small, vertical or slanting rock, are things which have no meaning for anyone who is not intending to surmount them, for a subject whose projects do not carve out such determinate forms from the uniform mass of the *in itself* and cause and orientated world to arise—a significance in things. There is, then, ultimately nothing that can set limits to freedom, except those limits that freedom itself has set in the form of its various initiatives, so that the subject has simply the external world he gives himself.[67]

Thoreau is giving himself an external world through "Ktaadn," and, upon finding that external world in the disorienting corporeal distinction of the savage mountain, Thoreau finds his footing and expresses the ethically saturated purpose of excursions into nature: "What a place to live, what a place to die and be buried in!"[68] We find, after an essay of searching for the myths of the moose and the Indian, that "the Indian still hunts and the moose runs wild."[69] Thoreau sets the limits to his freedom through his venture into the heart of wildness, to its foundational qualities and its terminus in the feeling of alienation, disembodiment, fear, inexpressible joy—in short, the feeling of being a spirit in a world of matter, being fated not to connection with unfamiliar savage nature but to feeling the freedom of one's own consciousness of the limits of one's most important properties.

"A Narrow Field": Reading "Walking"

Perhaps Thoreau's effective last word on the subject of wildness comes from his most mature essay, "Walking, or the Wild." The essay concerns a particular type of walking—sauntering—as a means of recreating one's own sense of wildness within. Of course, alongside most of Thoreau's celebrated essays, it includes overtures to politics, including one interesting passage: "Man and his affairs, church and state—and school, trade and commerce, and manu-factures and agriculture—even politics, the most alarming of them all—I am pleased to see how little space they occupy in the landscape. Politics is but a narrow field."[70] Thoreau allows that politics exists to serve a purpose but objects to the notion that politics occupies a privileged space in human conduct and concern. Noting that politics "has its place merely, and does not occupy all space," Thoreau offers the rationale for his persistent defense of the freedom of wildness. Politics extends itself beyond its parameters, enters into our discussion of personal and natural value, and becomes the means by which we measure our freedom. Arguing that politics is a narrow field, Tho-reau allows that political freedom has a place in human conduct, but that, for the individual, overvaluing its contribution to a full and natural life is "most alarming." Politics is "but as the cigar smoke of a man."[71]

In the first sentence of the essay, Thoreau alerts that he wants "to speak a word for Nature, for absolute Freedom and Wildness, as contrasted with a Freedom and Culture merely civil."[72] We might then ask the question, what is the word that Thoreau wishes to speak for wildness, contrasting that with the words that provide entrée into the machinations of polite society? Tho-reau's word, the word that will speak wildness, is *sauntering;* Thoreau is clear to use this word—or perhaps this meaning or interpretation of the word *walking*—to explain the force of wildness, the freedom inherent in nature and the freedom missing in culture. *Sauntering* is the word Thoreau wishes to speak, and he wishes to use its meaning as a way of endearing one to the demands of the saunterer and the expression of freedom felt in the act of sauntering. *Sauntering* is the word for Nature, for Freedom and Wildness—but it also opposes itself to civil Freedom and Culture. Interestingly, if we follow the construction of Thoreau's first sentence, we find that absolute and civil freedoms contrast with each other, but that wildness contrasts with cul-ture. Much of Thoreau's essay will dictate the consequences of this contrast and the subsequent means through which individuals can retain the absolute freedom of wildness in a time bent on exploiting the civil freedom of culture.

Thoreau offers two etymological derivations in the text, that of *saunter-ing* and that of *village*. We learn early that Thoreau's etymology leads him to locate *sauntering* "from idle people who roved about the country, in the middle ages, and asked charity, under pretence of going à *la sainte terre*—to the holy land."[73] Thoreau then allows another derivation, of "having no particular home, but equally at home everywhere."[74] The twin senses of holiness and homelessness ground Thoreau's employment of sauntering as a means toward understanding wildness. Thoreau names his essay "Walking," but it is clear that he gives value to a particular type of walking, defined by its insistent aimlessness. The aimlessness of the saunter locates the freedom of the walk literally in the legs of the saunterer; releasing oneself from a destination, the saunter itself becomes a holy practice, a practice of presence grounded in the experience of putting one's feet into the soil, the grass, the water. We are reminded of Thoreau's use of the fox in the early essay "A Natural History of Massachusetts": "When I see a fox run across the pond on the snow, with the carelessness of freedom, or at intervals trace his course in the sunshine along the ridge of a hill, I give up to him sun and earth as to their true proprietor."[75] The fox dazzles Thoreau with a running pattern that is delightfully unpredictable, intractable, driven by its instincts and responding to the challenges of the surrounding world. If Thoreau had the language in 1843, he would have described the fox as a saunterer. In this case Thoreau offers a notion of freedom as "carelessness," an absolute freedom grounded in the experiences of wildness.

To saunter is to speak a word for nature, to experience the freedom of wildness. Thoreau builds the concept of sauntering, mimicking it with the notion of practicing philosophy or going to battle, offering preparatory words that point to its rarity and its method: "If you are prepared to leave father and mother, and brother and sister, and wife and child and friends, and never see them again; if you have paid your debts, and made your will, and settled all your affairs, and are a free man: then you are ready for a walk."[76]

Thoreau meaningfully raises the stakes of the "walk" in this case, arguing that the walk must place itself above and beyond other, more important concerns. What Thoreau is driving at in this passage, however, is not that one need to sacrifice in order to walk, but that the saunterer is untethered. The detachment of self from personal, financial, and political relationships is the prerequisite for sauntering. Thoreau mentions this sentiment in the second chapter of *Walden*, arguing, "As long as possible live free and uncommitted."[77] Wildness comes only to those who can walk without pretense, without destination, without preoccupation. Thoreau mentions famously in "Slavery in Massachusetts," "The remembrance of my country spoils my walk."[78] Much of "Walking" also concerns itself with the ways in which a walk can be spoiled by attention to details beyond one's immediate surroundings. Many are willing to leave behind their wife, child, job, or friend, to take a walk—but how many can leave behind the memory of them? How many can truly leave behind the political world, that incessant maggot running through their heads, conditioning their thoughts?

Thoreau offers a second etymological derivation in "Walking," one that sets the stakes of his cause. "The village is the place to which the roads tend. . . . Varro derives from *veho* to carry, because the villa is the place to and from which things are carried. . . . Hence too apparently the latin word *vilis* and our *vile;* also *villain.* This suggests the kind of degeneracy villagers are liable to."[79]

Sauntering has to do with the holiness of walking aimlessly, and, fittingly, the village has to do with the degeneracy, the villainy, of purposive action. The first derivation refers to taking things to and from, suggesting that the village is a destination; of course, Thoreau is alerting the reader to the village as the destination of a kind of walking, the purposive walking that saturates experience with the anticipation of the outcome and the remembrance of business transactions. Thoreau supplies his critique with unnaturally strong language; the primary "degeneracy" of the villagers is not to respect the experience of walking, not to fill the vitality of the embodied moment, but to push it aside in favor of imagining outcomes and counting steps. The crime is to take away the "springs of life" and supplant this with instrumental goods—exercise, financial gain, social mores—and Thoreau's move to place these instrumental goods as a sort of villainy adds vitality to his attack on the village.

The two etymological derivations in "Walking" establish Thoreau as the patron saint of the fresh path, alerting others to the joys had in negating established centers of civilized life. Thoreau's next move is to identify the myth of the West with the notion of the wild, resigning the East to the past and its cultures, languages, arts, and impediments. As eastward is the past, Thoreau's concept of the West is placed in the future tense: "The future lies that way to me."[80] Thoreau does not refer to a particular westward point, but to the idea of the West as that which invites the new, the untouched, the visceral. The notion of westward movement marks a transition in Thoreau's valuation of wildness as a type of freedom: identifying wildness with westward expansion allows Thoreau to characterize wildness as the type of freedom that will prevail in the coming migration. "I should not lay so much stress on this fact, if I did not believe that something like this is the prevailing tendency of my countrymen."[81] Thoreau is completing the transcendentalist break with history, replacing its bonds with the sovereignty of the traveler, suggesting a human movement that mimics "the migratory instinct in birds and quadrupeds."[82]

Generally, the move westward is couched in the argument of advancing the privilege of property rights to more Americans. Indeed, many see the move westward as a way of establishing the same rights of property denied to individuals in the cultured East. Thoreau, however, does not argue that the move west is made for private property. Indeed, Thoreau is careful to oppose property rights to the spirit of wildness: "At present, in this vicinity, the best part of the land is not private property; the landscape is not owned, and the walker enjoys comparative freedom. But possibly the day will come when it will be partitioned off into so-called pleasure grounds, in which a few will take a narrow and exclusive pleasure only. . . . To enjoy a thing exclusively is commonly to exclude yourself from the true enjoyment of it. Let us improve our opportunities then before the evil days come."[83]

Thoreau's "Walking" presents wildness as an absolute freedom in order to reinforce his argument against commitments in *Walden:* westward expansion offers the opportunity to relieve the suffering of old institutions on new land, offering instead an expanse that can belong to none and all, a wild paradise that encourages the "true enjoyment" of the unpropertied. Once one takes property, one begins to enjoy primarily the having of that property and not the opportunities and surprises the property offers to the self. Walking offers a microcosm of the American Revolution itself; this time, however, it is a philosophical revolution aimed to realize a more fully nurtured notion of absolute freedom. "Walking" is Thoreau's essay on wildness, but wildness appears here as the type of freedom endemic to a more positive and more comprehensive manifest destiny of the United States.

Thoreau clearly puts great hope in the United States, and the substance of this hope is both existential and philosophical: "If the heavens of America appear infinitely higher, the stars brighter, I trust that these facts are symbolical of the height to which the philosophy and poetry and religion of her inhabitants may one day soar."[84]

The West—the uninhabited (and thus unspoiled) part of the United States—offers not only the promise of America, but takes in the promise of the world itself. Thoreau values the West for its possibility, its openness to new configurations of freedom, value, identification, and experience. American philosophy, similarly, needs to imbibe the wild surroundings and become a philosophy that is equal to the task Thoreau hands it. The West as the land of imagination and of clarity lends a philosophical credence to Thoreau's configuration of wildness's place of purpose; we see, through this understanding of the West as the place of wildness, that Thoreau is in fact no longer writing about walking (if he ever was), but writing about the space that makes philosophy possible again. Walking, sauntering, are ways of doing philosophy; however, as Thoreau is at pains to remind readers throughout his writings, walking is increasingly less peaceful, less conducive to philosophy.

The West can potentially solve the ills that plague a comprehensive reflection on life. Thoreau finds value in the West for this reason; in fact, one could argue that it is the only value of the West: "Else, to what end does the world go on, and why was America discovered?"[85] But Thoreau is torn between the wildness of the *idea* of the West and the fear of its becoming a part of the past. This relationship between a hoped-for future and a dreary past establishes wildness once again within the sphere of myth, where it resides within *The Maine Woods*. Nature, as the myth that comes to life through engagement, promises the pure freedom of wildness: "There is plenty of genial love of nature, but not so much of Nature itself."[86] Thoreau deftly distinguishes between nature and Nature, recalling the experience of "Ktaadn" when he comes to love the vast and inhuman wildness that Nature displays, opening the possibility of a similar wildness within himself. The wild is given mythological value, and Thoreau's most important characterizations of the United States are also built on this promise of the possibility of myth becoming life: "Perchance, when in the course of ages, American Liberty has become a fiction of the past—as it is to some extent a fiction of the present—the poets of the world will be inspired by American mythology."[87]

How does myth solve the problems of nineteenth-century Concord? Thoreau alludes to the idea of future myth as a sort of truth: "The wildest dreams of wild men, even, are not the less true, though they may not recommend themselves to the sense which is most common among Englishmen and Americans to-day."[88] Wildness conforms to its own standards of truth, becoming a means of transcending the "common sense" toward the use of the senses to appeal to a higher understanding of Nature. Thoreau does not denigrate the senses; indeed, he yearns for the sound of the wood thrush, the smell of the trapper's coat, the look of the tanned skin.[89] The difference between the common sense and the wild sense, however, is in the degree of life imbued through the sensual encounter. Thoreau notes famously, "Life consists with Wildness. The most alive is the wildest."[90] The common sense relies on the stock interpretation of phenomena filtered through a civilizing process of pleasure and distaste, entirely disengaged from the enchanting and mesmerizing powers of the moment of meeting between the object and the subject of wildness.

Civilization caters to some, but not to all, Thoreau argues: "Because the majority, like dogs and sheep, are tame by inherited disposition, this is no reason why the others should have their natures broken that they may be reduced to the same level."[91] Thoreau is arguing not so much for wildness as a universal value as for universal freedom as a value to those whose nature is attuned to its precepts. Civilization is marked by Thoreau not for its brutality but for its ubiquity. "Here is this vast, savage, howling Mother of ours, Nature lying all around, with such beauty, and such affection for her children, as the leopard—and yet we are so early weaned from her breast to society—to that culture which is exclusively an interaction of man on man."[92]

The process of "weaning" from Nature occurs primarily due to the danger that Nature provides—and Thoreau is keen to highlight its "vast, savage, howling" properties. But perhaps the civilizing device of shielding children from the trouble, the fright, and the challenge of Nature comes at too great a cost. Thoreau would that the greater part of us (and by "us" he means the wild ones) be "meadow and forest."[93] Wildness offers one the freedom of carelessness, which concretizes in the "Society for the Diffusion of Useful Ignorance," a mock proposal Thoreau makes to amplify the value of *not* knowing certain alienating topics. To Thoreau, useful ignorance is a "Beautiful Knowledge," the knowledge of the world experienced not through its various categories or learned aversions, but through entrenchment in the changing seasons, the smells, sounds, and sights of the animals around us and inside of us.

The argument that wildness occupies a privileged space in Thoreau's political thought rests, perhaps fittingly, on the concept's ability to present a theory of freedom that transcends political boundaries. Wildness preserves Thoreau's sense of hope but also serves as a foil for political liberty, a catch-all for the experience of nature, and a way of describing the immanent character embedded within the landscape. The disparate functions of the term reveal wildness as a more or less wild concept, one that refuses to reduce itself to a simple characterization. In this sense we can see wildness performing the functions of Thoreau's "freedom from all plaintiveness," following the morning joy that is the purpose of *Walden* and Thoreau's broader excursions.[94] The phenomenological character of wildness suggests that it is a preparatory disposition, one that exercises the self's instinctual (and, as Thoreau might argue, natural) tendencies toward a lived aesthetic. Pushing oneself away from the scientific characterization of nature and the political characterization of freedom opens the space for a broad appreciation of the natural world, revealed through turning toward the realization of myth as reality and the subsequent demotion of reality to myth.

That the broader purpose is aesthetic is clear from Thoreau's closing paragraph in "Walking": "So we saunter toward the Holy Land; till one day the sun shall shine more brightly than ever he has done, shall perchance shine into our minds and hearts, and light up our whole lives with a great awakening light, so warm and serene and golden as on a bank-side in Autumn."[95] We walk toward the light, appreciating the substance of nature as we step on the earth and imbue ourselves with the sensory delights of an uncommitted appreciation of that which surrounds. In a sense, Thoreau's wildness is preparatory to the highest Aristotelian knowledge, wherein Aristotle's higher purpose (coming from years of trained study) is to acknowledge that "all physical reality and the entire universe are sacred. There is something marvelous and divine about even the most humble beings."[96] The aesthetic of natural appreciation arises for Aristotle out of years of comprehensive study; for Thoreau, on the other hand, we arise to this aesthetic valuation with the aid of a rigorous process of unlearning, of becoming the animal we are underneath the excesses of culture.

5

How to Mind Your Own Business

Thoreau's work toward developing a philosophical self culminates in its ultimate test: the ability to withstand the seductions of democratic political participation and concern. In this sense, the criticisms—from Emerson's famous
argument that Thoreau was too content to lead a huckleberry party, to Alfred
Tauber's diagnosis of Thoreau's "failed" politics—approach Thoreau's corpus
with a good bit of legitimacy. Emerson is essentially correct to state, "He
declined to give up his large ambition of knowledge and action for any narrow craft or profession, aiming at a much more comprehensive calling, the
art of living well."[1] It is unfortunate that Thoreau's reputation as a political theorist suffers from an unimaginative and narrow reading of his reform
papers, instead of reading his political theory into his broader vision.[2] If we
make light of Thoreau's broad work as a sort of *askesis*, what then can we
make of his political theory?

This chapter argues that a close reading of Thoreau's work, particularly
his reform papers, alongside his journals and letters evokes an understanding
of his political thought that runs counter to the prevailing literature. I argue,
in fact, that Thoreau's reform papers read as "fits" or "starts" of transient political interest, generated by the proximity of political issues to the daily life of
Concord. While we may attempt to read Thoreau's defense of John Brown or
his critique of the Fugitive Slave Act as victories over his entrenched individualism, Thoreau's comprehensive vision leads us to see these momentary
interludes as failures to properly craft and care for an insulated self. This
rather dramatic retelling of the story of Thoreau's political engagement helps
us to understand his persistent critiques of mass democracy and his trenchant
unwillingness to dedicate his life to the eradication of evil.

Thoreau's intermittent political participation highlights the tensions
involved in developing a modern update of Epictetus's philosophy of own-

ness. Thoreau's criterion for engagement is not the *popularity* or even the *importance* of an issue, but the issue's *proximity* to his own life. Thoreau's major goal, in this case, is to distance himself from the problem so as to go on crafting himself and apprehending nature. Any desire Thoreau carries for a different world is driven by a desire to be rid of the concern with everyday politics, to be able to realize the carelessness of freedom and journey through life dedicated only to his own art of living.

To return to Emerson's famous eulogy, "Wanting this, instead of engineering for all America, he was the captain of a huckleberry party. Pounding beans is good to the end of pounding empires one of these days, but if, at the end of years, it is still only beans!"[3] Interestingly, Emerson centers on Thoreau's cultivation of beans, clearly a remark on *Walden*'s insufficiency as a directive text for America. As mentioned above, however, Thoreau responds to Emerson through "The Bean-Field," suggesting that pounding beans is in fact *not* "still only beans," but the means by which one carries a philosophical personality capable of engendering indifference. Emerson quickly turns away from the criticism toward a broader appreciation of Thoreau's singular vision: "But these foibles . . . were fast vanishing in the incessant growth of a spirit so robust and wise, and which effaced its defects with new triumphs."[4] Emerson's conceptualization of Thoreau's growth veers from the political toward the natural, revealing an acute understanding of Thoreau's economy of energy and its important valuative aspects. Thoreau's dedication to botany, entomology, and the reflective simplification of provincial philosophical life displaces our sense of the valuable, revealing not a curmudgeon who is so much dissatisfied with politics as one who repeatedly and willfully refers the political to its rightful place below individual consciousness and concern.

This aspect of Thoreau's thought is perhaps the most difficult to defend, but I will do so in this chapter. Thoreau makes a virtue out of political indifference, and that virtue becomes the crowning achievement of his privatist vision. In some ways Thoreau's tension between his thought and his intermittent political action is indicative of the place of American transcendentalism within the wider world of reform movements in the nineteenth century. Thoreau's defense of political indifference contributes to the debate between the individualism of the new market economy and the vitalist individualism of the American Renaissance. This chapter argues that political indifference, the elective detachment of the self from matters of the public, survives an uneasy tension with the desire to participate partially in the antislav-

ery activities of the antebellum period. Thoreau's connection between philosophical selfhood and political participation is most clearly established in
his correspondence with Harrison Blake, a follower and admirer. To properly gauge Thoreau's political interest, we must understand the fullness of
this relationship.

Thoreau as Teacher: Becoming a Sage in Letters

Thoreau's correspondence is not particularly noteworthy, with one major
exception. Thoreau's letters to Harrison Blake serve as "the record of his
inner biography," according to Robert Richardson.[5] Thoreau's letters to Blake
are a necessary source for understanding the development of his philosophy
and Thoreau's sense of philosophy's importance to his life. The letters take
the form of a sage teaching a student the basic principles of a Stoic strain of
thought, with an emphasis on apprehending the real, embracing indifference, and accepting voluntary poverty as a condition of the philosophical
life. Reading Thoreau's letters to Blake in the context of his political theory
allows the force of the correspondence to be felt in the way that Thoreau felt
it, having taken upon himself a student amidst the great personal failures of
the late 1840s (his disappearing relationship with Emerson, the failure of *A
Week on the Concord and Merrimack Rivers*, and his post-Walden ennui). Thoreau's letters to Blake serve as his first experience as philosophical sage.

Thoreau's first letter to Blake opens with an isolating presence, reducing
Blake's existential realm to the intensely private, finding distance between
oneself and one's environs: "If any should succeed to live a higher life, others
would not know of it; that difference and distance are one . . . To set about
living a true life is to go a journey to a distant country."[6] To write that "difference and distance are one" suggests Thoreau's mind-set about philosophical journeying—that he inherits Socrates's vision of himself in *Theaetetus:* "I
am utterly disturbing [*atopos*] and I create only perplexity [*aporia*]."[7] Thoreau
prepares Blake for the long work of creating a philosophical self, a "journey
to a distant country." Speaking from experience, Thoreau finds that the philosopher will become a stranger, decried within the community and full of
self-doubt and crippling opposition. Thoreau wants Blake to feel the necessity and importance of maintaining a solid grip on his private affections; in
fact, at the close of the first letter, Thoreau offers this counsel: "In what concerns you much do not think that you have companions—know that you

are alone in the world."[8] Thoreau makes Blake feel the effects of the philosophical apprenticeship he proposes with the first letter. Importantly, this is
precisely the advice Blake wishes to glean from Thoreau. In his first known
letter to Thoreau, Blake summarizes Thoreau's thought: "You would sunder
yourself from society, from the spell of institutions, customs, conventionali-
ties, that you may lead a fresh, simple life with God."[9] Blake opens his correspondence for Thoreau with the desire to simplify his life.

Thoreau's call for the intensification of private life aids the prevalent
mood of the text: admonishing Blake to simplify his commitments. "I do
believe in simplicity. It is astonishing as well as sad, how many trivial affairs
even the wisest man thinks he must attend to in a day."[10] This is familiar
advice from Thoreau, but in this case Thoreau pushes Blake to investigate
his commitments and come to a fuller sense of their requirements: "So simplify the problem of life, distinguish the necessary and the real. Probe the
earth to see where your main roots run . . . why not see,—use your eyes?"[11]
As mentioned previously, simplification is the first step in the apprenticeship of philosophy. The counsel Thoreau gives to himself in the early *Journal*
comes forward in his correspondence with more force and self-assurance. In
the letters to Blake, simplification plays a very specific role: allowing Thoreau to abandon social and political cares. Later in the first letter, he writes:
"I have sworn no oath. I have no designs on society—or nature—or God. I
am simply what I am, or I begin to be that."[12] Thoreau first offers simplification and now approaches the fruits of that work on the self. Simplifying his
existence allows him to abandon broad social care, a necessary step on the
road toward political indifference. Thoreau's words—"I have no designs" on
society, nature, God—read as a very particular sort of release from the trouble of taking trouble with another's life. Toward the end of this statement,
Thoreau offers that he accepts himself as he is, "or I begin to be that." Thoreau's placement of the latter qualifier has the effect of reminding Blake (and
other readers) that his work is to accept life as it presents itself, a particularly
privatist sort of working ethic.

Thoreau continues to caution Blake against involvement in the existential worlds of others: "If you would convince a man that he does wrong do
right. But do not care to convince him."[13] Thoreau removes the proselytiz-
ing aspect of the philosophical life from the table of possibilities, invoking
(again) his strong preference for a privatist leaning away from the public.
Instead of remedying others, Thoreau suggests to Blake, "Know your own

bone; gnaw at it, bury it, unearth it, and gnaw it still. Do not be too moral. . . . Aim above morality."[14] Thoreau's counsel that Blake take constant care to look after himself, to make himself the primary subject of his own existence, verifies the movement away from a "democratic individuality" toward a project of progressively radicalizing egoism that demands a constant watch over the self. What is curious, for Thoreau, is the problem of the substance of his retreat: does Thoreau retreat into the self out of frustration with the public, or does his philosophical vision (as relayed to Blake) render any politics valueless?

The letters to Blake do not demonstrate the sense of frustration that Thoreau evinces in his *Reform Papers*. In the public speeches and writings, Thoreau appears in a guise of indignation, frustration, offense, animation, and moralization. While I will argue, later in the chapter, that these readings neglect important passages in these texts, Thoreau does not demonstrate the same prevailing mood in his correspondence. Thoreau establishes a place for political engagement within his overall sphere of self-making. Placing politics within the context of the art of living is necessary for Thoreau. Richardson writes: "On May 24 John Brown and a small band of followers killed five unarmed proslavery settlers along Pottawatomie Creek. Kansas and Kansans bled all summer. Thoreau was aware of these events, but his day-to-day interests continued overwhelmingly in botany."[15] Thoreau writes to Blake in May 1848: "'We must have our bread.' But what is our bread? It is baker's bread? Methinks it should be very *home-made* bread."[16] This lesson situates social and political concern within Thoreau's notion of an insulated self or "inner citadel."[17] Thoreau's primary concern is with creating a philosophy of home, an aesthetics of existence that privileges the private, both accelerating and expanding the everyday concerns of average life, even in the face of historically significant injustice.

Thoreau's thorough provincialism and his inward isolation affect his ability to feel common emotions we associate with human life: "You ask if there is no doctrine of sorrow in my philosophy. Of acute sorrow I suppose that I know comparatively little. My most genuine sorrows are apt to be but transient regrets. The place of sorrow is supplied, perchance, by a certain hard and proportionably barren indifference. I am of kin to the sod, and partake largely of its dull patience."[18] Thoreau's ideal of a natural life requires that one absolve oneself of the common emotions of social life—instead taking upon oneself the mantle of the long view of nature and resolving to live as a Stoic.

Thoreau admits that he knows no regret but also uses that as a principle for Blake to follow. Notice, importantly, that Thoreau demonstrates how a hard and barren indifference replaces sorrow, admonishing Blake to cure himself of these emotions as well. Thoreau claims himself "kin to the sod," providing stark evidence of a self-transformation that culminates in an authentically natural life. As Thoreau moves forward in this portion of his letter, he writes that his "happiness is a good deal like that of the woodchucks."[19]

Thoreau's natural life is indeed, as David Robinson claims, a "worldly transcendentalism," particularly in the correspondence as he connects his meager life to a higher calling. In a letter from November 1849, Thoreau compares his own life to the yogin: "'The yogin, absorbed in contemplation, contributes in his degree to creation: he breathes a divine perfume, he hears wonderful things. Divine forms traverse him without tearing him, and united to the nature which is proper to him, he goes, he acts, as animating original matter.' To some extent, and at rare intervals, even I am a yogin."[20]

Beginning the letter, Thoreau notes, "I am subsisting on certain wild flowers which Nature wafts to me," giving Blake a sense of Thoreau's kinship with the natural order of things.[21] At this point it is important to note that Thoreau is settling his philosophical credentials by comparing himself with forest animals, creating a kinship with nature, and declaring himself an occasional yogin. Thoreau establishes these principles early in order to allow Blake to be prepared for the thrust of the letter's message, which appears to be one of strict political indifference. Thoreau, the thing-of-nature who masquerades as yogin and feeds on what nature provides, is the natural and the transcendent ideal for Blake.

Thoreau follows this setup with one of his most stark declarations of political indifference; in this case, Thoreau renders the recreational politics of international news and gossip meaningless to the natural philosopher: "I know little about the affairs of Turkey, but I am sure that I know something about barberries or chestnuts of which I have collected a store this fall. When I go to see my neighbor he will formally communicate to me the latest news from Turkey, which he read in yesterday's Mail. . . . Why, I would rather talk of the bran, which, unfortunately, was sifted out of my bread this morning and thrown away. It is a fact which lies nearer to me."[22]

This is perhaps Thoreau's most direct statement not only on his indifference to politics but on the conditions of political engagement anywhere in his correspondence. Thoreau's natural orientation prepares him to reject political participation, particularly the satellite participation of a burgeoning mass democracy. But there is more here than Thoreau's critique of the newspaper. Thoreau's argument that he would rather meditate on the bran that was "sifted out of my bread this morning" appears flippant, but it in fact signals an important aspect of Thoreauvian privatism that Blake needs to hear. Thoreau qualifies his statement and gives it depth by arguing on behalf of proximity: "It is a fact which lies nearer to me." We are to understand here that Thoreau replaces *importance*, a conventional indicator of political value, with *proximity*, suggesting that political participation is valid for the privatist only when it comes near enough to one's own life to prompt action. Bran is not more important than politics necessarily, but it is to Thoreau on that day and at that time. The privatist, living a natural life, does not seek political participation or information but leaves politics alone until directed to it by the closeness of a particular situation.

Thoreau's critique of political participation and his value of political indifference arise out of the exuberance of life, and Thoreau's earnest desire to understand the question he asks in the first week of his two years at Walden Pond: "Life! who knows what it is—what it does?"[23] He counsels Blake, "I am not afraid that I shall exaggerate the value and significance of life, but that I shall not be up to the occasion which it is."[24] Thoreau then connects this statement to his earlier critique of the news: "If there is anything more glorious than a congress of men a-framing or amending of a constitution going on, which I suspect there is, I desire to see the morning papers. I am greedy of the faintest rumor."[25] In this counsel, we get a sense of the purpose of Thoreau's philosophy, to define and exhaust what he calls "life." Thoreau's individualism places extraordinary demands on political engagement—politics must be near to him but also must contribute to the burgeoning sense of life that is inside of him.

Thoreau's longest letter to Blake exorcises the languishing mood in which it begins, with Thoreau laboring to pay the debt from the failure of *A Week on the Concord and Merrimack Rivers*. Thoreau describes to Blake his having reached a philosophical plateau, though not in a negative sense: "I have had but one *spiritual* birth (excuse the word,) and now whether it rains or snows, whether I laugh or cry, fall farther below or approach nearer to my standard, whether Pierce or Scott is elected,—not a new scintillation of light flashes upon me, but ever and anon, though with longer intervals, the same surprising and everlastingly new light dawns to me, with only such variations as in the coming of the natural day, with which indeed, it is often coincident."[26]

Thoreau reaches a point of stasis in this letter, having worked himself into a philosophical personality that transcends temporality and apprehends the infinite within the everyday. He writes in the next paragraph, "As to how to preserve your soul from rotting, I have nothing to learn but something to practice."[27] This is Thoreau's admission of having reached a point of the sage, the impoverished and natural self who has conquered circumstances and the seductions of the public. Importantly, Thoreau does not gain knowledge through experience but uses experience as practice for a set of principles that aim to reduce his reliance on externals. Thoreau's perfected Stoicism occurs only through the negation of the value of the political; this political indifference, as a contributing factor to Thoreau's philosophical serenity, is a challenging political theory that takes the relation of the self to the state as the primary theoretical problem of democratic politics.

How to Mind Your Own Business

Thoreau's major expression of life philosophy, that one "mind one's own business," highlights the coordination of political and economic themes in his work. The "business" one should mind includes the project of getting a living as well as the cultivation of an inward check on the importance of external events. While Thoreau's narrowing of economics consists in his lifelong pursuit of getting a living, Thoreau's political attachments are much more sporadic and uneven. The notion of minding one's own business as a declaration of political indifference helps us to understand why Thoreau engages slavery primarily as it approaches his own life (literally, it appears, with the Anthony Burns Concord case in 1854 and with Thoreau's acquaintance with John Brown in 1859). This section uses the concept of "minding one's own business" to ground Thoreau's political indifference as a particularly unique response to the mass democratization and economic liberalization of New England in the antebellum period.

Before we begin with Thoreau's understanding of minding one's business, it is fitting to recognize that the concept does not originate with Thoreau, but with Plato. Book IV of Plato's *Republic* establishes the baseline definition of individual justice as a keeping to oneself, using one's own nature as an indicator of value and pursuit: "'Well, then, my friend,' I said, 'this—

the practice of minding one's own business—when it comes into being in a certain way, is probably justice.'"[28] Plato also describes justice as "not being a busybody," holding close to the notion that one obeys that to which one is intended. The value one gives to a city, in Plato's *Republic*, depends first upon the psychological affirmation of one's nature and its place within the city's structure. Indeed, the difficult work of becoming an effective member of a polity appears to exist primarily in accepting one's limitations, whether they are the limitations of the desiring masses or the limitations of the intellect called to rule. To identify oneself as a philosopher is to love truth—and Emerson lays this praise at Thoreau over and again—but to love truth one has first to love the truth of oneself, to exercise and practice the philosophical work of naked introspection and collective education necessary to establish one's horizon.

Minding one's own business works as a theory of individual justice because it creates the harmony necessary to ground a sound individual life. It is important to note, however, that this notion does not originate in keeping oneself away from the affairs of others necessarily, but to devote oneself to the cultivation of a soul that is respectful and attentive to that which it owns. The work of developing a solid inner life is not an easy task; indeed, we can look at Thoreau's *Walden* as well as his journals for testimony to this truth. Thoreau constructs a broad philosophy of conduct that he hopes will deliver him to a more natural life—indeed, Thoreau hopes to infuse himself with nature's lessons on fate and freedom—and thus uses every facet of his existence to fashion a self capable of living naturally. Minding his own business springs from the affirmative font of ownness. To carry one's own within oneself is to dedicate and rededicate one's life to crafting that which lies as potential within itself.

Minding one's own business, in Plato's thought, is based primarily on the theory of "ownness," wherein one takes value in what belongs to the self. This involves the expansion of the concept of property to include not only one's holdings but one's personality, predilections, aversions—in short, one's nature. The strain of self-possession on which Thoreau hinges his philosophy is not based in capitalist acquisition but within the simplification and experimentation necessary to establish one's horizon. Plato's work in *Republic* is similar: one has to first establish one's ground; then the work of making and releasing attachments culminates in the character of minding one's own affairs. The philosophically damning effects of attaching oneself to things that are not within the self's power animate Plato's attempt at a government without politics; that is, Plato is so afraid of the externalization of democratic politics that he is willing to erase the possibility of politics from the ideal in order to preserve one's ability to stay within one's horizon, both in design and in execution. Similarly, Thoreau remains suspicious toward democratic processes, fearing the loss of control evoked through the drama of vicarious importance and knowledge more than the possibility of domination through nondemocratic processes.

As commentators have long understood, Thoreau's radical individualist political philosophy is fundamentally at odds with his intermittent participation in the antislavery movement of the antebellum United States. Mid-twentieth-century scholars who attempted to account for that discrepancy were largely hostile, with critics such as Hannah Arendt and Vincent Buranelli branding Thoreau's politics a failed brand of egoism or anarchism.[29] Later in that century and early in the present, other analysts have sought to rehabilitate Thoreau's reputation by arguing that he was an exemplar of liberal democratic individualism, and they have characterized him as bent on cultivating "conscience," a unifying concept that aligns recent research on his influence as a moral philosopher with his highly selective involvement in political activities. Even among those adhering to this explanation, however, there is little consensus, with one critic calling Thoreau's conscience "militant,"[30] and another "democratic,"[31] and a third asserting that Thoreau exhibits a "moral sensitivity and therefore a political irritability that are exceptionally keen."[32]

Economics, however—specifically Thoreau's brand of "home economics"—may be a more useful context than moral philosophy for reconciling Thoreau's political thought with his sporadic political action. Philosophers and ordinary citizens alike struggled to accommodate themselves to the early nineteenth century's rapid economic transformations, and they did so through such institutions as the state, the church, and social movements. Others, however, chose a principled withdrawal, a stance Thoreau endeavored to articulate and to maintain. In *Walden* he instructs, "Let every one mind his own business."[33] This notion of minding one's own business suggests the ways in which politics and economics intersect and intertwine in Thoreau's thought. The "business" one should mind includes not only the lifelong pursuit of making one's living but that of cultivating a serene inner self in defiance of one's neighbors', and the nation's, busyness. In this second regard, minding one's own business can be taken as a declaration of political indifference—that is, of the elective detachment of the self from public matters.

And yet the fact of Thoreau's political engagement remains. By closely reading his personal writings—private journals and letters to friends, especially Harrison Blake, an acquaintance and devotee of Thoreau's thought who received Thoreau's best letters (and, indeed, the best expression of his philosophy)—we can see that even in private Thoreau was not disengaged from but, rather, attuned to political subjects, albeit in a different register from that of his speeches and public writings. Despite this difference, however, it is evident in both private and public writings that even as Thoreau is compelled by political issues, he is extraordinarily uncomfortable with his attachment to them. Thus, the private journals and letters do not really support or discredit the politically active Thoreau; instead, they highlight his persistent misgivings as well as the terms under which he is willing to participate in political affairs or, alternatively, to retreat once more into his privatist political philosophy.[34]

Thoreau's preference for what we might call a "home economics" is a direct response to mid-nineteenth-century America's industrial concept of "business." For Thoreau the "business" of others includes both the labor performed for them and an undue interest in their concerns, such as newspapers' gossipmongering, quite literally a business of other people's business. In an August 1854 letter to Blake, Thoreau reflects on what he considers to be the better course: "Only think for a moment, of a man about his affairs! How we should respect him! How glorious he would appear! Not working for any corporation, its agent, or president, but fulfilling the end of his being! A man about *his business* would be the cynosure of all eyes."[35]

Minding one's own business is, in Thoreau's view, an antidote to the market revolution, which has radically transformed the lives of the nation's citizens, indebting them to corporations or to other persons with more power than they. As he notes in "Life without Principle," "the world is a place of business."[36] Denying the virtue of industriousness and elevating personal choice, Thoreau, for his part, values work insofar as it promotes the well-being of the individual, well-being as the individual himself defines it. "'What!' exclaim a million Irishmen starting up from all the shanties in the land, 'is not this railroad which we have built a good thing?' Yes, I answer, *comparatively* good, that is, you might have done worse; but I wish, as you are brothers of mine, that you could have spent your time better than digging in this dirt."[37]

The woeful status of wage laborers prompted a number of American transcendentalists, including Orestes Brownson, Theodore Parker, and, to a lesser degree, Thoreau, to comment on how the process of getting a living was irrevocably changing in nineteenth-century America.[38] Thoreau's *Walden*, particularly the first two chapters, attempts to reclaim the economic and philosophical components of minding one's own business, a task best accomplished, he believes, when the individual withdraws both physically and intellectually from outward circumstances.

Attention to political matters that are not vital to one's self-interest can also alienate the individual from important personal matters. In a striking late letter to Parker Pillsbury on the subject of the coming Civil War, Thoreau notes: "I do not so much regret the present condition of things in this country (provided I regret it at all), as I do that I ever heard of it. I know of one or two who have this year, for the first time, heard a President's message; but they do not see that this implies a *fall* in themselves rather than a *rise* in the President."[39]

By holding himself aloof, Thoreau does not deny that it is an area of expertise the world requires, but he does reject it as a means by which the individual gains vitality. For Thoreau the self should be engaged in the business of discovering its own interests and its own properties, and his philosophy, to some extent, exhibits both the pleasures and pitfalls of finding one's business and single-mindedly pursuing it.[40]

Although Thoreau seems to cordon off politics as a specialized area, his point is, more accurately, that most individuals should be nurturing their own talents rather than involving themselves in political issues that do not require their attention or yield to their desires. How, then, should the individual conduct himself? Thoreau offers a suggestion in a famous passage from "Resistance to Civil Government": "As for adopting the ways which the state has provided for remedying the evil, I know not of such ways. They take too much time, and a man's life will be gone. I have other affairs to attend to. I came into this world, not chiefly to make this a good place to live in, but to live in it, be it good or bad."[41]

When confronted with the problems of government, each individual must look to his own taste and time to gauge the appropriateness of his participation, and in this instance, Thoreau strips his own political obligations down to the dictates of his mood and circumstances. By choosing to mind his own business, he declines responsibility for society's affairs and suggests that he owes himself (and his society) no further explanation than that reform would "take too much time." Minding his business is, then, Thoreau's means of simplifying his life and supplying an internal check on the external obligations a democracy would seem to impose. Read in this way, "Resistance to Civil Government" is not an anarchic piece, nor is it necessarily an essay decrying government's involvement in its citizens' lives; it is, first and foremost, a privatist statement of disdain for the ways in which "everyday politics" draws the individual's imagination outward from its proper inward focus.

Thoreau's dismissal of everyday politics is not novel for his time period, nor is it exceptional among his transcendentalist cohort; in fact, one could argue that Emerson and Parker wrote equally powerful denunciations, as did conservative minister Horace Bushnell.[42] What makes Thoreau's defense of political indifference unique is the emphasis he places on the efficacy of the individual's narrowing the scope of his interest, cultivating what lies near, and maintaining that limited focus not simply as a periodic tactic for deflecting unwanted commitments but as a sustained strategy for life. As Thoreau learns (and relearns) to "mind his own business," he makes himself—and his project of getting a living—the paramount concern of his life. He does not dismiss politics altogether; rather, he places a premium on matters closest to hand, those affairs that are, quite literally, his business. In radicalizing individual choice, he reduces the costs of egoism; in other words, by assigning the determination of worth to the self alone, he places the self beyond criticism, thus freeing himself to perform the "experiment" of his life without worry or guilt. Noting that bran lies nearer to one than global affairs is a way of contrasting the insignificant but personal intricacies of private life with the significant but impersonal affairs of the world. Thoreau values most highly, then, not that which is most "important" but that which is most personal.

The readiest means of focusing the individual on those matters that are vitally important to him is simplification, simplification in all its forms—political indifference being but one expression of it: "By simplicity, commonly called poverty, my life is concentrated and so becomes organized."[43] Offering one response to the busying tendencies of a rapidly advancing society, *Walden* presents a plan for breaking the bonds of complexity. "Our life is frittered away by detail. An honest man has hardly need to count more than his ten fingers, or in extreme cases he may add his ten toes, and lump the rest. Simplicity, simplicity, simplicity! I say, let your affairs be as two or three, and not a hundred or a thousand; instead of a million count half a dozen, and keep your accounts on your thumb nail."[44] In Thoreau's personal accounting, political participation is not vital to him, although it might be to the next man or woman.

Whether in nature or in politics, Thoreau sees indifference not as a hollow, negative characteristic but as a positive, useful virtue. In a *Journal* entry from 1851, he describes an incident in which he snatches a toad from the jaws of a snake: "I thought, as the toad jumped leisurely away with his slime-covered hind quarters glistening in the sun, as if I, his deliverer, wished to interrupt his meditations—without a shriek or fainting—I thought what a healthy indifference he manifested."[45]

The toad's indifference to the world around it strikes Thoreau as a tremendous benefit, for it allows the creature to live in the world as it comes to him. The main factor separating animal and human is, in Thoreau's estimation, the latter's moral sense, which generally gives him the advantage, but not always. "Why always insist that men incline to the moral side of their being?" Thoreau asks. "Our life is not all moral."[46] Later he comments: "A wise man is as unconscious of the movements in the body politic as he is of the processes of digestion and the circulation of the blood in the natural body. The processes are *infra*-human."[47]

Not prepared to deny that the workings of politics and society are, in some sense, vital, Thoreau nonetheless suggests that they should, like human digestion, operate below the level of consciousness. Later in the same entry, he notes: "As for society, why should we not meet, not always as dyspeptics, but sometimes as eupeptics?"[48]

The Challenge to Political Indifference

It is not possible to isolate the precise moment at which Thoreau provisionally committed himself to the antislavery movement of his time. His mother and sisters, lifelong antislavery activists, no doubt had been encouraging him to do so. In 1850 Congress had passed the Fugitive Slave Act, which made the North complicit in the institution of slavery by requiring that any slave who had escaped from his or her master and was subsequently apprehended in a free state be returned to the South. Although Thoreau had alluded to antislavery from time to time throughout his literary career and had helped escaped slaves evade capture, the Anthony Burns affair in the summer of 1854 stirred him to action. On May 24, 1854, nineteen-year-old Burns, who had escaped slavery in Richmond, Virginia, and traveled to Boston, where he worked, was apprehended while walking along the city's Court Street. Attempts to free him were unsuccessful and ended in violence. Burns was tried, convicted, and returned to his master. The event, which had the effect of consolidating antislavery sentiment in the commonwealth, apparently concentrated Thoreau's thought and prompted him to speak out at an antislavery rally in July.

In the speech that became the essay "Slavery in Massachusetts," Thoreau's self-satisfying ethics meets its limits in the public sphere, as he concedes his newfound willingness to become involved in political matters at the same time as he reiterates his reluctance to dedicate himself (or, indeed, much of his time) to their resolution. Although a strong declaration of abolitionist principle, the essay demonstrates the fundamental difference between Thoreau's concept of politics and the politics that the antislavery movement requires. He does not treat slavery per se, but, rather, the North's acquiescence to it, which, he insists, violates *his* sovereignty: "I feel that, to some extent, the State has fatally interfered with my lawful business. It has not only interrupted me in my passage through Court street on errands of trade, but it has interrupted me and every man on his onward and upward path, on which he had trusted soon to leave Court street far behind."[49]

The assertion that the Fugitive Slave Act's primary crime is its interference with the daily life of a free individual strikes many readers as offensive, but the remark captures the essence of Thoreau's temporary engagement with slavery and with politics. Thoreau is alarmed by slavery, to be sure; however, his philosophy of minding his own business dictates that the Fugitive Slave Act (and indeed slavery altogether) must necessarily become a matter of *his* business—that is, that slavery encroach upon him personally, that for him to take an interest in it, it must violate the liberal individualism he hopes to take for granted. As Thoreau mentions toward the end of the essay, "The remembrance of my country spoils my walk."[50] The point bears further emphasis: Thoreau's impetus to engage with the polity aligns with the ways in which the polity adversely affects him, not others.

The vital importance of the quote falls toward the end, where Thoreau remarks that the state interrupts him "on his onward and upward path, on which he had trusted soon to leave Court street far behind." The pull back to political engagement redirects Thoreau's energy but also interrupts his desire to transcend the political altogether. From this quote, Thoreau allows that acts of the state defy his desire to leave it behind, which leads us to conclude that Thoreau's desire is not to be pushed toward a type of political engagement, but to disavow the entrancing gaze of the political altogether. Thoreau's critique of the state contracts around his ability to stand aloof from it.

People have neglected the task of cultivating self-respect, he claims, and relied instead on the surety of public values. Each and every citizen should be engaged in the lifelong pursuit of creating and sustaining his or her personal set of values and should appeal to such institutions as society and government only insofar as they will better the life of the individual according to his or her unique standards. All too often, however, policy becomes a stand-in for morality, and individuals externalize their private opinions by giving them over to the press, whose role as a value-creating machine Thoreau disparages. Burns's return to slavery, mandated by state and federal law, awakens Thoreau to the larger problem of how each citizen's indolence has allowed legality to be equated with morality: "Will mankind never learn that policy is not morality—that it never secures any moral right, but considers merely what is expedient?"[51] Not only does Thoreau separate policy from morality, but he contends that the two spring from different sources. Morality, he explains, is an abiding internal response to the question of how one should live, not a code of conduct enforced by external authority. The moral life comes about through experimentation, through the experience of life as it is lived in the first person. Policy, on the other hand, derives its tenets from mere ease of custom.

Although morality carries much more weight than policy in Thoreau's scheme of the universe, he does not wholly dismiss politics. Instead, he believes that "the effect of a good government is to make life more valuable,—of a bad one, to make it less valuable."[52] The quotation is key to understanding why slavery serves as a limit case for his brand of political indifference. Thoreau is not an anarchist but a privatist—one who accepts government but does not participate in its workings—who prefers political matters to be "infra-human." Government is supposed to ensure the well-being of the individual, but whereas most Northerners thought that returning Burns to slavery was immoral, the opinion of the majority in this case did not trump the policy put in place by the state. In acting on the policy it had established, the government failed to make the lives of those individuals more valuable and, instead, denigrated their morality.

Most interestingly, Thoreau signals his withdrawal from politics in each of his "reform papers." In "Slavery in Massachusetts," we gain a clean break through the final two pages, which begins with Thoreau's startling shift of attention: "But it chanced the other day that I scented a white water-lily, and a season I had waited for had arrived."[53] Thoreau's abrupt shift signals his retreat from the issue toward a rededication to the natural world. Of course, Thoreau explains, the shift is encouraged by nature's absence from petty political bigotry: "Nature has been partner to no Missouri Compromise. . . . The foul slime stands for the sloth and vice of man, the decay of humanity; the fragrant flower that springs from it, for the purity and courage which are immortal."[54] Thoreau seeks the sweetness of the flower and yearns for that sweetness in human beings; he is not, however, asking all human beings to retain the sweetness of the flower in themselves, as he is explaining the source of his retreat is couched in the moral impossibility of human sweetness engaged by political means. Going beyond morality *and* policy, nature gives off the scent of life—vitality—while the servility of politics signals the death, the stink and decay, of the human relationship of power.

On October 30, 1859, two weeks following John Brown's failed assault on the federal arsenal at Harpers Ferry, Virginia, Thoreau defended the captain's action to his fellow citizens at Concord. As Jack Turner persuasively argues, Thoreau's "A Plea for Captain John Brown" should be viewed as a form of political participation,[55] but even as he delivers the address, Thoreau removes himself—despite his obvious interest—from fully committing to the issue at the heart of Brown's crusade: the abolition of slavery. Thoreau's hyperbolic statements on Brown's behalf suggest that he is grieving for a friend at the same time as he is shoring up the reputation Brown enjoyed in transcendentalist circles as a hero and a saint. Beyond that, however, Thoreau declines to embrace the cause that Brown espoused. Toward the end of the essay, he admits—for the second time; he had done so earlier, in "Resistance to Civil Government"—"I do not think it is quite sane for one to spend his whole life in talking or writing about this matter, unless he is continuously inspired, and I have not done so. A man may have other affairs to attend to."[56]

With this statement, Thoreau defends his wholly partial and temporary engagement with antislavery politics. He does not characterize the "other affairs" in which he may engage, for they are important only to himself, and the self alone assigns value to its endeavors. Thoreau chooses to involve himself in antislavery politics only when it becomes his business, and thus it becomes the limiting case for his political indifference. That certain people *are* inspired to take on political causes is not a goad to action but, rather, a further justification for him to withdraw his interest, just as he had dismissed philanthropy in *Walden:* "As for Doing-good, that is one of the professions which are full. I have tried it fairly, and . . . am satisfied that it does not agree with my constitution."[57]

As mentioned above, Thoreau recuses himself from political involvement in each of his famous "reform papers." This recusal is perhaps the most important part of the essays; in effect, Thoreau offers a fitful engagement with a political issue that encroaches upon his personal space, only to redirect that issue back toward those who are "continuously inspired" so that he may attend to his other affairs. That Thoreau never qualifies the "other affairs" suggests that he is not moralizing political indifference but offering a vitalist principle of political participation. If, then, we make too much of Thoreau's temporary "political action" as it is articulated in his speeches about John Brown and Anthony Burns, we risk losing sight of his more comprehensive contribution to an understanding of the role of an individual in a democratic society: the sacrosanct duty of the self is to vitalize that with which it is surrounded.

The Business of Others

Thoreau cultivates political indifference in the midst of tremendous political agitation, most prominently over slavery and the Mexican–American War. In "Resistance to Civil Government," he declares, "The government does not concern me much, and I shall bestow the fewest possible thoughts on it. It is not many moments that I live under a government, even in this world."[58] In his private letters, especially those to Harrison Blake, he describes over and over the detachment he yearns to achieve. In his first letter to Blake from March 1848, Thoreau explains: "I have no designs on society, or nature, or God. I am simply what I am, or I begin to be that. I live in the present."[59] Later, in a letter to Blake from September 1855, he insists, "I have no scheme about it—no designs on men at all," and again, in December 1856, he stresses that he does "not think much of America or of politics."[60] Thoreau's letters to

Blake constitute a sort of "inner biography," which reveals a thinker intensely concerned with the principles of individuality—freedom and simplicity—but unwilling to commit to a political platform, party, or cause.[61]

American transcendentalism coincides with the first wave of American reform. From 1815 until 1860, Americans vigorously campaigned against slavery, alcoholism, emergent capitalism, the unfair treatment of women, and other societal ills. In many ways, the two movements were different, but they often shared a common goal as well as a common membership. Orestes Brownson advocated for labor reform; Margaret Fuller grounded women's rights in feminist philosophy; Theodore Parker crusaded against slavery and impure labor practices; and, one might add, both Emerson and Thoreau made brief forays into the abolitionist movement. Thus, Thoreau has often been branded by association with the early nineteenth century's "spirit of reform."[62] But he, more than any other in the transcendentalist cohort, resists such a label.

Although a number of transcendentalists were deeply involved with collective-living experiments as an avenue toward social reform—from George and Sophia Ripley's mildly successful Brook Farm to Bronson Alcott and Charles Lane's disastrous Fruitlands—and although many more flirted with the idea, Thoreau entertained not a moment of doubt. "As for these communities," he unambiguously stated, "I think I had rather keep bachelor's hall in hell than go to board in heaven."[63] Indeed, one could view Thoreau's retreat to Walden Pond as an individualist response to collective living practices. In "Reform and the Reformers," his critique of the spirit of communitarianism in his time, he writes: "Most whom I meet in the streets are, so to speak, outward bound, they live out and out . . . I would fain see them inward bound, retiring in and in, farther and farther every day, and when I inquired for them I should not hear, that they had gone abroad anywhere . . . but that they had withdrawn deeper into the folds of being."[64]

Reform movements draw the individual outside of himself, outside his own business, and into that of others. In short, Thoreau rejects the Kantian notion adopted by many transcendentalists that individuals come to know themselves discursively through a shared moral community.

More often than not, society plays the enemy in Thoreau's thought. For him, insight into how one ought to live in a rapidly industrializing economy comes through individual self-study alone. His privatist response to the challenges of his time is merely the most radically individualist of the transcendentalist theories of self-cultivation, and it carries with it an almost pathological distrust of society's proclaimed values. As a rule, politics, while providing important tools and services for the self, extends the self beyond its own mind toward a world of seductive interest but little inward promise.

Thoreau's cultivation of political indifference stems in part from his lack of faith in the power of reform, especially the collective reform of an individual life. Dismissing the assumption that people improve when they are coerced to do so by their peers, he instead regrets our influence on one another, wishing to place all freedom in the individual. In his first book, *A Week on the Concord and Merrimack Rivers*, he describes a chance meeting and, in the process, introduces us to his theory of interpersonal relations: "He was, indeed, as rude as a fabled satyr. But I suffered him to pass for what he was, for why should I quarrel with nature? and was even pleased at the discovery of such a singular natural phenomenon. I dealt with him as if to me all manners were indifferent, and he had a sweet wild way with him."[65]

Our desires for reform prompt us to romanticize our influence on one another, Thoreau understands, and so he strives for a purer relation: to appreciate others in their singularity rather than feebly attempting to normalize them according to his own dictates. Later in *A Week*, he adds: "We must accept one another as we are."[66] In doing so, we value each individual as a unique center of expression and respect his or her appropriate remoteness from us. "They want all of a man but his truth and independence and manhood," Thoreau complains.[67] And as he states succinctly in the late essay "Reform and the Reformers," "inward is a direction which no traveler has taken. Inward is the bourne which all travelers seek and from which none desire to return."[68]

Viewing Thoreau within a reform tradition, scholars have described *Walden* as an American prophecy[69] or a democratic advice manual,[70] but Thoreau would have disdained such characterizations, however flattering, of the book: "I would not have any one adopt *my* mode of living on any account; for, beside that before he has fairly learned it I may have found another for myself, I desire that there may be as many different persons in the world as possible; but I would have each one be very careful to find out and pursue *his own* way, and not his father's or his mother's or his neighbor's instead."[71]

In *Walden* Thoreau defends a particular life as but one among a host of other viable, indeed laudatory, options; therefore, the book is not an instruction manual except in the largest possible sense. Stanley Cavell explains, "It would be a fair summary of the book's motive to say that it invites us to take an interest in our lives, and shows us how."[72] Ultimately, however, it is we ourselves who must take interest in ourselves, and interest in ourselves properly keeps us vitally separated from the interests of, and an interest in, others. We can wish, desire, or hope to change others—as Thoreau himself hopes from time to time—but we must keep our actions focused on ourselves. Even if we were to achieve all of our political dreams, Thoreau notes, we would be left with the question "What then?"[73]

For Thoreau, indifference is, in essence, a manifestation of pluralism. If we respect ourselves as singular individuals, we will not fight for the rights of others but ignore them, because, quite simply, we cannot know what they consider to be their rights, that is, what they value. He notes, "You may know what a thing costs or is worth to you; you can never know what it costs or is worth to me."[74] Thoreau's political indifference is, then, at least in one sense, a response to the strained pluralism of liberal politics, which mandates personal restraint insofar as it legislates recognition of others' individual rights and interests. But Thoreau is unwilling to sacrifice his own hard-won values to the immediate and expedient utility of the public sphere. He would rather ignore his fellow citizen than, to his detriment, be forced to accommodate his interests to the rights of the other.

Thoreau's argument that pluralism is best achieved through indifference suggests that he distrusts the discursive power of democratic politics. The major instrument for disseminating political information in his time, the newspaper, leaves individuals ill prepared to debate the issues closest to themselves, Thoreau argues, and sharing that external and ineffectual information does little to promote understanding. In fact, he asserts, discursive politics is a kind of "gossip" wherein people indulge themselves in other people's lives at a safe distance, using political knowledge to maintain separation. In that regard, discursive politics becomes a sort of coping mechanism, one Thoreau does not hold in very high esteem. In politics, we either hold fast to ideas that are of no interest to us, or, if we happen to believe passionately in an idea, we feel compelled to fight for its recognition with others who do not understand it, why we might value it, or our own measure of self-importance.

Remarking that "one can never be too vigilant about the narcissism that individualistic societies tend to engender,"[75] Brian Walker claims that Thoreau is among those democratic advice writers who advocate democratic individuality as a socially and economically progressive ideal to curb the natural excesses of democratic life. Thoreau, however, does not support that assertion. "I am not responsible for the successful working of the machinery of society," he insists.[76] Not only is he not responsible; he is not at all interested. Indeed, what could be a stronger assertion of that position than "I would not run round a corner to see the world blow up"?[77] Disinterest in political problems and the individuals who experience them permeates every element of Thoreau's philosophy, even his definition of helping the poor: "Be sure you give the poor the aid they most need, though it be your example which leaves them far behind."[78] While Nancy Rosenblum sees this passage as an exception to "Thoreau's show of indifference to others," it is in fact a perfect declaration of it.[79] Thoreau's dedication to self-reform may have public consequences, but those consequences are not part of his design. The design is, quite simply, to cultivate the self—nothing more, nothing less: "If you aspire to anything better than politics, expect no cooperation from men. They will not further anything good. You must prevail of your own force, as a plant springs and grows by its own vitality."[80] Reform will not make a better individual of the recipient or the executor and instead will drain the inner vitality of each.

In a letter to Blake, Thoreau roundly disavows that he possesses any instinct for reform, any intention of "doing good": "What a foul subject is this of doing good! instead of minding one's life, which should be his business; doing good as a dead carcass, which is only fit for manure, instead of as a living man. . . . If I ever *did* a man any good, in their sense, of course it was something exceptional and insignificant compared with the good or evil which I am constantly doing by being what I am."[81]

Thoreau may commit acts of goodness toward others, just as he may step on their toes or cause them harm. But such effects are merely circumstantial, unintended consequences of his proper attention to his own personal matrix of cares and concerns. Thoreau envisions political participation as a measure of "doing good," but not according to one's own dictates. When we consciously do good for others, we are outside of ourselves, alienated and driven by external motivations, quite simply, as he suggests, "dead" to ourselves. The proper posture for the individual in a democratic society is, on the contrary, indifference: he should mind his own business and let others mind theirs.

Quotidian Politics: Thoreau and the Measure of Engagement

Thus far we have explored both Thoreau's reticence with and Thoreau's engagement in politics; we are left, however, with the question of how

Thoreau's political indifference transmits a positive theory of political engagement. I argue that one of Thoreau's major innovations in political theory comes from his provincialism, in particular the quotidian value of politics that engages the self in political issues based on the proximity to one's own daily life. In this sense, Thoreau's articulation of proximity as a value of engagement replaces the more traditional political virtue of importance.

Thoreau's quotidian politics reveals itself throughout his canonical political writings, but it also appears in other registers. One of Thoreau's most poignant pieces of writing, the beginning of *Cape Cod*, in which he surveys the damage after a shipwreck, unhinges this valuative statement of importance: "I saw that corpses might be multiplied, as on the field of battle, till they no longer affected us in any degree, as exceptions to the common lot of humanity. Take all the grave-yards together, they are always the majority. It is the individual and private that demands our sympathy."[82]

In terms of the importance of the event, the shipwreck and subsequent body count dwarf the death by accidental choking, the death from old age, and the death of an infant whose body is not constituted for extended life. If we view our existential and temporal dedications in terms of overall importance, we are drawn to the large events; indeed, it is the "bigness" of an event that carries us forward to attention. Thoreau's articulation of value is starkly different—he mentions that the "individual and private" are the events, situations, tragedies, and joys to which we ought to devote our attention.

If we consider Thoreau's conceptualization of value politically, we find that Thoreau is committed to valuing events and persons that strike an existential chord within the small purview of his everyday life. This is the purpose for calling Thoreau's political engagement "quotidian," insofar as it refers to the everydayness of Thoreau's commitments. Thoreau clarifies Cavell's notion that "ordinariness . . . speaks of an intimacy with existence," because we attune ourselves as individuals to that which we can touch, see, smell, change, and locate.[83] Thoreau's consistent uneasiness with technological change (the telegraph, the locomotive) is a critique of the power of remoteness in pulling oneself away from those changes that are happening under one's feet: "Our inventions are wont to be pretty toys, which distract our attention from serious things."[84] What are these "serious things" to which we owe our attention? Nothing but the business of living a private life, of watching one's commitments to ensure their vital pertinence, of hoeing beans, housekeeping, writing, pencil making, eating supper, resting, keeping oneself free of direct engagement with slavery. For Thoreau, political engagement threads itself into a fabric of engaged everydayness, in which we find ourselves in a world of comfort and discomfort, challenged by the attention to which we give the smallest things.

Thoreau's critique of importance centers on the triumph of means over ends. We are quick to assume that because we can be concerned with the world beyond our outstretched arms, we ought to concern ourselves with that world. Take his famous refrain in *Walden:* "We are in great haste to construct a magnetic telegraph from Maine to Texas; but Maine and Texas, it may be, have nothing important to communicate."[85] Allowing ourselves to take in the advances of disengaged and merely recreational values speaks to the majesty of the important, the feeling of being in-the-know that accompanies recreational interest. But Thoreau's larger purpose, realized in his later life in the chronicling of wild fruits in the Concord region, offers the benefits of rekindling oneself with one's own world as an investment in time and dedication: "Such is the inevitable tendency of our civilization, to reduce huckleberries to a level with beef-steaks; that is, to blot out four-fifths of it or the going a-huckleberrying, and leave only a pudding, that part which is the fittest accompaniment to a beef-steak."[86]

Recreational democracy reduces, rather than expands, the existential engagement of oneself with the wider world. Taking Thoreau's emphatic case for huckleberrying, we can envision a closely engaged individual who chooses commitments through their proximity: "The crop grows wild all over the country—wholesome, bountiful, and free, a real ambrosia. And yet men, the foolish demons that they are, devote themselves to the culture of tobacco, inventing slavery and a thousand other curses for that purpose, with infinite pains and inhumanity go raise tobacco all their lives, and that is the staple instead of huckleberries."[87]

Thoreau's taste for huckleberries comes from his proximity to them, rather than from any distinct flavor or other aesthetic quality they may hold. This is an important criterion of interest for Thoreau; indeed, he devotes countless hours of his life to understanding and appreciating the various things directly around him, rarely venturing past Concord to study flora or fauna. Thoreau's criticism of tobacco in this instance reflects the dangers of an externalized, nonpersonal interest. People's interest in tobacco, an object not identified with their surroundings, replaces their knowledge of the land

and its people with complicity in "slavery and a thousand other curses," thereby pursuing the guilt that is native to the southerner. Thoreau's argument for proximity is based not only on familiarity, but with an expertise that assumes responsibility for one's surroundings and does not go in search of adopting the guilt of others.

In Thoreau's mind, huckleberries are compromised by the exploitation brought about from the cities, which send pickers from their burgeoning offices to take the berries from locals (who pick for nourishment, but also for merriment) and sell them back to the locals at a heavy price. Thoreau's strict provincialism suggests that these berries do not belong to the outsiders, because they have their own berries in their own localities from which to choose. Thoreau is coming to philosophical maturity during the market revolution, keenly aware of the loss of provincial identity and value soon to transform New England. "This is one of the taxes which we pay for having a railroad. All our improvements, so called, tend to convert the country into the town. But I do not see clearly that these successive losses are ever quite made up to us. This suggests, as I have said, what origin and foundation many of our institutions have."[88] We know from *Walden* that Thoreau is not willing to pay the existential tax for the railroad, but that it comes anyway. The railroad (alongside the newspaper) signals the transformation of local values and interests to a cosmopolitan vision of recreational politics played out through the new value of importance, broadly conceived.

Under this view, Thoreau's choice to engage political issues such as the poll tax, the Anthony Burns case, and John Brown's memory fit the profile of engagement offered in *Wild Fruits* and elsewhere. Thoreau's primary position of political indifference holds the value of political engagement hostage, hoping to locate an understanding of one's actual, existential investment in political issues prior to consenting to political action. Furthermore, Thoreau offers only temporary engagement, holding on to the belief that one requires only that the issue not "touch" one's existential reach, that one be able to go about his daily business without the stench of the issue ruining his walk. Craving local culture, local knowledge, and inner value, Thoreau offers political engagement only in the case of proximal interest.

The dominant interpretive lens on Thoreau's political philosophy centers on the term *conscience*, which is interpreted as his abiding sense of responsibility for the polity at large. But conscience, as defined by recent Thoreau scholars, is the application of one's moral code to the polity at large, an activity he was quick to disavow. Thoreau's overarching mission of minding his own business, with political indifference being its operative social component, thrives only insofar as the individual declines to reduce himself to the moral claims or projects of the peers of his time.

The recently published *A Political Companion to Henry David Thoreau* collects sixteen essays on the American individualist, each bent on evaluating his position as a political thinker—a democratic political thinker, in particular. Of the sixteen, only one is disapproving (in Harry Jaffa's essay, Thoreau's reputation suffers when posed against the towering example of Lincoln), and only two are ambivalent (Leigh Kathryn Jenco's essay on Thoreau's moral critique of institutionalized democracy and Melissa Lane's comparison of Thoreau to Rousseau).[89] The remaining essays praise Thoreau as a champion of a healthy form of individuality appropriate to an advancing democracy. George Kateb sets for Thoreau's legacy as such: "What makes . . . politics of resistance individualist is the presence of conscience, which means, in this context, the courage to stand for what all the advantaged profess but many do not follow. Thoreau, more than any other, has crystallized the sentiments of resistance for the sake of others."[90]

In other words, although Thoreau remained a somewhat ambivalent "reformer," his writings constitute political participation and demonstrate that he was heavily invested in teaching individuals how to live in a democracy.[91] Such lionization of Thoreau comes at the expense of his contemporaries, some of whom developed a much more thoroughgoing defense of individual liberties with regard to the state. Theodore Parker, in particular, is a better fit for Kateb's laudatory description, and it is Parker, not Thoreau, who fashions himself a prophet of conscience in the sense Stanley Cavell assigns to *Walden*.[92]

Conscience, of course, has a long and important history in American political thought. The Framers identified conscience and prudence as the mind's formative rational powers, a benign psychology that underwrites the concept of limited government. As historian Daniel Walker Howe explains, "in the moral philosophy Thoreau had learned at Harvard . . . the highest faculty was conscience, or the moral sense; then came prudence, the faculty that calculated one's rational self interest. Below these were ranged the passions, needing to be kept under rational control."[93]

Howe argues that in demonstrating that "the individual conscience could and must be empowered to act, and not only for the individual him-self, but also upon the body politic,"[94] as was evident in his refusal to pay the poll tax or his speeches on behalf of John Brown, Thoreau made a signifi-cant contribution to the American self. David Robinson likewise asserts that Thoreau showed his fellow Americans that "moral dissociation from evil is the first step in recognizing that it is not a necessary evil, that political insti-tutions and policies that have been created in the process of history can also be changed in that same process."[95]

Recent interpretations of Thoreau, most of which are admiring but some of which pronounce his political philosophy a "failure" for its inability to appropriate liberal values,[96] neglect to come to terms with the uniqueness of his approach. Thoreau's letters and journals, in particular, offer insight into the mind of a theorist who transcends the boundaries of political duty as he focuses on cultivating a self; indeed, Thoreau takes his personal free-dom (awarded by the state) to its logical conclusion: a life determined by its own horizons, creating and sustaining its own limits. Thoreau, ultimately, is not defined by his conscience but by his yearning for indifference, achieved through a sustained attention to "minding his own business."[97]

Thoreau's political indifference, however, met its limit in the encroach-ment of American slavery in his life, and his understanding of that constraint is revealed in a poignant *Journal* entry of June 16, 1854, not long before he delivered the speech that would become "Slavery in Massachusetts":

> I had never respected this government, but I had foolishly thought that I might manage to live here, attending to my private affairs and forget it. . . . For my part, my old and worthiest pursuits have lost I cannot say how much of their attraction, and I feel that my investment in life here is worth many per cent less since Massachusetts last deliberately and forcibly restored an innocent man, Anthony Burns, to slavery. I dwelt before in the illusion that my life passed somewhere only *between* heaven and hell, but now I cannot persuade myself that I do not dwell wholly within hell.[98]

After June 17, though, antislavery gives way to his major preoccupation that summer: the heat. The heat kept him from his attic study and forced him to congregate with the family downstairs. Craving privacy, he lamented, "Soci-ety seems to have invaded and overrun me. . . . I have made myself cheap and vulgar."[99] Thoreau's political interest may have been drawn to certain *events*, but he never developed that interest into a theoretical framework for effective political participation. Quite simply, he chose not to.

To those who would congratulate Thoreau as a defender of resistance, hear his words on the subject: "The attitude of resistance is one of weakness, inasmuch as it only faces an enemy; it has its back to all that is truly attractive. You shall have your affairs, I will have mine."[100] And to those who would praise his morality, he replies: "The best thought is not only without somberness, but even without morality. . . . The moral aspect of nature is a jaundice reflected from man. . . . There is no name for this life unless it be the very vitality of *vita*."[101]

Finally, those who see him as a reformer should reread "Resistance to Civil Government," in which he writes: "It is for no particular item in the tax-bill that I refuse to pay it. I simply wish to refuse allegiance to the state, to withdraw and stand aloof from it effectually. . . . In fact, I quietly declare war with the State, after my fashion, though I will still make what use and get what advantage of her I can, as is usual in such cases."[102]

Thoreau "quietly declare[s] war" after his own fashion, which is to say, he rids himself of concern. He wants to withdraw from the state, to "stand aloof from it," not to change it through voluntary negation. The most important part of the passage, however, is the last, in which Thoreau unapologetically announces that he will "make what use and get what advantage of [the state] as I can, as is usual in such cases." Although abstaining from participation, he insists on his right to the benefits of a democratic society. This underrated Thoreauvian construct, which demolishes the concept of a social contract, propounds the radical notion that the state exists for the individual, not vice versa. In this sense, Thoreau weathers the political storms of the early and mid-nineteenth century differently from many of his colleagues and fellow travelers, for whom social and economic forces figure decidedly in their moral and political theories. For his part, for better or worse, Thoreau simply strives to mind his own business.

6

The Fullness of Life

We locate Thoreau's political philosophy amidst the turn toward a cosmopolitan vision, a transformation made possible through increasingly savvy news and communications revolutions. Thoreau's thought stands out as a (last?) defense of the small, local, primitive life within the nature provided for the independent and self-seeking. Perhaps Thoreau is the quintessential American, appropriating the histories that suit him and abandoning the rest, stubbornly holding on to the individualism that, while characterizing his age, is also outstripped by forces beyond its control. My argument here is that Thoreau's privatism is the result of a hard-won victory for philosophy over anxiety, contentedness, and the vicissitudes of partiality. Thoreau engages with himself in a serious and repetitive way in order to put to rest the hauntings of an unreflective existence—one ripe with conformism and everyday democratic participations. Put simply, Thoreau offers a defense of the provincial and the small, and his privatism expresses that preference through its neglect of large and abstract problems in favor of the basic problems of individual life and the problems that invade that very small space.

Thoreau's final manuscript, *Wild Fruits*, pays homage to the small at nearly every turn. "How can we expect to understand Nature unless we accept like children these her smallest gifts . . . I love to get my basket full, however small and comparatively worthless the nut."[1] Turning our attention to the local lends Thoreau the deep sensory attention necessary to come to an appreciation of life for its own vitality. Thoreau's attention to the minute solves the (often fictitious) problems of modern life: "Who could believe in prophecies of Daniel or of Miller that the world would end this summer, while one milkweed with faith matured its seeds?"[2] Attending to that which surrounds him, Thoreau lends to readers of all times the opportunity of simplification, realized through intensified study of one's immediate environs and their vicissitudes. There is wonder in the small, not only for its assumption of the large but for its smallness, its stillness, its basic constitution: "If I could, I would worship the parings of my nails."[3]

Thoreau's *Wild Fruits* comes to a fever pitch as he defends the sanctity of individual labor in an extraordinary passage:

> If you would really take a position outside the street and daily life of men, you must have deliberately planned your course, you must have business which is not your neighbors' business, which they cannot understand. For only absorbing employment prevails, succeeds, takes up space, occupies territory, determines the future of individuals and states, drives Kansas out of your head, and actually and permanently occupies the only desirable and free Kansas against all border ruffians. The attitude of resistance is one of weakness, inasmuch as it only faces an enemy; it has its back to all that is truly attractive. You will have your affairs, I will have mine. You will spend this afternoon in setting up your neighbor's stove, and be paid for it; I will spend it in gathering the few berries of the *Vaccinium oxycoccus* which Nature provides here . . . and be paid for it also, after another fashion.[4]

There is perhaps no better description of Thoreau's engagements and their justifications than this passage. Thoreau argues that authentic selfhood requires a break from one's neighbors, that one's own labor and life must become puzzling to others. One has to find a work that removes ancillary concerns, facilitating that self's own growth by persistent attention. Thoreau finds himself moving away from the "resistance" he is famous for, supplying instead the directive that one pursue one's own path without attention paid to its social configurations or evaluations. Thoreau's *Wild Fruits* chronicles dozens of small excursions, the "cheap and private expeditions that substantiate our existence and batten our lives."[5] Our goal should be to drive Kansas out of our heads, a goal accomplished solely through robust individuality.

I have argued throughout this work that Thoreau's comprehensive philosophy serves his development of a privatist political theory. Entrenched in wonder, Thoreau's personal studies, walks, occupations, and preoccupations intensify the inward relationship he carries with his radically individualist ideals. Thoreau's lifelong interest in his surrounding space transfigures the concept of an intellectual life from its cosmopolitan pedestal to a provincial ideal that is startling in its comprehensiveness. Thoreau engages Concord throughout his life—indeed, upon leaving for one of few extended stays outside of Concord, Thoreau laments in a letter to Richard Fuller, "I expect to leave Concord, which is my Rome, and its people, who are my Romans"— in a way that the town and country seep into his very thought.[6] Thoreau's inward relationship strains to place itself beyond Concord's boundaries, and we get the sense that the town's horizon appears to be Thoreau's horizon as well. But this is not meant to criticize Thoreau, whose provincialism is one of the many points of interest for those who seek an honest and original voice of nineteenth-century America.

Thoreau's critique of politics is not the center of his thought, but it does occupy privileged space, primarily because politics appears to be the target of Thoreau's most biting criticism. "Politics is, as it were, the gizzard of society, full of grit and gravel, and the two political parties are its two opposite halves, which grind on each other. Not only individuals but states have thus a confirmed dyspepsia, which expresses itself, you can imagine by what sort of eloquence. Our life is not altogether a forgetting, but also, alas, to a great extent a remembering, of that which perchance we should never have been conscious of—the consciousness of what should not be permitted to disturb a man's waking hours."[7]

The primary source of Thoreau's critique of politics is an economy of energy that needs to vitalize itself, to find outlets that enhance the intimate feeling of life. Thoreau never neglects the necessity of government's function, nor does he displace politics altogether. Thoreau merely argues that politics is ideally a digestive process that does not "disturb a man's waking hours." Contrary to moral outrage or victimhood, this is a curious and brave assertion of disinterest out of vitalist concerns—this is why, of course, Thoreau uses the term *waking*, playing on his long-held interest in theorizing wakefulness as vitality. Thoreau refers to politics as a digestive process throughout his thought, consistently returning to the metaphor to put politics in its proper place. We learn from the defense of political indifference that the distance between our lives and political matters accounts for the detachment, that it is not only a detachment from politics but a replacement for politics. Thoreau's privatism is thus shaped by his having other lives to live, other affairs to attend to, than by the political life that finds itself expressed in newspapers and through gossip in the town square.

Thoreau's case for privatism hinges on an understanding that political life fosters a self-interpretation as a member of a group. This group identification, in its mission to hold the self sacred, bases its understanding of freedom, autonomy, and justice on commonly held assumptions and rights granted through a collective process. The subsequent dedication to the state, for Thoreau, requires the replacement of "the individual" with "individuals" as frame of reference for rights and responsibilities: "Nations! What are nations? Tartars! And Huns! And Chinamen! Like insects they swarm. The historian survives in vain to make them memorable. It is for want of a man that there are so many men. It is individuals that populate the world."[8] What appears as a strict liberal understanding of political identity yields something more radical in Thoreau. He is absolving himself not of national identification, but of any historical identification that transposes the individual's corporeal, local life into something else. Thoreau views himself as a Concordian and holds up that personality because it is not obstructive—it makes no demands upon him. This is the source of Thoreau's affirmation of provincial identity, made manifest in its refusal to guarantee a certain quality to personal identity through manufactured histories and spurious individual affiliations.

The loss of identity is not the sole problem in this case. Thoreau views the expense of life involved in maintaining historically grounded political institutions as a waste of energy:

> How much of the life of certain men *goes* to sustain, to make respected, the institutions of society. They are the ones who pay the heaviest tax. . . . Certain men are always to be found—especially the children of our present institutions—who are born with an instinct to perceive them. They are, in effect, supported by a fund which society possesses for that end, or they receive a pension and their life *seems* to be a sinecure—but it is not. . . . What an array of gentlemen whose sole employment—and it is no sinecure—is to support their dignity, and with it the dignity of so many indispensable institutions.[9]

Thoreau does not lampoon the dignified public service of individuals whose livelihood is bound up in preserving institutions. He refers to them as paying the "heaviest tax," that is, the tax of their vitality and the energy that encapsulates their lives. Thoreau twice refers to this work *not* being a sinecure, meaning that there are steep prices to pay, although the benefits appear to outweigh the costs. One can gain from a cursory reading of *Walden* that Thoreau is a thinker perpetually concerned with cost; existential costs, however, are the ones to which Thoreau devotes most of his attention. A supposed sinecure of dignified individuals who make their livelihood through the institutions that give them their name and stature expend terrible costs upon themselves in maintaining these institutions. The cost, in this case, is freedom, simplification, vitality, care.

The costs of political life are not limited to those who work on behalf of the state. Thoreau harbors a belief in a necessary chasm between any individuals, a distance that is unconquerable but, perhaps, does not feel as far as it truly is. Striving to live within even a polite, amenable society provides pitfalls; as an alternative Thoreau crafts an intricate inner world that submits to the outside only when the integrity of the self prompts engagement. "It is worth the while to live respectably unto ourselves. We can possibly *get along* with a neighbor, even with a bedfellow, whom we respect but very little; but as soon as it comes to this, that we do not respect ourselves, then we do not get along at all, no matter how much money we are paid for halting . . . I believe that it is in my power to elevate myself this very hour above the common level of my life."[10]

The life of self-respect is more difficult to achieve than the life of respectability. In this sense, Thoreau harks back to the Stoics with whom he shares the concern over cultivating ownness. Becoming one's own, living a life that one can respect, requires constant vigilance, careful attention to one's own commitments, and a sense of immanent vitality of life that outstrips moral and political engagements and tendencies. Thoreau's privatism is a means toward this ultimate end of a joyful life lived according to its own merits, within its own temporal and spatial boundaries. Thoreau connects the internal contradictions that lead to crippling self-doubt with the external contradictions that seem necessary for polite social life.

Our relations to others should end in relations back to ourselves. If we live with integrity, our inward table of virtues should govern our actions such that encounters with others should strengthen us; as a result, Thoreau finds that we can limit the number of relations we have with others if we increase the intensity by applying a privatist's strategy to the relationships themselves. In an early letter to Blake, Thoreau argues that "it is nothing (for us) permanently inherent in another, but his attitude or relation to what we prize, that we admire."[11] Even our best relationships—and one has to think here Thoreau is referring to his relationship with Emerson—reflect only what we desire from life, our own "prize." Every personal relationship engages the possibility of introspection; indeed, every love of another human being offers insight into what one desires himself to be. This useful device, however, also has its shortcomings. One can begin to identify himself with the other (who has the prize he so desires), thereby lessening his own commitment to himself in favor of a transitive sort of fulfillment. For Thoreau, this possibility is what makes average social and political life so very difficult to manage—we are always on the edge, teetering toward losing identity to identification.

Social and political life would not be a harrowing project if the existential offering were more palatable. Thoreau finds himself from time to time taking stock of his social value, a value he generally calibrates through his labor. Feeling the sting of an unsuccessful *A Week on the Concord and Merrimack Rivers,* and still needing to pay for the unsold copies of the book, Thoreau remarks to Blake, "I have earned just a dollar a day for seventy-six days past."[12] Making his living through surveying, Thoreau feels himself devaluated by the public evaluation of his labor through wages. We can read Thoreau in this case as someone deeply hurt by the social rejection of his genius, a person feeling the pain amidst the extraordinary success of his closest friend (who, it should be noted, did not like the book either). Perhaps Thoreau is striking back—a defiant act from a man somewhat prone to defiance. "The whole enterprise of this nation, which is not an upward, but a westward one, toward Oregon, California, Japan, etc., is totally devoid of interest to me, whether performed on foot, or by a Pacific Railroad. It is not illustrated by a thought; it is not warmed by a sentiment; there is nothing in it which one should lay down his life for, nor even his gloves—hardly which one should take up a newspaper for."[13] The stakes of Thoreau's privatism require that one ask the question of the worthiness of his critique. Thoreau maintains a solid line of critique against the burgeoning mass culture of the newspaper throughout his life and always critiques the paper on the same terms—that is, that the news takes energy away from one's commitment to one's own life projects. In this case Thoreau argues that he has no interest in the larger movement of the time—the movement westward—by digging into himself and demanding that a worthwhile social cause be "illustrated by a thought." There is more than mere priggishness here, to be certain. Thoreau uses colorful language to describe a basic case of alienation from social values, and that alienation is magnified by his own internally developed table of values.

Thoreau's concern for "growth" animates his self-development. In another letter to Blake, Thoreau notes, "True, a man cannot lift himself by his own waistbands, because he cannot get out of himself; but he can expand himself (which is better, there being no up nor down in nature), and so split his waistbands, being already within himself."[14]

Thoreau's sense of self, the self that grounds the privatist political philosophy, is guided by the belief that self-overcoming in the service of life can and does continue to affirm life, amidst the processes of decay, and that selves are inwardly constituted such that self-valuation and finite self-perfections are possible. Thoreau's political philosophy thus reveals its affirmative side. Thoreau makes the case for privatism by allowing the self to engage itself meaningfully, through projects that enhance it and a valuative measure that guides experience according to its ability to enhance vitality. Taking radical separation as a virtue, Thoreau's privatism works on and cultivates a self that is a challenge to the conceptions of the individual as grounded by historical processes or created by collective values.

The Fullness of Life

No more satisfying deathbed utterance can be imagined for Thoreau than his reply to a question put gently to him by Parker Pillsbury a few days before his death. Pillsbury was an old abolitionist warhorse, a former minister who left his church over slavery, a man of principle and proven courage, an old family friend who could not resist the urge to peer into the future. "You seem so near the brink of the dark river," Pillsbury said, "that I almost wonder how the opposite shore may appear to you." Thoreau's answer provides a neat summary of his life: "One world at a time."[15] Prior to Thoreau's death, Harrison Blake asked him how he felt about the future, to which Thoreau replied that it was "just as uninteresting as ever."[16] Thoreau's emphasis on presence even in the face of death signifies his dedication to his own virtues, the necessity of personal experience, and his steadfast resistance to placing more emphasis on the life of the self than that self can justify. Thoreau's attitude toward his own death magnifies his experience of presence by embracing finitude; even in the face of its looming horizon, Thoreau maintains an interest only in the world he currently inhabits—the world of personal experience. Thoreau's profound disinterest toward the sentimentalities of personal finitude grasps privatism's realism.

The self's uses of the infinite are designed to provide comfort when facing existential problems. Thoreau's response, coincident with the principles of privatism, is to dismiss the illusory benefits of infinitude: "Some of his more orthodox friends and relatives tried to prepare him for death, but with little satisfaction to themselves. When an old friend of the family asked 'how he stood affected toward Christ,' he replied that 'a snow-storm was more to him than Christ.' When his Aunt Louisa asked him if he had made his peace with God, he answered, 'I did not know we had ever quarreled, Aunt.'"[17]

The examples taken from Thoreau's major contemporary biographies establish the value of private experience as a guiding principle of his life. Thoreau's death resonates with the principles of identity laid out in the affirmative portion of his philosophy. Thoreau's indifference toward the resolutions of finitude advances beyond the stability and security of the individual self to the virtue of simplification with respect to its own life. Thoreauvian simplification, in which the self valuates its own experiences according to its immanent principles, denies the influence of those compensations that do not originate in the self's own desires, experiences, or imagination. When Thoreau argues that "a snow-storm was more to him than Christ," he establishes that this collective valuation of life is a compensation for the failure of finitude.

Thoreau's privatism insists on the validity of living "one world at a time." The long project of self-mastery and self-understanding is always an unfinished product, since our moods, circumstances, and life cycles present to us different challenges and opportunities as we grow older. What remains constant for Thoreau is the value of inner life constituted through persistent reflection. From his earliest journal entries in 1840, Thoreau stands on his privatist ground: "I am freer than any planet; no complaint reaches round the world. I can move away from public opinion, from government, from religion, from education, from society."[18] The affirmation of private life is Thoreau's benchmark achievement, the ground of his affirmative philosophy and the source of his critique of the changing shape of individuality in the nineteenth century. And this celebration of self-isolation is echoed in his late *Journal* entries as well: "You may know what a thing costs or is worth to you; you can never know what it costs or is worth to me. All the community may scream because one man is born who will not do as it does, who will not conform because conformity to him is death—he is so constituted. They know nothing about his case; they are fools when they presume to advise him. The man of genius knows what he is aiming at; nobody else knows. And he alone knows when something comes between him and his object."[19]

Thoreau's call for the value of private life is one of philosophical courage and joyful exuberance. Creating a valuative gulf between the self and the
other unfortunately damages Thoreau's critical reception. Thoreau's politics is
an undeniably distant, deliberating, and calculating individualism; this critique, however, is necessary for Thoreau to establish the value of self-directed
exuberance, the finite perfections of private life obscured by satellite attachments. Thoreau's genius demonstrates the stakes in the cultivation of the self,
the value of simplifying one's life, attaching meaning to the immanent projects of personal existence, rekindling the existential concept of freedom, and
loosing the bonds of collective life. Thoreau's privatism expands individual
life by connecting it to its most necessary components, yearning toward a
fullness of life bathed in the joy of the private moment.

Acknowledgments

I would like first to recognize the existential support of my wife, Christina, whose constant companionship has given me the vitality to live well. Because of her, I do not put more emphasis on the completion of an academic text than it deserves. Christina has given me a life with principle—and has ventured with me on a journey to raise our two incomparable children, Ezra and Annika. I'm grateful to her for her vision, her clear mind, and her powerful intellect. I dedicate this book to her in earnest.

I'm grateful to my son, Ezra, whose love of nature provides me with endless joy. I hope he always remains the boy who will examine anything that moves with curiosity and respect. I'm grateful to my daughter, Annika, the most interesting person I know. She truly contains multitudes, in the words of Whitman, and she leaves me perpetually in awe.

My parents, Pat and Paula McKenzie, encouraged me through every avenue of my life. Their constant support and sacrifice cannot be appreciated enough.

The book is also dedicated to my mentor, Frederic Homer, whose exacting mind encouraged me to look for questions in unexpected places and to concentrate on the application of philosophy to the practice of life. My intellect came alive that fall semester in 1998 when he introduced me to political theory via William James.

The book was made possible by the guidance of Michael Weinstein, whose courses and guidance refined my mind in the best possible way. Michael remains a source of intellectual and existential inspiration to me. I'll always be happy to have known him so well intellectually.

Many others provided intellectual support to the work. I'd like to thank Shannon Mariotti, who improved the text at every turn and provides an example of a truly humane and exacting scholar. Christopher Dustin helped me to refine my argument by continually finding opportunities for nuance and complexity. The book is much better for it. I've also received help from Daniel W. Smith, Leigh Raymond, Sam McCormick, Kevin Anderson, and Lynn Rhoads.

Steve Wrinn and Allison Webster at the University Press of Kentucky are superb editors. I'm not certain how to put into words my appreciation for their kindness, patience, professionalism, and commitment.

Notes

Introduction

1. Henry D. Thoreau, *The Writings of Henry D. Thoreau: Journal (1837-1854)*, ed. Elizabeth Hall Witherell et al., 8 vols. (Princeton: Princeton University Press, 1981–2009), 3:104; hereinafter, Thoreau, *Journal* (Princeton).

2. As my argument will clarify below, my decision to use a more or less pedestrian conception of politics is not meant to critique readings of Thoreau that advance a more contemporary view of the political. For alternative views of Thoreau's use of the political, see Jane Bennett, *Thoreau's Nature: Ethics, Politics, and the Wild* (New York: Sage, 1994), and Shannon Mariotti, *Thoreau's Democratic Withdrawal: Alienation, Participation, Modernity* (Madison: University of Wisconsin Press, 2010).

3. Plato, *Apology*, trans. Harold North Fowler, Loeb Classical Library (Cambridge: Harvard University Press, 1914), 117.

4. This is the argument of Ellen Meiksins Wood and Neal Wood, "Socrates and Democracy: A Reply to Gregory Vlastos," *Political Theory* 14, no. 1 (1986): 73–74.

5. Plato, *Apology*, 115.

6. Ibid.

7. Dana Villa, *Socratic Citizenship* (Princeton: Princeton University Press, 2001), xii.

8. Ibid., 5.

9. Ibid., 9.

10. Ibid., 24.

11. Ibid., 32.

12. Ibid., 54.

13. Ibid., 55.

14. George Kateb, "Socratic Integrity," in *Patriotism and Other Mistakes* (New Haven: Yale University Press, 2006), 216.

15. Ibid.

16. Ibid., 241.

17. Stanley Cavell, *In Quest of the Ordinary: Lines of Skepticism and Romanticism* (Chicago: University of Chicago Press, 1988), 10.

18. Henry D. Thoreau, *The Correspondence of Henry David Thoreau*, ed. Carl Bode and Walter Harding (New York: New York University Press, 1958), 247.

19. Ibid.

20. See, for instance: George Kateb, *The Inner Ocean: Individualism and Democratic Culture* (Ithaca: Cornell University Press, 1992); Bob Pepperman Taylor, *America's Bachelor Uncle* (Lawrence: University Press of Kansas, 1996); Jack Turner, ed., *A Political Companion to Henry David Thoreau* (Lexington: University Press of Kentucky, 2009).

21. Michel Foucault, *The Hermeneutics of the Subject,* trans. Graham Burchell (New York: Palgrave Macmillan, 2005), 16.

22. See Foucault's "Self Writing," in *Ethics, Subjectivity and Truth,* ed. Paul Rabinow (New York: Free Press, 1998), 207–22.

23. Ibid., 209.

24. Thoreau, *Journal* (Princeton), 2:136.

25. Ibid.

26. Robert Richardson, *Henry Thoreau: A Life of the Mind* (Berkeley: University of California Press, 1986), 273.

27. Thoreau, *Journal* (Princeton), 4:259.

28. Thoreau was a reader of the Stoics, having read (or read of) Zeno and Epictetus while in college. See Richardson, *Henry Thoreau,* 70.

29. A. A. Long, *Epictetus: A Stoic and Socratic Guide to Life* (New York: Oxford University Press, 2002), 58.

30. Richardson, *Henry Thoreau,* 104–15.

31. Thoreau, *Journal* (Princeton), 4:259.

32. Ibid.

33. Ibid., 4:260.

34. Ibid.

35. Ibid.

36. Ibid.

37. Ibid., 4:270.

38. Epictetus, *Discourses,* trans. W. A. Oldfather, Loeb Classical Library (Cambridge, MA: Harvard University Press, 1998), 1:123; hereinafter, Epictetus, *Discourses* (Loeb).

39. Thoreau, *Journal* (Princeton), 1:297.

40. Ibid., 4:141.

41. Bennett, *Thoreau's Nature,* xx.

42. Ibid.

43. Ibid., 8.

44. Ibid., 42.

45. Ibid., 17.

46. Ibid., xxii.

47. Examples of the moralist interpretation of Thoreau's thought abound. Mid-

century critics such as Hannah Arendt and Vincent Buranelli harangue Thoreau for his moral stiffness, while George Kateb restores the value of morality behind the recuperative lens of "democratic individuality." Leigh Kathryn Jenco's article "Thoreau's Critique of Democracy" (in Turner, ed., *A Political Companion to Henry David Thoreau*) articulates a moral critique of democratic institutions, without defining what "moral" or its variants mean in the text.

48. Bennett, *Thoreau's Nature*, 76fn20.

49. Brian Walker, "Thoreau on Democratic Cultivation," *Political Theory* 29 (April 2001): 155.

50. Brian Walker, "Thoreau's Alternative Economics: Work, Liberty, and Democratic Cultivation," *American Political Science Review* 92, no. 4 (1998): 849.

51. Ibid., 850.

52. Ibid., 851.

53. Walker, "Thoreau on Democratic Cultivation," 159.

54. Mariotti makes a strong case for reading Thoreau as a theorist of alienation. Incidentally, she argues that *alienation* is not a term Thoreau uses to "describe the loss of self and dilution of experience" (12). Thoreau approaches this use in *Walden:* "It is very evident what mean and sneaking lives many of you live, for my sight has been whetted by experience; always on the limits, trying to get into business and get out of debt, a very ancient slough, called by the Latins *aes alienum*, another's brass." Henry D. Thoreau, *Walden* (New Haven: Yale University Press, 2006), 5; hereinafter cited as *Walden* (Yale).

55. Ibid., xiii.

56. Ibid., xvii.

57. Ibid., 15.

58. Ibid., 93.

59. Ibid., 121.

60. In particular, Mariotti politicizes Thoreau's walks in the same spirit as Bennett adds an ethos to the suspension of temporal and spatial location in enchanting experiences in *The Enchantment of Modern Life* (Princeton: Princeton University Press, 2001). Bennett's employment of enchanting experiences recalls Thoreau's reveries of silence in "Sounds" and "Solitude." In each case, the onus is on the author's ability to sufficiently place these activities as forms of political critique or ethical reformation.

61. Mariotti notes: "Thoreau uses the practice of huckleberrying to model his own particular version of democratic politics. Thoreau contrasts huckleberrying with the jail, the judicial system, and politics as it is commonly understood to highlight the unique nature of his own version of politics and of democratic political practices. He leaves the jail to practice another kind of politics, in the huckleberry fields, to enact a new kind of politics that he seems to think will be more conducive

to creating the kind of citizens who can relate to the state as individuals and neighbors, not as machines" (*Thoreau's Democratic Withdrawal*, 129). What is lacking in this analysis is any discussion of "another kind of politics" or Thoreau's "particular version of democratic politics." Thoreau retreats in "Walking," and elsewhere, and reconstitutes political terms through natural examples (the "stately pines," the freedom of the fox, et cetera) but does not use these conceptions in the village itself. Thoreau does not seem to source nature for its democratic potential but uses the distancing of wildness to improve his own understanding of these concepts for himself. See Johannes Voelz, "Alienation Revisited," *American Literary History* 24 (2012): 618–30.

62. Sharon Cameron, *Writing Nature: Henry Thoreau's* Journal (Chicago: University of Chicago Press, 1989 [1985]), 4.

63. Ibid., 11.

64. H. Daniel Peck, *Thoreau's Morning Work: Memory and Perception in* A Week on the Concord and Merrimack Rivers, *the "Journal," and* Walden (New Haven: Yale University Press, 1990), 43

65. Ibid., 15.

66. Ibid.

67. Thoreau, *Walden* (Yale), 119.

68. Cameron, *Writing Nature*, 24.

69. Ibid.

70. Ibid., 31.

71. Ibid., 60.

72. Ibid., 75.

73. Ibid., 49.

74. Ibid., 16.

75. Peck, *Thoreau's Morning Work*, 43.

76. Ibid., 47.

77. Ibid., 68.

78. Ibid., 71.

79. Interestingly, Cameron comes to the opposite conclusion: "Quotation from Thoreau's *Journal* is further rendered suspect by Thoreau's aggressive attempt to disorganize the categories and conventions by which we customarily conceive of natural phenomena" (Cameron, *Writing Nature*, 20).

80. Peck, *Thoreau's Morning Work*, 107.

81. Ibid.

82. Ibid., 77.

83. Ibid., 88.

84. Ibid., 100.

85. Thoreau, *Walden* (Yale), 119.

86. Quoted in Cameron, *Writing Nature*, 19. Originally appeared in Thoreau, *Journal* (Princeton), 4:53–54.

87. Cameron, *Writing Nature*, 19.

88. Thoreau, *Journal* (Princeton), 4:53.

89. Ibid., 4:52.

90. Ibid., 4:53.

91. Ibid., 4:54.

92. Ibid., 4:55.

93. Ibid., 4:54.

94. Peck, *Thoreau's Morning Work*, 100.

95. Henry D. Thoreau, *The Journal of Henry David Thoreau*, ed. Bradford Torrey and Francis Allen, 14 vols. (Boston: Houghton Mifflin, 1906), 9:32; hereinafter, Thoreau, *Journal* (Houghton Mifflin).

96. Ibid.

97. When I write "philosophical exercise," I refer to Foucault's rethinking of Hellenistic thought in *The Hermeneutics of the Subject*. I make more of the connection between Thoreau and *askesis* in chapter 2 of the text.

98. Thoreau, *Journal* (Houghton Mifflin), 9:33.

99. Of course, I pull the notion of inwardness as a citadel from Pierre Hadot, *The Inner Citadel: The Meditations of Marcus Aurelius* (Cambridge: Harvard University Press, 1998).

100. Nancy Rosenblum, *Another Liberalism: Romanticism and the Reconstruction of Liberal Thought* (Cambridge: Harvard University Press, 1987), 85.

101. Ibid., 86.

102. Ibid.

103. Ibid., 89.

104. Ibid., 99–100.

105. Cameron, *Writing Nature*, 3.

1. Reflective Simplification

1. This is largely the view of Pierre Hadot. See *Philosophy as a Way of Life*, trans. Michael Chase (Oxford: Blackwell, 1995), and *What Is Ancient Philosophy?* trans. Michael Chase (Cambridge: Harvard University Press, 2002).

2. Thoreau, *Journal* (Princeton), 1:469.

3. Richardson, in *Henry Thoreau*, makes the persuasive case that Thoreau was one of the foremost readers of ancient thought in America at the time of his life.

4. Pierre Hadot, "There Are Nowadays Professors of Philosophy, but Not Philosophers," trans. J. Aaron Simmons and Mason Marshall, *Journal of Speculative Philosophy* 19, no. 3 (2005): 233.

5. Hadot, *Inner Citadel*, 10.

6. Hadot, *Philosophy as a Way of Life*, 150.

7. Thoreau, *Journal* (Princeton), 1:121.

8. Ibid.

9. Foucault, "Self Writing," 208.

10. Thoreau, *Journal* (Princeton) 1:34.

11. Ibid., 1:73.

12. Michel Foucault, *The Hermeneutics of the Subject: Lectures at the Collège de France, 1981–1982,* trans. Graham Burchell (New York: Palgrave Macmillan, 2005), 359.

13. Foucault, "Self Writing," 208.

14. Thoreau, *Journal* (Princeton), 1:295.

15. Ibid., 1:11.

16. Ibid., 4:309–10.

17. Foucault, *Hermeneutics of the Subject*, 37.

18. Marcus Aurelius, *Meditations,* ed. and trans. C. R. Haines, Loeb Classical Library (Cambridge: Harvard University Press, 1930), 193.

19. Henry D. Thoreau, *The Writings of Henry D. Thoreau: Reform Papers,* ed. Wendell Glick (Princeton: Princeton University Press, 1973), 171; hereinafter, Thoreau, *Reform Papers.*

20. Marcus Aurelius, *Meditations,* 5.

21. Ibid., 325.

22. Ibid., 293.

23. Ibid., 223.

24. Thoreau, *Reform Papers,* 3.

25. Marcus Aurelius, *Meditations,* 211.

26. Ibid., 161.

27. Ibid., 145.

28. Ibid., 331.

29. Hadot, *Inner Citadel,* 239.

30. Foucault, *Hermeneutics of the Subject*, 295.

31. Ibid., 297.

32. Ibid., 298.

33. Ibid., 304.

34. Stanley Cavell, *The Senses of Walden* (Chicago: Chicago University Press, 1992), 5.

35. Ibid., 13.

36. Ibid.

37. Ibid., 17.

38. Ibid., 20.

39. Ibid., 22.

40. Ibid., 25.

41. Ibid., 32.

42. Ibid., 119.

43. Edward McGushin, *Foucault's Askesis: An Introduction to the Philosophical Life* (Chicago: Northwestern University Press, 2007), 10.

44. Ibid.

45. Thoreau, *Walden* (Yale), 14.

46. Thoreau, *Journal* (Princeton), 3:97.

47. Ibid., 1:34.

48. Ibid., 2:177.

49. Ibid., 2:324.

50. Ibid.

51. Ibid.

52. Sherman Paul, *The Shores of America: Thoreau's Inward Exploration* (Champaign: University of Illinois Press, 1958 [1972]), 175.

53. Thoreau, *Journal* (Princeton), 1:361.

54. Ibid., 1:343.

55. Ibid., 7:503.

56. Ibid.

57. Henry D. Thoreau, *Familiar Letters of Henry David Thoreau* (Boston: Houghton Mifflin, 1906), 199.

58. Ibid., 211.

59. Ibid., 201.

60. Ibid., 202.

61. Thoreau, *Walden* (Yale), 48.

62. Daniel Walker Howe, *What Hath God Wrought: The Transformation of America, 1815–1848* (New York: Oxford University Press, 2007), 623.

63. Thoreau, *Journal* (Princeton) 2:355.

64. Peck, *Thoreau's Morning Work*, 71.

65. Ibid., 72.

66. Thoreau, *Journal* (Princeton), 3:384.

67. Ibid., 4:440.

68. Ibid., 8:67.

69. A. A. Long, *Epictetus: A Stoic and Socratic Guide to Life* (New York: Oxford University Press, 2002), 61.

70. Thoreau, *Walden* (Princeton), 2–3.

71. Ibid., 3.

72. Ibid., 6.

73. Ibid., 2.

74. Brian Walker (1998, 2001) argues convincingly that Thoreau aims to model himself after advice-giving manuals popular in the nineteenth century, while also keeping an eye on the role of advice giving in Stoic philosophy.

75. Epictetus, *Discourses* (Loeb), 3:171–73.
76. Thoreau, *Walden* (Yale), 24.
77. Ibid.
78. Ibid., 144.
79. Ibid., 181.
80. Ibid., 169.
81. Ibid., 168.
82. Ibid., 354.
83. Ibid.
84. Ibid., 7.
85. Ibid., 22.
86. Ibid., 24.
87. Ibid., 157.
88. Ibid., 181.
89. Ibid., 357.
90. Ibid., 16.
91. Ibid., 17.
92. Ibid., 298.
93. Ibid., 165.
94. Ibid., 120.
95. Ibid., 139.
96. Ibid., 158.
97. Ibid., 159.
98. Ibid., 160.
99. Ibid., 162.
100. Ibid., 222.
101. Ibid., 224.
102. Ibid., 225.

2. Poverty Eternal

1. Thoreau, *Journal* (Princeton), 1:255. I found this quotation in Alfred I. Tauber, *Henry David Thoreau and the Moral Agency of Knowing* (Berkeley: University of California Press, 2001), 38.

2. Thoreau, *Journal* (Princeton), 3:305–6.

3. I do not employ *vitalist* in my discussion of Thoreau in the same way the term is used by Jane Bennett, particularly in her *Vibrant Matter*. I am more interested in the way in which Thoreau uses the term and its variations to refer to an evaluative criterion of life from the standpoint of the feeling of life itself.

4. Thoreau, *Journal* (Princeton), 156.

5. Thomas M. Allen, *A Republic in Time: Temporality and Social Imagination*

in Nineteenth-Century America (Chapel Hill: University of North Carolina Press, 2008), 142.

6. Thoreau, *Journal* (Princeton), 2:378.

7. Henry D. Thoreau, *The Writings of Henry D. Thoreau: Excursions*, ed. Joseph J. Moldenhauer (Princeton: Princeton University Press, 2007), 223; hereinafter, Thoreau, *Excursions*.

8. Richardson, *Henry Thoreau*, 380–81.

9. Thoreau, *Journal* (Princeton), 4:6.

10. Ibid., 4:390.

11. Ibid., 5:412.

12. Ibid.

13. Ibid.

14. Ibid., 5:215.

15. Ibid., 5:120.

16. Ibid.

17. Ibid., 2:5.

18. Cavell, *Senses of Walden*, 10.

19. Thoreau, *Walden* (Yale), 362.

20. Sarah Allan, *The Way of Water and Sprouts of Virtue* (Albany: SUNY Press, 1997), 10–11.

21. Thoreau, *Walden* (Yale), 106.

22. Marcus Aurelius, *Meditations*, 39.

23. Ibid., 67.

24. Tauber, *Henry David Thoreau*, 35.

25. Ibid.

26. Ibid.

27. Ibid., 40.

28. Ibid.

29. Thoreau, *Walden* (Yale), 105.

30. Ibid.

31. Ibid.

32. Ibid., 229.

33. Ibid., 191–92.

34. Ibid., 358.

35. Ibid., 361.

36. Ibid., 321.

37. Ibid., 105.

38. Allan, *Way of Water and Sprouts of Virtue*, 83.

39. Thoreau, *Walden* (Yale), 358.

40. Ibid., 354.

41. Ibid., 355.

42. Ibid., 245.

43. Ibid.

44. Ibid., 224.

45. Ibid.

46. Ibid., 226.

47. Thoreau, *Journal* (Houghton Mifflin), 10:326.

48. Ibid., 10:146.

49. Ibid.

50. Ibid., 9:306.

51. Thoreau, *Walden* (Princeton), 5.

52. Ibid.

53. Ibid., 6.

54. Thoreau, *Journal* (Houghton Mifflin), 11:227–28.

55. Thoreau, *Walden* (Princeton), 7.

56. Ibid., 8.

57. Ibid., 10.

58. Ibid., 34.

59. Ibid.

60. Ibid., 81.

61. Ibid., 84.

62. Thoreau, *Walden* (Yale), 107. Later, Thoreau mentions that "to read well, that is, to read true books in a true spirit, is a noble exercise, and one that will task the reader more than any exercise which the customs of the day esteem" (108).

63. Ibid., 120.

64. Ibid.

65. Ibid., 121.

66. Thoreau, *Walden* (Yale), 119.

67. Ibid., 126.

68. Ibid., 139.

69. Thoreau, *Correspondence*, 247.

70. Thoreau, *Walden* (Yale), 356.

71. Ibid., 357.

72. Ibid., 242.

3. Life near the Bone

1. Michael T. Gilmore, *American Romanticism and the Marketplace* (Chicago: University of Chicago Press, 1985), 35–36.

2. Thoreau, *Familiar Letters*, 83. This particular letter is from Thoreau to his

mother and father shortly after his arrival in Staten Island, where he served as tutor to the sons of William Emerson.

3. Thoreau, *Walden* (Yale), 348–49.

4. Ibid., 349.

5. Ibid., 350.

6. Ibid., 348.

7. In a *Journal* entry from August 14, 1840, Thoreau writes, "I cannot attach much importance to historical epochs—or geographical boundaries—when I have my Orient and Occident in one revolution of my body" (Thoreau, *Journal* [Princeton], 1:172).

8. Martin Heidegger, "Why Do I Stay in the Provinces?" in *Heidegger: The Man and the Thinker*, ed. Thomas Sheehan (Chicago: Precedent, 1981), 27.

9. Ibid., 28.

10. Thoreau, *Walden* (Princeton), 318–19.

11. Heidegger, "Why Do I Stay in the Provinces?" 28.

12. Thoreau, *Walden* (Princeton), 223.

13. Ibid., 224.

14. Ibid., 225.

15. Heidegger, "Why Do I Stay in the Provinces?" 29.

16. Thoreau, *Journal* (Princeton), 1:151.

17. Ibid., 1:150.

18. Ibid., 1:158.

19. Ibid., 1:164.

20. Ibid., 1:166.

21. Thoreau, *Walden* (Yale), 17.

22. Thoreau, *Journal* (Princeton), 1:170.

23. Ibid., 1:178.

24. Ibid., 1:179.

25. Epictetus, *Discourses*, trans. Robert Dobbin (New York: Oxford University Press, 1998), 7; hereinafter, Epictetus, *Discourses* (Oxford).

26. This reading of Roman Stoicism is indebted to Pierre Hadot, whose *The Inner Citadel* and *What Is Ancient Philosophy?* remain the key texts in this school; Thoreau, *Walden* (Princeton), 31.

27. Richardson, *Henry Thoreau*, 150–52.

28. For an excellent analysis of Epictetus and Socratic invulnerability, see Christopher Gill, *The Structured Self in Hellenistic and Roman Thought* (New York: Oxford University Press, 2006), esp. 74–126.

29. Epictetus, *Discourses* (Loeb), 4:245.

30. Ibid., 4:251.

31. Thoreau, *Walden* (Yale), 89.

32. Epictetus, *Discourses* (Loeb), 4:267.

33. Thoreau, *Walden* (Yale), 87.

34. Carl J. Guarneri, *The Utopian Alternative: Fourierism in Nineteenth-Century America* (Ithaca: Cornell University Press, 1991), 43.

35. Ibid., 8–9.

36. Richard Francis, *Transcendental Utopias: Individual and Community at Brook Farm, Fruitlands, and Walden* (Ithaca: Cornell University Press, 1997), 42.

37. Ibid., 1–34.

38. This provides us with just one of the countless Socratic tendencies within transcendentalist thought, particularly its Thoreauvian vein. The question of parts and wholes not only defines Plato's *Meno* but could be said to be one of the hallmark concepts of Socratic philosophy altogether.

39. Ralph Waldo Emerson, *Essays and Lectures*, ed. Joel Porte (New York: Library of America, 1983), 54.

40. Guarneri, *Utopian Alternative*, 108.

41. Ibid., 49.

42. Nathaniel Hawthorne, *The Blithedale Romance*, ed. Seymour Gross and Rosalie Murphy (New York: W. W. Norton, 2010), 16.

43. Sterling Delano, *Brook Farm: The Dark Side of Utopia* (Cambridge: Harvard University Press, 2004), 120–22, 145.

44. Ibid., 165.

45. Ibid., 125.

46. Ibid., 208–9.

47. Ibid., 254–56.

48. Francis, *Transcendental Utopias*, 137.

49. Richard Francis, *Fruitlands* (New Haven: Yale University Press, 2010), 236–39.

50. Lane's defense of libertarianism is collected in a series of letters entitled *A Voluntary Political Government*.

51. Francis, *Fruitlands*, 81.

52. Ibid., 163.

53. Thoreau, *Walden* (Princeton), 40–41.

54. Ibid., 84.

55. Quoted in Richardson, *Henry Thoreau*, 101.

56. Walker, "Thoreau's Alternative Economics," 40.

57. Ibid., 55.

58. Rudiger Safranski, *Martin Heidegger: Between Good and Evil*, trans. Ewald Osers (Cambridge: Harvard University Press, 1998), 1.

59. Thoreau, *Walden* (Princeton), 14.

60. Walker, "Thoreau's Alternative Economics," 849.
61. Epictetus, *Discourses* (Loeb), 1:71.
62. Ibid., 1:105.
63. Ibid., 1:123.
64. Epictetus, *Discourses* (Loeb), 2:39.
65. Ibid., 2:57.
66. Ibid., 2:101.
67. Thoreau, *Walden* (Princeton), 15.
68. Epictetus, *Discourses* (Loeb), 1:225.
69. Ibid., 1:247.
70. Ibid., 1:321.
71. Thoreau, *Correspondence*, 247.
72. Epictetus, *Discourses* (Loeb), 1:409.
73. Thoreau, *Reform Papers*, 74.
74. Epictetus, *Discourses* (Loeb), 2:325.
75. Thoreau, *Correspondence*, 221.
76. Thoreau, *Reform Papers*, 90.
77. Ibid., 5.
78. Ibid., 6.
79. Ibid., 5.
80. Ibid., 6–7.
81. Ibid., 7.
82. Thoreau, *Walden* (Yale), 6.
83. Thoreau, *Reform Papers,* 18.
84. Ibid., 19.
85. Ibid., 9.
86. Ibid., 10–11.
87. Ibid., 9–10.
88. Ibid., 10.
89. Ibid., 71.
90. Ibid., 14.
91. Ibid., 74.
92. Ibid., 78.
93. Ibid., 75.
94. This is discussed at length in Laura Dassow Walls's *Seeing New Worlds: Henry David Thoreau and Nineteenth-Century Natural Science* (Madison: University of Wisconsin Press, 1995).
95. Thoreau, *Reform Papers*, 146.
96. Ibid., 210.
97. Ibid.

98. Melissa Lane makes a similar argument in her essay "Thoreau and Rousseau: Nature as Utopia," in *A Political Companion to Henry David Thoreau*, ed. Jack Turner (Lexington: University Press of Kentucky, 2009).

99. Thoreau, *Reform Papers*, 146.

100. Ibid., 148.

101. Ibid., 150.

102. Ibid.

103. Thoreau, *Walden* (Yale), 172.

104. Ibid., 176.

105. Thoreau, *Reform Papers*, 205.

106. Ibid., 129.

107. Ibid., 111.

108. Ibid.

109. Ibid., 321.

110. Ibid., 322.

111. David Robinson, "'Unchronicled Nations': Agrarian Purpose and Thoreau's Ecological Knowing," *Nineteenth-Century Literature* 48, no. 3 (1993): 326–40.

112. Thoreau, *Journal* (Princeton), 2:202.

113. Thoreau, *Walden* (Princeton), 52.

114. Ibid., 131.

115. Thoreau, *Journal* (Princeton), 2:200–201.

116. Thoreau, *Journal* (Princeton), 2:203.

117. Thoreau, *Walden* (Princeton), 328.

118. Ibid., 329.

4. Wildness

1. Thoreau, *Reform Papers*, 174.

2. That is, wildness incorporates Jane Bennett's characterization but does not stop there. Its primary purpose remains the disposition that prepares description, not the critical capacity of the self's social world. See Bennett, *Thoreau's Nature*, xxi.

3. Thoreau, *Journal* (Princeton), 4:34.

4. Sherman Paul, *For Love of the World* (Iowa City: University of Iowa Press, 1992), 7.

5. Bennett, *Thoreau's Nature*, 42.

6. Thoreau, *Reform Papers*, 93.

7. George Kateb, *Patriotism and Other Mistakes* (New Haven: Yale University Press, 2006), 247–48.

8. Ibid., 250.

9. Ibid., 257.

10. Ibid., 264.

11. Ibid., 266.

12. Ibid., 270.

13. Thoreau, *Journal* (Princeton), 4:258–59.

14. Ibid., 3:133.

15. Ibid., 5:10.

16. Ibid., 4:249.

17. Ibid., 8:139–40.

18. Ibid., 4:482.

19. Ibid., 5:411.

20. Mariotti, *Thoreau's Democratic Withdrawal*, 121.

21. Ibid.

22. Ibid., 122.

23. Ibid., 125.

24. Thoreau, *Reform Papers*, 86.

25. Thoreau, *Journal* (Princeton), 2:171–73.

26. Thoreau, *Excursions*, 4.

27. Ibid.

28. Ibid., 5.

29. Ibid., 22.

30. Ibid., 5.

31. Ibid., 22.

32. Alan Hodder, *Thoreau's Ecstatic Witness* (New Haven: Yale University Press, 2001), 21.

33. Thoreau, *Familiar Letters*, 255.

34. Thoreau, *Correspondence*, 15.

35. Ibid., 20.

36. That is to say, Thoreau's major concern, even in the early correspondence mentioned, is with rearticulating political terms for his own vital use. Thoreau does not reemploy them as critical responses to the state so much as he appropriates them from the state for himself. This is the difference between what I see as a privatist articulation of wildness and the critical or agonic vision of wildness established by Bennett and Mariotti.

37. Thoreau, *Correspondence*, 45.

38. Walt Whitman, *Poetry and Prose*, ed. Justin Kaplan (New York: Library of America, 1982), 87.

39. David Robinson, *Natural Life: Thoreau's Worldly Transcendentalism* (Ithaca: Cornell University Press, 2004), 150.

40. Thoreau, *Correspondence*, 68.

41. Thoreau, *Walden* (Yale), 158.

42. Ibid., 164.

43. Henry D. Thoreau, *The Writings of Henry D. Thoreau: The Maine Woods*, ed. Joseph J. Moldenhauer (Princeton: Princeton University Press, 1972), 206; hereinafter, Thoreau, *Maine Woods*.

44. One could examine Thoreau's disdain for Polis's desire to kill a moose alongside Thoreau's encounter with Louis Neptune in "Ktaadn," in which Neptune steadfastly inquires into only one topic: what Thoreau killed on the trip. Death is a signal of a refined, civilized style, no doubt reflected in Thoreau's critique of the American Indian's adoption of ultracivilized notions and mores.

45. Thoreau, *Maine Woods*, 197.

46. Ibid., 235.

47. Ibid., 185.

48. Ibid., 77–78.

49. Ibid., 78.

50. Ibid., 244.

51. Ibid., 193.

52. Peck, *Thoreau's Morning Work*, 7.

53. Thoreau, *Maine Woods*, 224.

54. Ibid., 224–25.

55. Thoreau, *Maine Woods*, 203.

56. Bennett, *Thoreau's Nature*, 40.

57. Thoreau, *Maine Woods*, 296.

58. Ibid., 55.

59. Ibid., 57–58.

60. Richardson, *Henry Thoreau*, 389: "In his last sentence, only the two words 'moose' and 'Indian' were audible."

61. Thoreau, *Maine Woods*, 66.

62. Ibid., 70.

63. Ibid., 71.

64. Ibid.

65. Ibid.

66. Ibid., 81.

67. Maurice Merleau-Ponty, *Phenomenology of Perception*, trans. Colin Smith (New York: Routledge, 2003), 507.

68. Thoreau, *Maine Woods*, 82.

69. Ibid.

70. Thoreau, *Excursions*, 192.

71. Ibid.

72. Ibid., 185.

73. Ibid.

74. Ibid.

75. Ibid., 16.
76. Ibid., 186.
77. Thoreau, *Walden* (Princeton), 84.
78. Thoreau, *Reform Papers*, 108.
79. Thoreau, *Excursions*, 192.
80. Ibid., 195.
81. Ibid., 196.
82. Ibid., 197.
83. Ibid., 194–95.
84. Ibid., 200.
85. Ibid.
86. Ibid., 208.
87. Ibid., 209.
88. Ibid.
89. Ibid., 202–3.
90. Ibid., 203.
91. Ibid., 211.
92. Ibid., 213.
93. Ibid., 214.
94. Ibid., 221.
95. Ibid., 222.
96. Hadot, *What Is Ancient Philosophy?* 85.

5. How to Mind Your Own Business

1. Joel Myerson, ed., *Emerson and Thoreau: The Contemporary Reviews* (New York: Cambridge University Press, 1992), 419.
2. Of course, as I mention in the introduction, Bennett, Mariotti, and Walker go a long way toward remedying this problem.
3. Ralph Waldo Emerson, "Thoreau," in *Emerson and Thoreau*, ed. Myerson, 428.
4. Ibid.
5. Richardson, *Henry Thoreau*, 208.
6. Thoreau, *Correspondence*, 214.
7. Plato, *Theaetetus*, 149a. Quoted in Hadot, *What Is Ancient Philosophy?* 30.
8. Thoreau, *Correspondence*, 217.
9. Ibid., 213.
10. Ibid., 215.
11. Ibid.
12. Ibid., 216.
13. Ibid.

14. Ibid.

15. Richardson, *Henry Thoreau*, 344.

16. Thoreau, *Correspondence*, 219.

17. Pierre Hadot's magnificent book on Marcus Aurelius is titled *The Inner Citadel.*

18. Thoreau, *Correspondence*, 221.

19. Ibid., 222.

20. Ibid., 251.

21. Ibid., 250.

22. Ibid., 251.

23. Thoreau, *Journal* (Princeton), 2:156.

24. Thoreau, *Correspondence*, 258.

25. Ibid.

26. Ibid., 296–97.

27. Ibid., 297.

28. Plato, *Republic,* ed. and trans. Allan Bloom (New York: Basic Books, 1968), 111 (433b).

29. Hannah Arendt, *Crises of the Republic* (New York: Mariner Books, 1972); Heinz Eulau, "Wayside Challenger: Some Remarks on the Politics of Henry David Thoreau," *Antioch Review* 9, no. 4 (1949): 509–22; Vincent Buranelli, "The Case against Thoreau," *Ethics* 67, no. 4 (1957): 257–68.

30. Nancy Rosenblum, "Thoreau's Militant Conscience," *Political Theory* 9 , no. 1 (1981): 81–110.

31. Jack Turner, "Performing Conscience: Thoreau, Political Action, and the Plea for Captain John Brown," *Political Theory* 33 (2005): 448–71.

32. Kateb, *Patriotism and Other Mistakes,* 250.

33. Thoreau, *Walden* (Princeton), 13.

34. Richardson, *Henry Thoreau*, 186–87.

35. Thoreau, *Familiar Letters,* 277.

36. Thoreau, *Reform Papers,* 156.

37. Thoreau, *Walden* (Princeton), 54.

38. Howe, *What Hath God Wrought,* 525–69; Philip Gura, *American Transcendentalism: A History* (New York: Hill and Wang, 2007), 124–49.

39. Thoreau, *Familiar Letters,* 438.

40. The same can be said for Emerson. A striking passage from "Self Reliance" summarizes it well: "Expect me not to show cause why I seek or why I exclude company. Then, again, do not tell me, as a good man did today, of my obligations to put all poor men in good situations. Are they *my* poor?" (Ralph Waldo Emerson, *The Collected Works of Ralph Waldo Emerson,* ed. Alfred Ferguson and Jean Ferguson Carr, 9 vols. [Cambridge: Harvard University Press, 1979], 2:230).

41. Thoreau, *Reform Papers,* 74.

42. Ralph Waldo Emerson, *The Political Emerson*, ed. David Robinson (New York: Beacon, 2004); Dean Grodzins, *American Heretic: Theodore Parker and Transcendentalism* (Chapel Hill: University of North Carolina Press, 2002), 469–72; Daniel Walker Howe, *Making the American Self* (New York: Oxford University Press, 1997), 182.

43. Thoreau, *Journal* (Houghton Mifflin), 10:246.

44. Thoreau, *Walden* (Princeton), 91.

45. Thoreau, *Journal* (Princeton), 2:243.

46. Ibid., 1:140.

47. Ibid., 3:103.

48. Ibid. Thoreau's insistence on our ability to get beyond politics and toward something more substantial to human life is echoed in Nietzsche's declaration from the preface to *The Anti-Christ:* "You need to be used to living on mountains—to seeing the miserable, ephemeral little gossip of politics and national self-interest *beneath* you. You need to have become indifferent. . . . Respect for yourself; love for yourself; an unconditional freedom over yourself" (Friedrich Nietzsche, *The Anti-Christ, Ecce Homo, Twilight of the Idols, and Other Writings*, trans. Judith Norman [New York: Cambridge University Press, 2005], 3).

49. Thoreau, *Reform Papers*, 107.

50. Ibid., 108.

51. Ibid., 104.

52. Ibid., 106.

53. Ibid., 108.

54. Ibid., 108–9.

55. Turner, "Performing Conscience," 465–68.

56. Thoreau, *Reform Papers*, 133.

57. Thoreau, *Walden* (Princeton), 73.

58. Thoreau, *Reform Papers*, 86.

59. Thoreau, *Familiar Letters*, 196.

60. Ibid., 306, 347.

61. On Thoreau's letters to Blake as an "inner biography," see Richardson, *Henry Thoreau*, 208.

62. One could look at the Princeton University Press edition of Thoreau's sociopolitical essays *Reform Papers* for evidence of this connection.

63. Quoted in Richardson, *Henry Thoreau*, 100–101.

64. Thoreau, *Reform Papers*, 194.

65. Henry D. Thoreau, *The Writings of Henry D. Thoreau: A Week on the Concord and Merrimack Rivers*, ed. Carl Hovde, William L. Howarth, and Elizabeth Hall Witherell (Princeton: Princeton University Press, 1980), 206; hereinafter, Thoreau, *Week*.

66. Ibid, 283. This quotation complicates Bob Pepperman Taylor's major thesis that Thoreau's abiding interest was in a cohesive moral community and that his writings reflect his desire to reform individuals and society along moral lines. See Taylor, *America's Bachelor Uncle*, 55–57.

67. Thoreau, *Journal* (Houghton Mifflin), 11:329.

68. Thoreau, *Reform Papers*, 193.

69. Stanley Cavell, *Senses of Walden*, 19–21; George Shulman, *American Prophecy: Race and Redemption in American Political Culture* (Minneapolis: University of Minnesota Press, 2008), 39–87.

70. Walker, "Thoreau on Democratic Cultivation."

71. Thoreau, *Walden* (Princeton), 71.

72. Cavell, *Senses of Walden*, 67.

73. Thoreau, *Week*, 127.

74. Thoreau, *Journal* (Houghton Mifflin), 11:379–80.

75. Walker, "Thoreau's Alternative Economics," 45.

76. Thoreau, *Reform Papers*, 81.

77. Ibid., 170.

78. Thoreau, *Walden* (Princeton), 75.

79. Nancy Rosenblum, "Thoreau's Democratic Individualism," in *A Political Companion to Henry David Thoreau*, ed. Jack Turner (Lexington: University Press of Kentucky, 2009), 21.

80. Thoreau, *Journal* (Houghton Mifflin), 11:351.

81. Thoreau, *Familiar Letters*, 255.

82. Henry D. Thoreau, *The Writings of Henry D. Thoreau: Cape Cod*, ed. Joseph J. Moldenhauer (Princeton: Princeton University Press, 2004), 9.

83. Cavell, *In Quest of the Ordinary*, 4.

84. Thoreau, *Walden* (Princeton), 52.

85. Ibid.

86. Henry D. Thoreau, *Wild Fruits*, ed. Bradley P. Dean (New York: W. W. Norton, 2000), 57.

87. Ibid., 51.

88. Ibid., 59.

89. Henry Jaffa, "Thoreau and Lincoln"; Leigh Kathryn Jenco, "Thoreau's Critique of Democracy"; and Melissa Lane, "Thoreau and Rousseau: Nature as Utopia," in *A Political Companion to Henry David Thoreau*, ed. Jack Turner (Lexington: University Press of Kentucky, 2009), 178–204; 68–98; 341–71.

90. George Kateb, *The Inner Ocean: Individualism and Democratic Culture* (Ithaca: Cornell University Press, 1992), 33.

91. Turner, "Performing Conscience"; Walker, "Thoreau on Democratic Cultivation"; Cavell, *Senses of Walden*.

92. Grodzins, *American Heretic*, 342, 492.

93. Howe, *Making the American Self*, 249.

94. Ibid., 250.

95. Robinson, *Natural Life*, 55.

96. Tauber, *Henry David Thoreau*, 5.

97. Thoreau, *Reform Papers*, 159.

98. Thoreau, *Journal* (Houghton Mifflin), 6:355–56.

99. Ibid., 6:436.

100. Ibid., 9:36.

101. Ibid., 1:265.

102. Thoreau, *Reform Papers*, 84.

6. The Fullness of Life

1. Thoreau, *Wild Fruits*, 218.

2. Ibid., 198.

3. Ibid., 169.

4. Ibid., 165.

5. Ibid.

6. Thoreau, *Correspondence*, 94.

7. Thoreau, *Journal* (Princeton), 3:103.

8. Ibid., 2:188.

9. Ibid., 2:465–66.

10. Thoreau, *Familiar Letters*, 262.

11. Thoreau, *Correspondence*, 259.

12. Ibid., 250.

13. Ibid., 252.

14. Ibid., 266.

15. Ibid., 389.

16. Ibid., 388.

17. Walter Harding, *The Days of Henry Thoreau: A Biography* (Princeton: Princeton University Press, 1992), 464.

18. Thoreau, *Journal* (Princeton), 1:129.

19. Thoreau, *Journal* (Houghton Mifflin), 11:381.

Bibliography

Abbott, Philip. "Henry David Thoreau, the State of Nature, and the Redemption of Liberalism." *Journal of Politics* 47, no. 1 (1985): 182–208.

Allan, Sarah. *The Way of Water and Sprouts of Virtue.* Albany: SUNY Press, 1997.

Allen, Thomas M. *A Republic in Time: Temporality and Social Imagination in Nineteenth-Century America.* Chapel Hill: University of North Carolina Press, 2008.

Arendt, Hannah. *Crises of the Republic.* New York: Mariner Books, 1972.

Aurelius, Marcus. *Meditations.* Edited and translated by C. R. Haines. Loeb Classical Library. Cambridge: Harvard University Press, 1930.

Bennett, Jane. *The Enchantment of Modern Life: Attachments, Crossings, and Ethics.* Princeton: Princeton University Press, 2001.

———. *Thoreau's Nature: Ethics, Politics, and the Wild.* New York: Sage, 1994.

Buranelli, Vincent. "The Case against Thoreau." *Ethics* 67, no. 4 (1957): 257–68.

Cafaro, Philip. *Thoreau's Living Ethics:* Walden *and the Pursuit of Virtue.* Athens: University of Georgia Press, 2004.

Cameron, Sharon. *Writing Nature: Henry Thoreau's* Journal. Chicago: University of Chicago Press, 1989.

Cavell, Stanley. *In Quest of the Ordinary: Lines of Skepticism and Romanticism.* Chicago: University of Chicago Press, 1988.

———. *The Senses of Walden.* Chicago: University of Chicago Press, 1992.

Delano, Sterling F. *Brook Farm: The Dark Side of Utopia.* Cambridge: Harvard University Press, 2004.

Emerson, Ralph Waldo. *Essays and Lectures.* Edited by Joel Porte. New York: Library of America, 1983.

———. *The Political Emerson.* Edited by David Robinson. New York: Beacon, 2004.

Epictetus. *Discourses.* Translated by Robert Dobbin. New York: Oxford University Press, 1998.

———. *Discourses.* Translated by W. A. Oldfather. Loeb Classical Library. Cambridge: Harvard University Press, 1998.

Eulau, Heinz. "Wayside Challenger: Some Remarks on the Politics of Henry David Thoreau." *Antioch Review* 9, no. 4 (1949): 509–22.

Foucault, Michel. *Ethics: Subjectivity and Truth.* Edited by Paul Rabinow. New York: Free Press, 1998.

———. *The Hermeneutics of the Subject: Lectures at the Collège de France, 1981–1982*. Translated by Graham Burchell. New York: Palgrave Macmillan, 2005.

Francis, Richard. *Fruitlands: The Alcott Family and Their Search for Utopia*. New Haven: Yale University Press, 2010.

———. *Transcendental Utopias: Individual and Community at Brook Farm, Fruitlands, and Walden*. Ithaca: Cornell University Press, 1997.

Garber, Frederick. *Thoreau's Redemptive Imagination*. New York: New York University Press, 1977.

Gill, Christopher. *The Structured Self in Hellenistic and Roman Thought*. New York: Oxford University Press, 2006.

Gilmore, Michael T. *American Romanticism and the Marketplace*. Chicago: University of Chicago Press, 1985.

Grodzins, Dean. *American Heretic: Theodore Parker and Transcendentalism*. Chapel Hill: University of North Carolina Press, 2002.

Guarneri, Carl J. *The Utopian Alternative: Fourierism in Nineteenth-Century America*. Ithaca: Cornell University Press, 1991.

Gura, Philip. *American Transcendentalism: A History*. New York: Hill and Wang, 2007.

Hadot, Pierre. *The Inner Citadel: The* Meditations *of Marcus Aurelius*. Cambridge: Harvard University Press, 1998.

———. *Philosophy as a Way of Life*. Translated by Michael Chase. Oxford: Blackwell, 1995.

———. "There Are Nowadays Professors of Philosophy, but Not Philosophers." Translated by J. Aaron Simmons and Mason Marshall. *Journal of Speculative Philosophy* 19, no. 3 (2005): 229–37.

———. *What Is Ancient Philosophy?* Translated by Michael Chase. Cambridge: Harvard University Press, 2002.

Harding, Walter. *The Days of Henry Thoreau: A Biography*. Princeton: Princeton University Press, 1992.

Hawthorne, Nathaniel. *The Blithedale Romance*. Edited by Seymour Gross and Rosalie Murphy. New York: W. W. Norton, 2010.

Heidegger, Martin. "Why Do I Stay in the Provinces?" In *Heidegger: The Man and the Thinker*, edited by Thomas Sheehan. Chicago: Precedent, 1981.

Hodder, Alan D. *Thoreau's Ecstatic Witness*. New Haven: Yale University Press, 2001.

Howe, Daniel Walker. *Making the American Self: Jonathan Edwards to Abraham Lincoln*. New York: Oxford University Press, 1997.

———. *What Hath God Wrought: The Transformation of America, 1815–1848*. New York: Oxford University Press, 2007.

Kateb, George. *The Inner Ocean: Individualism and Democratic Culture*. Ithaca: Cornell University Press, 1992.

———. *Patriotism and Other Mistakes*. New Haven: Yale University Press, 2006.

Lane, Ruth. "'Standing Aloof' from the State: Thoreau on Self-Government." *Review of Politics* 67, no. 2 (2005): 283–310.

Long, A. A. *Epictetus: A Stoic and Socratic Guide to Life*. New York: Oxford University Press, 2002.

Mariotti, Shannon. *Thoreau's Democratic Withdrawal: Alienation, Participation, Modernity*. Madison: University of Wisconsin Press, 2010.

McGushin, Edward. *Foucault's Askesis: An Introduction to the Philosophical Life*. Chicago: Northwestern University Press, 2007.

Merleau-Ponty, Maurice. *Phenomenology of Perception*. Translated by Colin Smith. New York: Routledge, 2003.

Myerson, Joel, ed. *Emerson and Thoreau: The Contemporary Reviews*. New York: Cambridge University Press, 1992.

Nabers, Deak. "Thoreau's Natural Constitution." *American Literary History* 19, no. 4 (2007): 824–48.

Neufeldt, Leonard N. *The Economist: Henry David Thoreau and Enterprise*. New York: Oxford University Press, 1989.

Nietzsche, Friedrich. *The Anti-Christ, Ecce Homo, Twilight of the Idols, and Other Writings*. Translated by Judith Norman. New York: Cambridge University Press, 2005.

Packer, Barbara L. *The Transcendentalists*. Athens: University of Georgia Press, 2007.

Paul, Sherman. *For Love of the World*. Iowa City: University of Iowa Press, 1992.

———. *The Shores of America: Thoreau's Inward Exploration*. Champaign: University of Illinois Press, 1958 (1972).

Peck, H. Daniel. *Thoreau's Morning Work: Memory and Perception in* A Week on the Concord and Merrimack Rivers, *the "Journal," and* Walden. New Haven: Yale University Press, 1990.

Plato. *Apology*. Translated by Harold North Fowler. Loeb Classical Library. Cambridge: Harvard University Press, 1914.

———. *Republic*. Edited and translated by Allan Bloom. New York: Basic Books, 1968.

Richardson, Robert D. *Henry Thoreau: A Life of the Mind*. Berkeley: University of California Press, 1986.

Robinson, David M. *Natural Life: Thoreau's Worldly Transcendentalism*. Ithaca: Cornell University Press, 2004.

———. "'Unchronicled Nations': Agrarian Purpose and Thoreau's Ecological Knowing." *Nineteenth-Century Literature* 48, no. 3 (1993): 326–40.

Rosenblum, Nancy. *Another Liberalism: Romanticism and the Reconstruction of Liberal Thought*. Cambridge: Harvard University Press, 1987.

———. "Thoreau's Militant Conscience." *Political Theory* 9, no. 1 (1981): 81–110.

Safranski, Rudiger. *Martin Heidegger: Between Good and Evil.* Translated by Ewald Osers. Cambridge: Harvard University Press, 1998.

Shulman, George. *American Prophecy: Race and Redemption in American Political Culture.* Minneapolis: University of Minnesota Press, 2008.

Tauber, Alfred I. *Henry David Thoreau and the Moral Agency of Knowing.* Berkeley: University of California Press, 2001.

Taylor, Bob Pepperman. *America's Bachelor Uncle: Thoreau and the American Polity.* Lawrence: University Press of Kansas, 1996.

Thoreau, Henry D. *The Correspondence of Henry David Thoreau.* Edited by Carl Bode and Walter Harding. New York: New York University Press, 1958.

———. *Familiar Letters of Henry David Thoreau.* Boston: Houghton Mifflin, 1906.

———. *The Journal of Henry David Thoreau.* Edited by Bradford Torrey and Francis Allen. 14 vols. Boston: Houghton Mifflin, 1906.

———. *Walden.* Edited by Jeffrey S. Cramer. New Haven: Yale University Press, 2006.

———. *Wild Fruits.* Edited by Bradley P. Dean. New York: W. W. Norton, 2000.

———. *The Writings of Henry D. Thoreau: A Week on the Concord and Merrimack Rivers.* Edited by Carl Hovde, William L. Howarth, and Elizabeth Hall Witherell. Princeton: Princeton University Press, 1980.

———. *The Writings of Henry D. Thoreau: Cape Cod.* Edited by Joseph J. Moldenhauer. Princeton: Princeton University Press, 2004.

———. *The Writings of Henry D. Thoreau: Excursions.* Edited by Joseph J. Moldenhauer. Princeton: Princeton University Press, 2007.

———. *The Writings of Henry D. Thoreau: Journal (1837–1854).* Edited by Elizabeth Hall Witherell et al. 8 vols. Princeton: Princeton University Press, 1981–2009.

———. *The Writings of Henry D. Thoreau: Reform Papers.* Edited by Wendell Glick. Princeton: Princeton University Press, 1973.

———. *The Writings of Henry D. Thoreau: The Maine Woods.* Edited by Joseph J. Moldenhauer. Princeton: Princeton University Press, 1972.

———. *The Writings of Henry D. Thoreau: Walden.* Edited by J. Lyndon Shanley. Princeton: Princeton University Press, 1971.

Turner, Jack. "Performing Conscience: Thoreau, Political Action, and the Plea for Captain John Brown." *Political Theory* 33 (2005): 448–71.

———, ed. *A Political Companion to Henry David Thoreau.* Lexington: University Press of Kentucky, 2009.

Villa, Dana. *Socratic Citizenship.* Princeton: Princeton University Press, 2001.

Voelz, Johannes. "Alienation Revisited." *American Literary History* 24 (2012): 618–30.

Walker, Brian. "Thoreau on Democratic Cultivation." *Political Theory* 29, no. 2 (2001): 155–89.

————. "Thoreau's Alternative Economics: Work, Liberty, and Democratic Culti-
vation." *American Political Science Review* 92, no. 4 (1998): 845–56.
Walls, Laura Dassow. *Seeing New Worlds: Henry David Thoreau and Nineteenth-Cen-
tury Natural Science*. Madison: University of Wisconsin Press, 1995.
Whitman, Walt. *Poetry and Prose*. Edited by Justin Kaplan. New York: Library of
America, 1982.
Wood, Ellen Meiskins, and Neal Wood. "Socrates and Democracy: A Reply to
Gregory Vlastos." *Political Theory* 14, no. 1 (1986): 55–82.

Index

www.ingramcontent.com/pod-product-compliance
Lightning Source LLC
Chambersburg PA
CBHW030506100426
42813CB00002B/360